Size Zero *and* Beyond

A personal study of anorexia nervosa

by

Jacqueline M Kemp

Augur Press

SIZE ZERO AND BEYOND:
A PERSONAL STUDY OF ANOREXIA NERVOSA
Copyright © Jacqueline M Kemp 2012

The moral right of the author has been asserted

British Library Cataloguing in Publication Data.
A catalogue record for this book is available from the
British Library.

ISBN 978-0-9571380-0-1

First published 2012 by
Augur Press
Delf House,
52, Penicuik Road,
Roslin,
Midlothian EH25 9LH
United Kingdom

Printed by Lightning Source

Size Zero and Beyond:
A personal study of anorexia nervosa

Author's note

The views and opinions expressed in this book are entirely personal. The names of most people and the names of some places have been changed.

This book is not a source of medical advice. If you are concerned by any of the issues raised, professional medical advice should be sought.

The author and the publisher do not accept any responsibility for loss or damage arising from reliance on this publication.

Cover image:

The artwork which appears on the front cover of this book is a detail of a painting entitled Masked Love by the artist Joyce Gunn Cairns MBE, reproduced with her kind permission.

Dedication

This work is dedicated to the Earth,
To the substance and being of the Earth,
To the creatures of the Earth,
To the vegetation of the Earth,
To the people that dwell upon the Earth,
And to the spirit beings involved with the Earth
On her evolutionary pathway.

Acknowledgements

It is impossible to thank everyone by name who has helped me with this book, as I have received support, affirmation and encouragement to put my story into writing from so very many sources. To those people I offer my heartfelt gratitude. However I wish to make a special mention of certain people and creatures without whose assistance, support and steady insistence of their confidence in me, I would never have persisted in my efforts to communicate my story to the world at large.

Many thanks to the staff of Augur Press, who have provided guidance and advice, and have given generously of their time and expertise in the production of this book. Garry Irvine of Mobile IT Experts has provided invaluable service in putting the book together. My sister Sylvia is a wonderful sister, kind, supportive and generous, and is there for me on the end of the phone whenever I need to share my troubles. Jerry Orr has supported and helped me in many practical ways in my daily life and supplied me with all sorts of electronic equipment to help with my book. Grant Jarvis has given me generous financial support, and looked after me in times of illness. My health practitioners, Brian Gardener, Charmaine Shepherd and Julie Osborne, have given me constant support, kindness and treatment, and encouraged me with their interest in my writing. The late Dr Frank Lake was the first person to affirm that I had something worthwhile to write about, and encouraged me to write a book. My departed friend, Watson, always believed in me and always encouraged me to write. My spiritual guide, Ruth White, has given me her unfailing support and encouragement in bringing this book into being. My cats have given me their furry companionship in the depths of my despair, without which I would not have survived to write this.

Contents

Poems by Jacqueline Kemp

Poem by Alfred Lord Tennyson

From Ancient Runes

Author's note:
The poems in this book are printed in the form in which they
flowed from me at the time of writing. Although in hindsight I
have thought of ways in which they might be improved, or
changed to adapt to my current outlook on life, I have resisted
the urge to alter them. I feel that to leave them as they stand
represents more authentically the stage I was at when I wrote
them.

Preface by Ruth White

It is an honour to have been asked to write an introduction to this book by Jacqueline Kemp, whom I have been privileged to know for many years. Jacqueline is a gifted person: a healer, musician, keen observer of life, and committed to spiritual growth and a love of all that constitutes the essence of Earth. She has consistently pursued these aspects of herself despite her life-time battle with anorexia nervosa – that demanding illness which is so difficult to define, and which is often misunderstood at all kinds of levels.

Soren Kiirkegaard, the philosopher, said: 'Life must be lived forward but it can only be understood backwards'. Socrates said: 'The unexamined life is not worth living'.

Jacqueline kept going forward with her life, despite the exigencies of her condition, and in this book she looks back on it in order to understand it. She examines it in order to bring meaning to it. The work and honesty here are an example to us all. Sometimes what we are asked to face alongside Jacqueline is challenging. It is sometimes tender to the point of being poetic. Often there is a humour that comes through, even from the depths of the struggle. Above all, this is a courageous book. It is completely self-revealing, and because of that, I believe it will be of great help to others who suffer or have suffered as Jacqueline has, with anything in their lives that leads to limitation and frustration, for as she shows, these things can also lead to moments of transcendence.

In her own introduction to the book, Jacqueline explains that this is a very personal story. It offers no solutions, no cures. It is an account of her life experience, written simply, movingly and with the utmost integrity. As we follow the story, we can all take the role of fellow travellers, even though our journeys may be very different to the one recorded here. We each have our own story, and when someone shares theirs, in the open and brave way that Jacqueline has accomplished in these pages, we can all learn from each other with humility and respect.

This is not an easy read, but it is a very rewarding one. Thank you Jackie, for what you have given here.

Ruth White

Ruth White is highly regarded as an author, transpersonal psychologist, therapist, spiritual teacher and guide. She has many years of experience and is internationally renowned as a workshop leader. She runs a private practice near Brighton, on the South coast of the UK. Further information about her work can be found on her website: www.ruthwhite-gildas.co.uk

Preface by Kenneth Clark

This is a story, very elegantly and beautifully written, of a very intelligent woman's lifelong struggle with anorexia nervosa. Coming originally from a financially comfortable middle class southern English family, Jacqueline comes to live much of her life in poverty and hardship in Scotland. Her story outlines a long journey to find a cure for the pain of her condition. She describes her obsessive preoccupation with food and the invariably tortuous path of starving, binging, purging, with consequent depression, despair and hopelessness. She traces the complex family dynamics of her childhood and of the effects of these upon her personality and on the development of her anorexic condition. Despite her severe difficulties, which included poor self worth, phobias, numerous extra anxieties, depression, lack of a sense of self, combined with her anorexia, Jacqueline nevertheless pursues a path aimed at relief and cure.

Although a complete cure is never found, a transformation of her anorexia and a setting free from her damaging self image is achieved. Her profound personal growth and learning on her path is very clearly portrayed. In her tenacious pursuit of a cure, Jacqueline engages with a truly formidable array of those involved in the fields of mental health and psychological difficulties. Those professionals expected to be most effective often show failures with their established treatments. However, her involvement with varied therapists often provides surprising growth in unexpected, apparently unrelated areas that still allow progress and personal development to occur, making those engagements very worthwhile and particularly rewarding for her. Her path involves her with psychiatrists, psychologists, psychoanalysts and those practising spiritual healing, past-life regression, dream work and homeopathy, to mention but a few. She clearly is a person of unusual sensitivity and self awareness and with considerable insights into her self. She is also, in her own words, 'thin skinned'.

Jacqueline portrays unusual relationships that develop throughout her life, and these sometimes involve abuse, or being used. But most involve care, concern and help that are naturally rewarding, and to her are especially important and valued in her life. Despite her many psychological handicaps, her inner drive for a cure never subsides. This leads her to an unusually diverse range of life experiences that are important ingredients for her path of learning, self awareness, self honesty and acquiring her philosophy of life. Jacqueline's creative poetry or prose in each chapter reflects her complex and intricate feelings surrounding different aspects of her life, as well as often reflecting her outlooks and philosophies that have progressively developed.

I first met Jacqueline as a patient in my clinic in 1972, at a time when she was very ill with anorexia nervosa. I engaged with her in psychotherapy for a number of years, until a change in circumstances made it impossible for her to continue treatment. Since then, she has kept in touch with letters, and occasionally by phone.

This is a life story from which professionals could well gain insights. People interested in unusual life struggles and life experiences will find this book engaging. Those with eating disorders may well find it particularly absorbing.

Kenneth Clark, MA, DCP member of BMA

Kenneth Clark studied psychology and philosophy at Bangor College, University of Wales, and subsequently obtained a Post Graduate Diploma in Clinical Psychology at Glasgow University. After completing the diploma he was employed by the NHS as the psychologist in the Professorial Department of Psychological Medicine at the Southern General Hospital in Glasgow. Following this he continued employment in the NHS as a clinical psychologist and has extensive experience of over thirty years. Since retiring from his position as Head of Department at Fairmile Hospital, near Reading, he has worked part time as Principal Psychologist at Prospect Park Hospital in Reading. He is currently involved in research with Dr Gordon Claridge, who was formerly a Professor within the Department of Psychology at Oxford University, and has published several papers in conjunction with him.

I would like to express my sincere thanks and appreciation to Ruth and Ken for their kind commendation of my book.

Introduction

This book is not about a cure, neither is it a self-help book. It is essentially a story, the story of a transformational journey – one that is still unfolding. In it I endeavour to share something of who I am as a human being, manifesting on both the spiritual and material planes in this incarnation. There are, of course, countless aspects of a human life, both seen and unseen, and so rather than attempt to tell the 'whole story', I have tried to focus on aspects relevant to anorexia nervosa – its suffering and its healing as I have experienced them.

Though I have expressed views, these are personal views and personal understandings, which I hope are always in the process of adjustment and enlargement. They are not intended to be definitive statements on the nature of things. I do not try to justify any of my experiences; their validity lies in the fact that I experienced them. As we move along the passage of time, often the colours and emotions attached to our experiences will change, and we will understand and interpret them differently. This does not nullify the initial experience in any way but merely shows it to be a living aspect of our personality, growing and changing with us. We can only act and interpret with the level of enlightenment that we possess at the time, and as that enlightenment spreads through the whole person, it gathers up with it and transforms all the experiences of life, creating a glorious tapestry of light and shadow which define the uniqueness of our individuality. This individuality is a feature of being incarnate, and though it may feel like separateness, it is underpinned by oneness with all creation.

As I pursue my way through my lifetime, I always want the answers, but I try to live the questions. I endeavour to be compassionate with myself – clumsy bungles included – in the task of living a human life. It is not easy to look at oneself with total honesty and be truly kind to oneself. When we come into this world, we quickly learn that our value depends on whether we can perform, produce or be competent at something, or whether we are attractive to look at according to current preferences of our society. This is especially true in our consumer-driven, noise-addicted, speed-worshipping Western society, where values such as compassion, community spirit, quietness and space seem in short supply.

I think that one of my reasons for wanting to write this book is that I have received so many gifts which embody the beautiful qualities of life, in a myriad of forms, in a myriad of ways and through a myriad of agencies. I want to tell you that the kind of world for which so many of us yearn is not lost, and that each one of us can manifest it, even if only in small ways, in our own lives.

Our collective character is not formed by the way we relate to the most powerful, the most competent and the most compelling aspects of life, but is shaped by the way we treat the weakest and neediest among us. For much of my life I have been one of the weak and the needy, and flowing through all the oppression, the marginalisation, the humiliation and the misunderstanding have come treasures which are of eternal value and are truly without price. Life affirming creativity and love arises from suffering, in the most extreme of circumstances, like the proverbial phoenix arising from the ashes.

I hope that whatever your feelings in relation to this work, you will find a gleam of light coming through it, especially for you, to touch you on your journey.

Foreword

Current descriptions of anorexia nervosa are usually focused primarily on a body weight that has been deliberately reduced such as to become persistently and dangerously low, such that physical health is compromised. This kind of situation is brought about principally by calorie restriction, but is frequently also associated with a variety of weight-reducing behaviours, such as bizarre or unhealthy eating patterns, 'rules' concerning the eating of food, purging by self-induced vomiting, and misuse of laxatives, diuretics or enemas. Excessive and compulsive exercising may also be a contributing factor to weight loss. Some experts believe that 'anorexia' is a misnomer, as appetite is *not* lost, and far more than eating is disordered. 'Obsessive Weight and Shape Disorder' or 'Body Image Related Disorder' could be more accurate names for the illness. Anorexia nervosa has been described by some specialists as a modern form of obsessive/compulsive disorder.

Bulimia nervosa has many similarities to anorexia nervosa, but is characterised principally by binge eating, in which a large quantity of food is consumed in short space of time. This is usually followed by attempts to compensate, such as by dieting, purging, vomiting, and also by excessive exercise, as is found in anorexia. In some cases bulimics will not become emaciated, but will remain at a relatively normal weight. Some sufferers will alternate between the two types of illness. Non-purging binge eating disorder is less likely to result in dangerous weight loss.

Preoccupation with body image is common to both bulimia nervosa and anorexia nervosa, and sufferers often have a distorted perception of their actual size. Shame and secrecy may compel sufferers to try to disguise their condition, and deny that there is anything wrong with them.

Certain consequences of both types of illness can be far-reaching and severe. For women and girls, a loss of menstruation is common when the weight reaches a certain low level, and fertility can be impaired. Distress concerning the illness can also cause menstruation to cease. Lanugo hair may appear on the body when at a very low weight. Starvation causes physical damage to the body, including poor repair and resistance to infection, stunting of growth, heart damage, bone loss, and disordered blood composition. The trauma imposed by starvation triggers the production of stress hormones, and this may lead to heightened irritability and arousal, and raised cholesterol levels. Purging may cause neurochemical disruption which can damage the brain and the heart, and the teeth may be adversely affected by persistent vomiting.

Psychosocial effects of both illnesses can vary widely, according to the personality, the physical constitution and the circumstances of the individual. Depression and anxiety are common, and obsessive/compulsive behaviours may radiate outwards from the focus on food and weight to affect many other areas of life. Inability to concentrate on anything but food is a symptom of a starving person. People who rely on an eating disorder to 'solve' problems may fail to develop other more creative ways to cope with life, and find themselves unable to tolerate distress, or to feel rewarded or fulfilled. In cases where the illness is severe and prolonged, career and financial circumstances may be negatively impacted, leading to social constraints in later life. Social relationships frequently present difficulties due to the demands of the illness, and this may lead to loneliness and social isolation. People who are ordinarily honest may be forced to lie, cheat and steal to maintain and protect their illness, and finding that relationships with other people can become an obstacle to the eating disorder, generally withdraw from contact. Anorexia nervosa in particular is a life-threatening illness, and even if treated may lead to severe and chronic health problems, and in some cases, to death or suicide.

Eating disorders have typically been more prevalent in Western society than the East, although as cultures become increasingly global in their influence, it may be that this distribution will change. With the advent of modern communication networks, traditional societies in the East are being increasingly penetrated by media influence, Western fashion and the Size Zero culture, which are thought to be factors in the development of eating disorders.

In Britain there has been a considerable rise in the number of reported cases of eating disorders, and the number of undiagnosed cases may be much higher. Obtaining accurate statistics presents difficulties, since many sufferers deny or hide their illness, and hospital admissions usually account for only the more serious cases.

Anorexia nervosa has been traditionally considered a 'women's disease', but eating disorder experts are now reporting a significant rise in the number of male anorexics referred to them. It may be that with a modern trend towards some degree of relaxation of traditional gender roles, males who have previously been unable to admit to their illness are coming forward to seek help. However this does not imply that men and boys who suffer from anorexia nervosa are likely to be homosexual, as a high proportion of males treated for anorexia nervosa are heterosexual.

It was previously believed that anorexia nervosa was linked to the onset of puberty in girls, but the illness is now being reported in children at a younger age than ever before – even as young as six years. Additionally the number of mature women seeking treatment has seen a recent increase. Some of these women developed anorexia nervosa in their teenage years and never managed to shake it off, with the illness being hidden or denied until some kind of trigger prompts its reappearance. Other women have developed anorexia nervosa or bulimia nervosa in later life, possibly triggered by work, social or family pressures, and exacerbated by the current trend of being expected to look much younger than their actual age. Certain professions, such as the model industry and ballet dancing, typically require women to be very slender, and this may prompt the onset of an eating disorder in vulnerable women.

The increase in numbers may be in part due to increased awareness of eating disorders, their nature and severity, and the recognition that it is not just teenage girls who are affected. There is more awareness amongst the medical profession, with GPs identifying eating disorders more readily and making more specialist referrals. Eating disorders are becoming more acceptable as a valid medical condition, and this may be encouraging more people to acknowledge their illness and seek treatment.

There is much discussion amongst the medical community and researchers as to the causes of eating disorders. Some have blamed the media as a powerful influence which promotes an ideal of unattainable physical perfection. Air-brushed and digitally-enhanced photographs of models and celebrities display unrealistic images of the human body, and the fashion and design industry has tended to glamorise excessive weight loss. Visual images can be very compelling, and people who are predisposed to eating disorders may be more susceptible to their influence.

For males, the social pressure on appearance is more difficult to understand as a factor in developing anorexia or bulimia nervosa. Traditionally, men have been required to be tall, lean, strong and muscular, with emaciation not being considered an attractive feature. However some experts believe that changes in the roles which males are expected to fulfil, and alterations in the balance of power between the sexes, may highlight tension and insecurity in males who do not have a stable, integrated sense of self. Additionally, increasing pressure on men to 'keep fit' and 'look good' may trigger some men into reaching for the 'false identity' of an eating disorder and the attendant over-identification with body image.

Today's children come under many pressures from the modern world that were not in existence a few decades ago. The screen culture of television and computers offers instant gratification and easy sensations, and if used excessively, can overload young minds with inappropriate stimulation. Busy parents may be tempted to use the TV or computer as a 'baby sitter', while children miss out on real play, real interactions and real physical exercise. Even more important, nourishing time spent with parents or other significant adults may be sacrificed in favour of time spent in front of the screen.

Academic pressures can contribute to a child's sense of needing to measure up to a certain standard, and promote anxiety if a sense of failure is experienced. Children are targeted at a young age by the fashion industry, and the playground can be an unhappy arena for those children who do not conform to the currently-favoured style of dress. Body image concerns can be observed at a much younger age than in previous years. It is my view that children are being drawn into enacting some forms of adult sexual behaviour at a much earlier stage of life.

All these factors can put pressure on a child's mental health, and may become focused in the form of vulnerability to an eating disorder.

Social deprivation has also been suggested as a contributing factor. Poverty, and also drug and alcohol abuse can harm a child's development, and the widening gap between rich and poor leaves more children than ever at risk from lack of essential resources for their healthy development.

Recent initiatives by the Government to promote healthy eating and to combat obesity have been described by some researchers as having a negative backlash. Although such campaigns are intended to raise public awareness of the importance of eating well and maintaining a healthy weight, people can become overloaded with information and become preoccupied with food, fuelling the development of eating disorders in vulnerable individuals. This may be especially applicable to children, who are likely to be bombarded by pro-health messages via their parents, their school and the media. Obese children may be ostracised and have to deal with bullying and teasing from peers, increasing the likelihood of developing an eating disorder.

A trend in cultural anxiety about the availability of food and its status on the healthy eating scale may provide a matrix which exacerbates the situation for people already overly preoccupied with eating. In the Western consumer society, where for many years there has been a surplus of food and commodities, there is a danger that the ability to demonstrate self-restraint can become an attitude of superiority. A moralistic tone may become attached to the healthy eating agenda, where giving in to 'base' desires – for chocolate or cream cakes for example – can be seen as weakness. Since self-regulation and control are primary features of anorexia nervosa, the healthy eating culture is not necessarily conducive to recovery from this illness, and may even have the opposite effect. For some, the overvaluation of self-control in respect of food can come to resemble a religious belief, with adherents being willing to sacrifice other highly valued aspects of life to the cause of weight loss, and engaging in self punishment or self harm if ' food rules' are broken.

Professionals are now recommending that the health message should be broadened to address wider implications, particularly including the emotional component of an individual's relationship with food.

Modern developments in science and technology have led to increased understanding of brain chemistry and information processing, and also of genetic coding. This has promoted interest in the possibility that some causative or predisposing factors of eating disorders are located in the brain or the genes. Recent research has shown that an inherited genetic code can create a neurotransmitter profile in the brain, which can be 'switched on' by dieting or hormonal changes in puberty. This pattern is thought to be a source of predisposition to eating disorders. Studies have revealed a higher correspondence for eating disorders in monozygous (identical) twins than in dizygous (non identical) twins. First degree relatives of patients with anorexia nervosa show an increased risk of developing the illness, and associations have been found with anorexia nervosa and families showing a history of obsessional personality, autism and anxiety disorders. These findings may indicate a genetic link in the development of anorexia nervosa.

Research involving brain scans of children with anorexia nervosa showed changes to the temporal lobe of the brain in a significant proportion of those examined. Other results suggested a possible functional lesion of the insula. Such biological lesions are thought to make the sufferer weak on central cohesion i.e. less able to see the bigger picture of events in life, and more likely to focus on small details. An obsessional focus on fine details related to food, weight and shape is characteristic of people with anorexia nervosa.

A proportion of sufferers of eating disorders have been found to be extremely sensitive to adrenaline, and therefore easily triggered into a heightened state of anxiety. Any stressful situation could put such people at risk of their illness becoming worse, or reappearing from a previously dormant state.

Psychological profiles, while not considered a cause of eating disorders, can help identify people who may be vulnerable to them. People who develop an eating disorder tend to be perfectionists, to have unrealistic ideals for themselves, to be overly self critical, and to have a high level of anxiety. Insecurity and lack of confidence are also common traits.

There are a wide variety of factors which can precipitate an eating disorder. Any kind of negative life event, such as abuse, neglect, bullying, or stress, can act as a trigger for the onset of the illness. Puberty has long been thought to be a precipitating factor, with not only the psychological response to bodily changes having an effect, but also the effects of hormonal changes on the brain. An initial 'sensible' diet may develop into an eating disorder, as may non-deliberate weight loss, for example after illness.

Once the eating disorder has become established, there are a number of perpetuating factors which can make recovery more difficult. The starvation syndrome itself tends to interfere with recovery programmes. Delayed emptying of the stomach, typical of starvation, causes a sensation of fullness, which may be interpreted as fatness by the sufferer. The changing of values, with food becoming the most salient stimulus, and a narrowing focus with avoidance of interpersonal interest, makes therapeutic intervention more difficult to establish. As the phobia of 'fat' increases, the related avoidance and obsessionality concerning it also increases. Similarly, body checking amplifies body image concern. Families with a high level of emotional expression may unwittingly delay the recovery of the sufferer, by over-protecting him or her from normal participation in life. Where medication is used to treat the condition, it has been found that depression when at very low weight rarely shows a positive response.

Today there are several different types of treatment for eating disorders. However the availability of these varies, according to the region and also the financial status of the sufferer and his or her family.

Hospitalisation is a possibility, but within the NHS this depends on the condition first being identified by a GP, and then a specialist referral being made. Usually only the most serious cases would be considered for hospital admission, while less serious cases may be offered out-patient treatment. For both options, the type of treatment available may be limited, due to the shortage of eating disorder specialists. In some cases this has led to patients being treated for depression, either on psychiatric wards or as out-patients, with no specialised help for eating disorders being given.

For males, this situation has been exacerbated in the past, with even fewer facilities available, owing to a rule according to which girls under the age of eighteen years are not allowed to occupy the same ward as men. This has resulted in some hospitals not being able to offer inpatient help to men, because of lack of ward space.

Doctors are now highlighting the shortage of help available to patients with eating disorders, and specialist eating disorder units are beginning to open in NHS hospitals. Until recently, people may have had to travel many miles to access specialist services, or pay for costly treatment in private centres.

Private centres specialising in the treatment of anorexia nervosa tend to focus on helping the patient to gain weight by strict supervision of food intake, with psychological support to help with the trauma that this necessarily involves. Drug treatment may be given to help the patient to tolerate weight gain. Patients are closely monitored to ensure that they do not avoid gaining weight by self-induced vomiting and purging, or by trying to burn off calories through exercise. In extreme cases, when a patient refuses to eat, feeding against consent, using a nasogastric tube, may be carried out. This requires the authority of a designated medical practitioner.

There are several types of psychological treatment available for help with eating disorders, such as private counselling or psychotherapy, which is usually on a one-to-one basis. Cognitive Behavioural Therapy is also used to treat eating disorders. The patient is helped to identify psychological reasons and triggers for unhealthy eating, and to devise alternative methods of coping. Problems and behaviours are broken down into component units to make their identification more manageable for the patient. However, within the NHS there are usually long waiting lists for this kind of treatment, due to a shortage of psychologists who are qualified to practice it. Family therapy and Cognitive Analytic Therapy are also used. Generally it has been found that continuity of treatment by an experienced specialist gives the most effective results in terms of long-term recovery.

Although it has been popularly thought that people with anorexia nervosa cannot gain weight until they have addressed the psychological roots of their difficulties, it has been found that, until a significant level of refeeding has been achieved, the sufferer is resistant to psychotherapeutic treatment. However, simply requiring a person with anorexia nervosa to gain weight against his or her will is unlikely to have any long term therapeutic effect, and the best results are achieved when the sufferer is personally motivated to seek help and pursue treatment. An adult cannot be obliged to have treatment for an eating disorder if they do not choose to do so, except if a medical practitioner deems compulsory detention under the Mental Health Act to be necessary in order to prevent deterioration and death.

Many more support groups are becoming available, through the internet and through the formation of local groups and organisations. Some websites, such as BEAT (Beat Eating Disorders, formerly the National Eating Disorders Association) offer excellent support and advice to sufferers seeking recovery, and to their helpers. Other websites, such as Pro Ana, provide sufferers with a means of contacting each other and sharing experiences, but actively encourage the pursuit of food control and losing weight. As such, they cannot be said to be offering any kind of support or impetus for recovery.

Some schools now recognise the need to address mental health issues, including eating disorders, and are providing 'safe places', where youngsters, who previously may have been afraid to speak out, can voice their concerns.

The concept of malnutrition as a factor in the development of anorexia nervosa did not emerge until around the 1980's, when scientists began to become aware of the similarities between the symptoms of zinc deficiency and anorexia nervosa. A deficiency of essential fatty acids was also thought to be linked to the anorexic condition. More recently, tryptophan, a neurotransmitter which helps control appetite and mood, has been identified as a possible factor, with evidence suggesting that anorexics and bulimics may be prone to tryptophan deficiency.

The interplay between nutrients and behaviour has become a fertile arena for research, not only in the field of mental illness, but also in other areas of concern such as delinquent and criminal behaviour, childhood ADHD, dyslexia and age-related memory decline.

This kind of research indicates that an effective treatment protocol for anorexia nervosa, and eating disorders in general, could include an optimum nutrition approach alongside skilled psychotherapy, emphasising the quality of food rather than the quantity, with the addition of supplements to ensure vitamin and mineral sufficiency.

A more detailed exploration of this topic with extensive references may be found at:
www.patrickhoford.com/100% Health/Eating Disorders

Recovery requires considerable effort, courage and determination on the part of the sufferer, and also from the carers and medical practitioners who are involved. Although full recovery is a real possibility, in many cases this is only partially achieved, or not achieved at all. When all things are considered, it is apparent that there is a huge community of people who are affected in one way or another by eating disorders. It is encouraging that there is increasing public recognition of this, and a growing concern to understand and treat these illnesses in effective ways.

Chapter One

How it all began

Alone. At home, with the Christmas Cake. All the family were out and she was left facing the monster that lurked in the larder. She had been playing with it all day, a gruesome game of desire and fear, the two forces equally matched and tearing her mind into writhing shreds. She knew exactly what would happen if she opened the cupboard.

The call of the cake ricocheted around in her tormented mind. Desperately she tried all manner of diversions. Add up the calories... How much would a slice cost?... Think of that nice skirt you want to wear that you can't do up... You would have to starve for days to get rid of the fat... The family would notice that you had eaten it, and I daresay they would be pleased to see you putting on a bit of weight... You could take a whole packet of laxatives afterwards and flush it out... Go and do something useful to take your mind off it. It was no use trying to take her mind off it. She knew the cake would triumph.

She crept towards the larder. Perhaps she could just take a few crumbs. That wouldn't be noticed, would it? She opened the door, ever so gently, and there it was, in all its rich sumptuous calorific glory. Bursting with moist dried fruits, laced with brandy, covered with lovely golden marzipan and topped with crunchy, sugary icing. Her heart beat rapidly as she gazed at it longingly. Will I, won't I, will I, wont I, will I, won't I? Holding her breath... Then... Can't bear it... help me... please, please, please God help me to stop. Will I... won't I... will I... won't I... will I... won't I... will I... won't I... willIwon'tIwillIwon'tIwillIwon'tIwillIwon'tIwillIwillIwillIwill. She knew the outcome was inevitable now.

Sniffing it, touching it, turning it round – what a heavenly

1

beauty it was. First a crumb, and the ecstatic wonder of its taste and texture. Then another crumb, and another, and then a small lump that had fallen off, followed by a very thin slice, a respectable slice, a huge slice and an even huger slice. She was feeling sick now. Another little piece, that will satisfy me, then I'll stop. But panic was rising. They would notice that she had eaten it. At least a third of the cake was gone and still she wanted more. Frantically she turned the cut side to the back. Maybe they wouldn't notice until tomorrow, she told herself. She could pretend she had put some out for the birds.

The disgust and shame rose like a swelling tide engulfing her whole being. Tricked again by the masquerading demon of the compulsion and her mind in total seizure, she tried desperately to blot everything out by grabbing at even more food – bread with slabs of butter and jam, biscuits, a lump of cheese, some stale sponge cakes...

At last, unable to stuff anything more into her stomach and feeling utterly revolting, she slammed the door of the larder and reeled into the sitting room, collapsing on the floor, overcome with despair and self loathing. She had done it again, and she had barely managed to diet off the last horrifying binge. Her stomach was bloated and full to bursting, and nausea enveloped her.

The pain and terror in her mind blotted out all awareness of self, all sense of reality. As she crumbled under the menacing flood of unbearable feelings, she craved oblivion. The years of suffering, without relief, weighed down, crushing her will to live. She dragged herself upstairs. There were a couple of full packets of paracetamol in the bathroom cupboard. If she took those along with her antidepressants and tranquillisers surely that would do the trick. But what would the family do, finding her lying there? Mum would be heartbroken. Will I go to heaven? she wondered. No, if I kill myself I will go to hell. It's a sin, isn't it?

There was a sound at the front door. The family was returning. She went and lay down on her bed.

2

This was a typical scenario in the history of my life's walk with anorexia nervosa – starving, dieting, bingeing, purging, while gripped by horror of my flesh and disgust with my body. There have been endless permutations of such events, with my ingenuity applied to a level of self-destructiveness that was surprising even to myself. It has been a lifetime of lonely desperation coupled with dismissive, uncomprehending attitudes towards the agony of my intense suffering – stretching day after day and year after year into the swirling mists of utter despair.

My mind has been tormented to the edges of insanity, and my personality stripped of all that clothed it as me. Yet I am still here to tell the tale, and as I look back down the road that I have travelled, I can see that all along it, Light has reached out to me and I have reached out to touch and absorb it. That is the only reason that I am still alive, somewhat sane and able to manifest something of my true self. When I say Light, I realise that I am only using a metaphor for something that is abstract and indefinable. It is a type of energy with a special quality, which comes through and makes itself known to me in an infinite variety of ways, for it is itself infinite. Sometimes I am so slow to perceive its presence that it is only in retrospect that I recognise it. In my life, the Light and the darkness are both part of the whole experience. They are not polarised but are woven together in a miraculous creation. Each one of us, and every living thing, is part of that creation.

*　*　*　*　*

I do not have very many clear memories of my childhood and early years of life. Those events which appear in my memory seem jumbled and non-linear, perhaps reflecting the bewilderment and confusion which has always been my essential inner experience. I think that for me, having to operate in a human body has never really made any sense. It feels all wrong – as if I have accidentally landed on the wrong planet.

It seems abhorrent to me that so much of life on earth is

3

based on eating or being eaten, or some other aspect of competition for survival. What kind of vile joke is this to which we are subjected? But then, even the stars 'eat' each other – when a powerful star with immense gravitational force comes within the range of a weaker star and begins to absorb its energy. Is this anthropomorphising the heavens perhaps, by seeing energy exchange in this way? Perhaps it could be seen as a co-operative merger, instead of aggressive consumption. In some conceptual frameworks the heavenly bodies are thought to have a consciousness, along with the idea that all that exists, from the infinitely small to the infinitely great, has awareness of some kind. Perhaps energy exchange is a given of existence itself, moving in paradox with a changeless state of pure being. Such philosophical and scientific concepts and explorations interest me greatly, but when in a state of tortured anorexic anguish they seem totally irrelevant.

It is difficult to write about my parents and family, in order to put over a picture of my life as I perceived it and experienced it, without doing injustice to the people concerned. I do not wish to excuse anyone from their choices and actions, least of all myself, as we are all fully responsible to ourselves and to each other. To try to make excuses prevents me from feeling the true force of what I experienced, and therefore prevents me from working through it fully – to a place of understanding and forgiveness of my mother and father.

In my opinion, forgiveness is a concept which is frequently much misunderstood. When I expressed pain and anger concerning my parents, I was often told to forgive them. What did this mean? I wondered in my heart. I tried hard, obedient as I was to the dogmas of certain belief systems, but I could never get rid of the wound, the shock, the rage and the anguish. It was no good saying to myself 'I forgive you' – these were only words, plastered like a band-aid over a mortal wound. I found that I had to be totally honest with myself about what I felt. Learning to hate was part of my salvation. Of course, I am not recommending hatred as a therapeutic tool or as an end in itself.

4

Yet if there is hate hidden in the soul, it must be brought to the Light in order for a transformational healing to take place and to become manifest in one's earthly life and personality.

In my early struggles with the concept and practice of forgiveness, I did not realise the power of thought forms, and I directed my hate vigorously towards its human focus. However, as I had some kind of religious framework in which to contextualise myself, I was also aware that this could somehow be part of a process of cleansing that would eventually clear the way for a realistic form of love to arise in my heart.

'What is love?' one may ask oneself. It is a word with such a very wide spectrum of interpretations, and is so often confused with need or desire. This is not to imply that need or desire cannot be the conveyance of love, but more that love, which has an abstract and eternal quality, is often incorrectly identified with need or desire, thus limiting its recognition. Love is so creative and infinite in its manifestation that it defies definition by the human mind, but it is recognised by the experience of the human heart – the heart which is intent on seeking it.

Later on in my life I could accept that while hatred must be experienced and given recognition, only love can transform the associated wound into a beautiful and powerful aspect of the whole being. There is a way of hating, but at the same time encapsulating the energy as something that is being worked upon, and redirecting it. I am still wrestling with true forgiveness. My understanding so far is that it has to reach to every part of my being – the sinews of my thoughts and attitudes, my emotions, the structure of my body, and the fabric of my life. Forgiveness is no easy work to accomplish on the earthly and spiritual journey!

As I proceeded along the tortuous road of facing up to myself and re-integrating forgotten parts of my humanity, I gradually became able to see my parents as human beings, just like myself, with their own baggage of wounds and struggles, conditioned as I am by the social milieu in which we existed side by side. Compassion and knowing began to seep through the tangled web of my relationships with them, and as it did so, started to set me free from the damaging image of myself that I had absorbed from them. This process is by no means complete, and will probably continue until the day I die. I hope that it does, for it brings life to my whole being, a life that will continue into other realms. Both my mother and my father have moved on to another level of existence now, and it has been my great privilege to assist each one to prepare for death in their own way, and to help them on their way with my prayers, thoughts and intercessions. Our relationships have continued to grow and change, and the healing process is still at work in the most wonderful and the most challenging ways.

*   *   *   *   *

To all outward appearances my childhood was very ordinary. There was nothing that would have been apparent to the casual onlooker that would have identified it as a breeding ground for anorexia nervosa. I had plenty of material advantages. We had a comfortable suburban house and good food, and I had nice clothes, pocket money, went to a good school, and had music lessons. Dad had a car – in the days when cars were much less of an everyday commodity – and although our family would not have been described as wealthy, in the financial climate of the time, by the time I was born, Dad had established himself in his profession as an accountant and had a good income.

Mum and Dad and my brother and sister all loved me, in their differing ways. So where did it come from, this monstrosity which grasped me in its terrible jaws and refused to let go, eating up my life with ravenous greed? I still do not think that I have found a definitive answer, but I do have certain clues and hypotheses. This is not strange, as anorexia nervosa is a disease of the whole person, body, mind, soul and spirit. It is not simply about dieting and a perilously low body weight, although alas it is often treated that way. Today the whole world suffers from severe imbalances in the availability and distribution of food, and attitudes towards its consumption, constituting an 'eating disorder' in its own right. Methods of food production can be exploitative of the earth's resources or of land rights, or of labour. Mass production and intensive farming or agriculture, coupled with excessive use of pesticides and herbicides, can rob food of its natural, health-giving energies. I believe that anorexia nervosa is one reflection of this current situation which relates not only to the eating of food but to the whole meaning and function of food. There are many others.

In reality my childhood was undergirded by constant fear and anxiety, and all my experiences and memories, even if not bad ones, are superimposed on that. From what I have picked up from family members, and what I have remembered in therapy, I didn't have a very good start in life, although I do not have any clear recollection of this. The relationship between my mother and father was very strained. They seemed to be such different people, and with such different agendas, that I often wondered what had drawn them to each other.

Mum was a gentle, compliant and loving person, given to self-sacrifice and meeting the needs of others. She came from a large, affectionate family and was apparently a bit of a tomboy at times in her youth, but also described herself as a 'good girl'. She was an intelligent and courageous woman, but unfortunately found very little outlet for this side of her nature. She was raised in an era of society where a woman's place was in the home, in the kitchen and with the children. This limiting and potentially degrading parameter of womanhood was certainly in part generated by religious attitudes of the time. By contrast, my father was an attractive, dynamic and very practical person, and though he worked hard to provide a decent living for us, his family, his emotional input was very negative in certain fundamental ways. His own upbringing had been rather harsh and devoid of gentleness, and he often described his own mother as a 'tyrant'. Within his family it seemed that there was little appreciation of anything 'feminine', and respect for women was in short supply. Perhaps his mother may have needed to be a 'tyrant', in an effort to uphold some measure of her dignity. Dad was selfish and irascible, critical and intolerant, and his cold hostile moods, which were mainly directed towards Mum, pervaded the atmosphere of the whole house. You couldn't get away from the heaviness. I lived in terror of these poisonous emanations, and felt helpless to comfort Mum in her despair and anxiety in the face of them.

A recent series of events which reawakened these feelings of being oppressed, invaded and degraded showed me how powerful the effect of Dad's attitudes and behaviour must have been on me, as a young child. The fear, constant anxiety and depression that I experienced in relation to these events was out of all proportion to the actual situation and to work through it all I had to face memories of the intimidation that my father had spread around him, and find ways to confront it in the present. This required a great deal of courage, effort and spiritual work.

For many years I feared my father, while at the same time yearning for his love and approval. I felt split in two by the strained dynamic between my parents, and it was a long time before I could begin to unify those polarised energies that I had absorbed. I used to see the situation as black and white, with him as the ogre and her as the suffering servant. Later on I came to see that it wasn't that simple by any means, and that it could be understood better as a kind of symbiotic pact, with each one using the shadow side of the other to give energy to an untransformed part of him or herself. I don't mean to imply that there was nothing of true love between them. However it lay hidden in the midst of the complex web of their visible and invisible relationship, as of course it does in all our human relationships.

No relationship is perfect. Perhaps the quality of a relationship springs from how truly each person knows themselves, as the more we have integrated the truth of ourselves, the more we truly love ourselves, and the more real love can shine through our relationships – including and blessing others as well. As I mentioned before, love is a difficult word. I have never really trusted it! Much of what we call 'love' is really need, projection, vicarious self-nurture or self-gratification. Yet for all that there is always authentic love hidden away in it somewhere, even if it is only its seeds.

With modern technology, it has become possible to understand much more of the life of the foetus in the womb. The developing human being is by no means insensitive to the emotional environment provided by its parents. And when does the incoming soul take up residence in the little body? Perhaps that varies with the individual in question. In any case, awareness definitely comes about at an early stage of the developing child, as can be seen by the wonderful *in utero* photography that is now available to us. When I was beginning to explore my anorexic illness in depth, this was a fairly new concept, and it was with some dubiety that I undertook primal therapy with the pioneering Dr Frank Lake. Several years of this kind of therapy, alongside my mother's sharing of her feelings concerning my conception and birth, helped me to piece together some kind of picture of my earliest beginning. How accurate it is I cannot say, but the most important aspect of it is that it formed for me the basis of an interpretation of my illness.

I was a late-comer to my parents' marriage. My brother and sister had been around for some while before I arrived, being respectively seventeen years and fifteen years older than I. They were of a different generation, and in many ways felt like an uncle and aunt, the age gap was so large. The Second World War had a profound effect on the everyday life of ordinary people, not least for my mother and father when my father was called up to go and fight. The parting was painful for them, as it must have been for so many couples – perhaps harder in some ways for the one left behind, not knowing if they would see their spouse again. My father was posted to Germany and Mum was left at home to cope with her two children and the repercussions of the war.

When the war ended – four years before I was born – and my father was demobbed, he returned to her a changed person. She was so looking forward to having him back, and so longing to be with him again, but he showed no sexual interest in her and was almost completely withdrawn from her. What dreadful anguish this must have caused her. At first she thought that it must be due to the stress of the war and all that he had gone through, but he later told her that he had met a German woman with whom he had fallen in love, and had had a child with her. My mother confided this to me when I was only about eight years old. Her grief was heavy on my young shoulders, but it was better to know than not to know.

Mum was constantly afraid that Dad would leave her and return to live in Germany with his lover. She did not often speak of this fear, but as I was very close to her as a child, I was aware of it as an undercurrent that affected the whole of our family's life. Although it must have been primarily the loss of my father that was the focus of her fear, there were other, more practical matters that must have been a source of great anxiety for her. In the era in which I grew up, employment for women was much more limited in scope than it is now. Questions about how she would earn a living, care for three children, and run a home single-handed if Dad left must have troubled her greatly.

It was a long time before I began to understand Dad's side of the story. Not until he was in his eighties and I in my forties was I able to make a space in my being to listen to his tale without judgement and anger. Up until then I had always felt the whole sad tangle that was meant to be a marriage was his fault. I have borne the weight of my parents' anger and sorrow for as long as I can remember, with an urgent insistence in my heart that somehow I must make it better for them. I suppose that the whole situation impacted so heavily on me because of my sensitive nature and perceptiveness, and because I was too young to have formed a sense of self that would have protected me from absorbing it all so profoundly. My parents were members of the Anglican Church, and in those days, illegitimate birth, adultery, divorce and such-like were much less commonplace than they are today. Certainly there seemed to be more guilt and shame around such matters, and they were generally not talked about.

My parents stayed together under one roof, but it seems to me that when the marriage of the heart broke down, they grew apart, each becoming more polarised in their personality roles. However, one cannot see everything that is hidden in the human heart nor the pathway of the soul. Perhaps they had something to work out together, on this earth, in this lifetime, and that in the mysteries of incarnation, the urge of love to perfect its manifestation was the force that kept them together.

Into this maelstrom of strife and unhappiness, I was born. I gathered that my conception was not the planned result of a joyful union, but that it resulted from my mother's pleading and my father's unwilling and resentful acquiescence. Apparently there was little of tenderness and communication but more a case of raw need. I still have the sad letter in which my mother confided this fiasco to me. Birth control was not widely used at that time and what unwelcome news it was when she found she was pregnant. She was alarmed and my father was angry. There were angry arguments, and abortion was considered. I have often wondered about the true nature of my mother's feelings about this. During the course of therapy, I gradually became aware of a confusing mixture of violent rage and utter desperation which seemed to be located somewhere in my abdomen. Could this have been an internalisation of my mother's emotions? Did she hate and resent the child growing inside her, as a living demonstration of her overwhelming need of my father's love, which he continued to deny her? Did her maternal instinct insist that she carry and bear the new life entrusted to her body? Whatever her feelings were, they must have given rise to a powerful conflict in her mind and heart. The family GP dissuaded my mother from having an abortion and gave her some pills instead, which were probably tranquillisers. Surely there must be a link between this and the repeated overdoses that I took in my early adulthood.

These troubled beginnings are the source of my sense of always being unwanted, feeling that I have no right to live and that I am nothing but an ugly nuisance – my body a shameful and disgusting blot on the copybook of human existence, my flesh a horrifying growth on my skeleton. I felt that I was not a valid person, but only existed as an extension of others, to serve their need of me, whatever that was. I had no shape. There was only one redeeming element. Many years later my mother told me that at the moment of her orgasm during my conception, she had had a vision of the gates of heaven opening and a great white angel swooping into her womb. Well, the heavenly stork brought her a bundle of trouble, but she said at times that if she hadn't had me to care for she would have gone mad. I nearly went mad instead.

As far back as I can remember I always felt odd – big and clumsy, trying to pack myself into a body that just didn't fit. It felt tight at the seams, and I felt I was gasping for air. At the age of about four years I developed bronchial asthma, and was often ill, wheezing and gasping for breath. I could not join in the vigorous activity of other children, for if I over-exerted myself with running, climbing or sometimes even walking too fast, I went blue in the face, wheezing and fighting against the tightness in my chest. I remember asking my mother, 'Mummy why are those children running?' – not understanding how anyone could run just for the joy of it. My impressions are that this condition was a discomfort to my parents. My mother seemed very anxious and over-protective towards me, and my father irritable and annoyed by my constant illness. Once again my body seemed to be causing upset and difficulty between my parents. I didn't like school and was only too pleased not to have to go because of my illness, and my father was angry when Mum kept me at home. A doctor whom I did not like would come to the house and sound my chest with his horrible cold stethoscope, and even then I felt embarrassed at having my flesh exposed. Usually some foul tasting medicine was prescribed. I have no idea what it contained, but it was red, syrupy and sickly, and I was often bribed to take it – with a two shilling piece or some other gift. Thus I learned that being ill and dependent brought me reward, and this, coupled with a lack of affirmation in other important areas of life, became a detrimental pattern that lay hidden in my unconscious mind for many years. It had a devastating and far-reaching effect in my adult life, and it was only with a great deal of anguish and regret that I was able to confront it and integrate it into my conscious awareness.

I was a lonely child, ill at ease with other children and frightened of adults, bewildered and alarmed by the world that I found I was obliged to live in. It seemed all wrong somehow, so confusing, and I could never work out what I was supposed to do to make it go right. I felt that I was in some kind of peculiar dramatic production and did not know my part. It was as if I had forgotten my lines and could not work out where to put myself. I was often ostracised and victimised by other children, as I was no good at standing up for myself, and I tended to make friends with other girls who were not part of the in-crowd. I was very fearful of boys, and did not know how to relate to them. I soon learned that it was safer to keep my thoughts and feelings hidden. I was also a child who could never take things lightly. Watching television became hazardous, and often I would go out of the room to find a quiet corner where I could try to cope with the anguish and fear that the images and sounds evoked. Those images and sounds would take root in my brain, and reappear to torment me at unexpected moments. Books, magazines and newspapers carried similar hidden dangers, and even now I have to be extremely careful of the material that I allow to enter my mind. In fact this is not a bad thing, for so much of that which is offered to the general public, including children, is pervaded with pernicious attitudes of competition, violence, greed, self-gratification, hostility and the like, or is pure junk – concealing the promulgation of current dogmas and social attitudes. I was terrified of the dark and could see 'eyes' looking at me from dark corners, something lying in wait at the top of the stairs, and a foreboding presence standing behind me. This latter state went on until my early thirties, its occurrence causing a barely contained panic, prickling at the back of my neck. I never did discover entirely what it was, but a clairvoyant friend once said that she saw it, a strange being with large ears.

I felt isolated in my family. There were not many people coming and going, just occasional visits from relatives or friends of Mum and Dad, and apart from my cousins, whom I saw only rarely, they were all adults. I clung to my mother as my main companion and she clung to me, no doubt for comfort. I was quiet and inward, very shy and fearful of situations outside of the 'security' of the family. As time went on I became more silent, and my diary became my confidante. I had no one but myself with whom to share the secret agonies and longings, and the pages were like a confessional, a listener who reflected me back to myself without judgement. I always felt old, unconsciously carrying the family's stress and unhappiness upon my shoulders, and attuned to a wider suffering of which I had no understanding at the time. My private thoughts were my refuge, and my belief in something beyond myself that was called 'God' was both my hope and my despair. I always felt a sense of being torn in different ways within my family. For example, I wanted to help Mum and make her happy, and lighten the burden that she seemed to carry. When I left home, to go to university and thereafter to join a community, I felt a sense of tearing and guilt every time I came and went from the family home. When I go to visit my sister who continues to live in the family home, I still experience that same feeling, although it is easier to recognise and deal with now. I can still feel, for a while, that I ought to be there, trying to make life better for her, trying to make things work right.

Food was a major preoccupation in Mum's life, both cooking it and eating it. Her life seemed to be centred on the kitchen, and although she often expressed the wish that she didn't have to cook, she couldn't seem to break free from it. It had a hold over her in some way. She was a good cook and made excellent meals, although she was always worrying about what food to prepare at each mealtime. I think that she was forever trying to please Dad with food, maybe as a way to win back his love.

When my grandfather on my father's side was very old he came to stay with us for two weeks at a time, alternating with my aunt, who lived close by. That was another worry for Mum, another mouth to please. She would feed everyone the food that they liked, when they wanted it – first Grandad and me, then my sister when she came in, and then my father when he came in. She always put herself last and ate when she could fit it in, which was usually with me. She liked her food and was quite well built, but not very much overweight, just a bit on the plump side. Mealtimes were not happy affairs and I remember them with great distress. Even now I absolutely hate and avoid sitting at a table with other people and eating food. Dad did not like sitting with the rest of us, and he preferred to sit in his own armchair with his food on his side table. When he did sit at the main table the atmosphere was no better. He was locked inside himself, unable and unwilling to open his heart to his wife and daughters, seeming aloof or overbearing with his likes and dislikes, his opinions and attitudes. He was never to my knowledge able to admit that he was wrong about anything, and apologise. If he did not like the food, Mum was unhappy and anxious. I don't know what it was like when my brother was still living at home. I have no memories of meals with him except when he and his own family descended on a Sunday for tea. It seemed that he was the only one that Dad was prepared to relate to, person to person – being another man, I suppose. I used to excuse myself early from the table and run down to the church to practise the organ. I forced myself to run all the way, trying to burn off the food that I had just eaten.

I spent a lot of time in the kitchen with Mum, helping her to prepare meals, and I know she wanted my company in this task of hers. We worked well together and I learned a lot about cooking. I liked food preparation and I think that I became fairly good at it. I loved making gorgeous cakes and decorating them, and experimenting with new recipes. At first I would allow myself a small sample of what I had created, but as my illness progressed, I concocted more and more magnificent delicacies for my family or other people to eat. None of it passed my lips and I only gazed at these creations, with longing and lust. I collected piles and piles of recipes, which I cut out from magazines, and I had a special file where I kept them. I spent ages perusing them, deciding what to make. Poor Mum worried about the expense of the ingredients of my culinary adventures, and dreaded having to ask Dad for more housekeeping money. As the breadwinner, he held the purse strings and gave Mum an allowance. She had to ask if she wanted anything extra, for me or for herself. Why did she allow herself to be put in such a powerless position? It had a profound effect upon my perception of womanhood.

I always wanted to be with Mum by myself, so that I didn't have to share her. Our family did not seem to be able to operate as a group: it was a collection of dysfunctional one-to-one relationships. It is difficult to know what kind of love I had for Mum, as when I started to eat compulsively, what I thought was love turned into a violent hate. On one hand, I have positive memories of being with her – going for walks together, shopping, sitting on her knee and talking, her comforting presence when I was ill or upset, her kindness and her laughter. I can't remember her ever saying 'no' to me, and the only time she became angry with me she apologised profusely, afraid I suppose, of losing my love and affection. However this was not altogether a good influence on my self-development. It led to a confusion of boundaries between her and me, so that I did not know where she ended and I began, and vice versa. I could not define myself in relationship to her, as she was too pliable, like dough that I could mould. I think that I was very manipulative in a subtle sort of way, which only served to reinforce my deep sense of not really being a person. Since I had no sense of self, this meant that I also could be manipulated, and ended up with the subconscious image of myself as an amorphous substance, that could be shaped into whatever another person desired. A complex battle of wills emerged between my mother and myself, rarely overt, and was usually effected by the transfer of guilt and reproach, or tears and unhappiness from one to the other. I feel very sad about the way in which I related to my mother. I know that my anorexia and the attitudes and behaviour which this generated hurt her deeply. Yes, she hurt and wounded me, albeit unknowingly, so that I was effectively crippled, but that does not make it all right. Although she died some years ago, our relationship still needs more healing.

On the other side of the coin I felt that Dad was lonely, and I tried to keep him company. I think that when I was a baby he was not at all interested in me and had little to do with me. The announcement of my conception had drawn no expression of joy from him, and there had been no welcome from him when I arrived in the world. When I was older and could help him and talk to him, he seemed to like me to be with him. I used to try to help him in whatever he was doing – decorating, fixing the car, or doing woodwork in his shed. He loved his shed and would disappear in there regularly, occupied with his projects and his own company. He was very good at DIY, and maintained the house and garden pretty much by his own initiative and skill. I wish that he had taught me more of his skills, but he was impatient and would rather do something himself than spend time teaching me how to do it. However I did pick up a few useful bits of knowledge as I watched and helped, passing this and that, holding things for him, running off to get something, and listening to him talking about what he was doing. He was probably talking to himself rather than to me, but at least it was some sort of communication. He often got very bad tempered if something didn't go right, and then his mood would waft through the whole family domain like a noxious vapour. I was so distressed by these moods: I tried to pacify Dad and absorb the anger, and prayed to God in my young mind to make it better. I loved Dad, and longed for him to recognise me as a person in my own right and to give me the affirmation and love that I craved. But my perception of myself in relation to him developed as that of an appendage, someone who was there conditionally, in order to make it better, whatever 'it' was.

In contrast to my relationship with Mum, I could find no inner connection with Dad, whereas with her, I could find no distinction. This conflict was embedded as a powerful polarisation in the structure of my personality. The approach/avoidance dynamic it created tore my mind to shreds as frantically I wove all sorts of complex thought patterns and compulsions to try to contain it. As the opposing drives fought with each other within my being, the intensity of each one grew stronger and stronger, until suddenly all would go dark and my self descended into an unfathomable blackness where my awareness was in total seizure. I will never know how I brought myself out of these unspeakable tortures, or indeed what brought me, for I don't think that I could have done it alone. Countless times, over and over again, a shaft of Light would reach down into my soul and revive me. There was never any pattern to it, and there still is not, as it does still happen from time to time. I could never follow a 'recovery routine' of any kind, devised either by myself or anyone else. The manifestation of divine Light is infinite in its precision, its beauty, and its effectiveness, as it reaches through to me in my life.

Until I was eleven years old, I only had one close friend of my own age – a very pretty and popular girl called Lillian. Beside her I always felt ugly, big and clumsy, and my clothes never felt right. They still do not feel right. We had some fun times together, but she could be very cruel, poking fun at me and deliberately excluding me from the circle of friends which she so readily drew around herself. I was always jealous of her other friends, and because I was so uncertain of myself and so sensitive, I was unable to mix with the general rough-and-tumble of childhood peer relationships. I will never believe that children are 'innocent' – whatever that is supposed to mean – in terms of behaviour. I think that they know very well what they are doing. Does awareness start from the cradle, I wonder? No doubt with my whining, endless fears and pestering I tested even my mother's patience. I still remember the pain of her once saying 'I wish you were like Lillian.' I too, wished I was like Lillian. How much, my mother would have never guessed. In my eyes Lillian was the gracious and beautiful fairy, and I the fat, ugly idiot.

Longing to be wanted was an abiding script in my life from as long as I can remember, and it still is, although now I am less willing to compromise my true nature for the dubious privilege of general social acceptance. I rarely did anything naughty, for I was so dependent on others' good opinion of me. I was afraid of upsetting my mother and afraid of my father's cold withdrawal and sour temper. At school I was always a 'good girl', eager to please the teachers and to do well in class. Words can be very formative in a child's life. I remember the anguish and shame of being called to the front of the class and told that I was stupid because I had made a silly spelling mistake. It only confirmed what I already believed.

I don't remember much about my brother in my early life. Being so much older than I he was like another adult in my life, an uncle, or even another father. My mother and sister told me that he was very fond of me and was the only one who could get me to sleep when I was fractious and wakeful. Mum told me that I cried a lot and that she used to get desperate. I can understand that. I hate the sound of babies and children crying, and instead of feeling sympathetic towards them, I feel angry. I wonder if she felt angry, and was afraid to admit it to herself. But this wailing creature, whom she hadn't really wanted, born of anger and desperation, making life difficult, was me.

My brother was lucky; he escaped the distaste and despising of femininity that emanated from my father's line. He left home to join the army when I was three years old, and I think that I must have missed him very much. Too young to understand why he had disappeared, I felt that he – the only warm and affirming male presence in my life – had abandoned me. In some ways, he must have felt like a second father, supplying the kind of demonstrative love that I needed so badly. My mother also must have missed him when he left home, as his absence would have intensified the effects of the rift between her and my father. This must served to increase her unhappiness, and her need of me as a focus of her attention. While in the army my brother met his future wife, and when he had finished his service they were married. I have a vague memory of being a bridesmaid, all dressed up in an uncomfortable dress, but the overriding impression was one of loss. The brother I had known as a comforting presence in my life had gone forever. Although he and his wife lived close by and visited us regularly, it was never the same. This sense of amputation pervaded all my relationships with men, until I began to recognise the projection of my infant search for my long lost brother.

Contrasted with this, my sister has always been a constant presence in my life. I believe that she looked after me quite a bit when I was growing up, and perhaps I perceived her as a second mum in some ways. In fact my mother told me that she had not really wanted Sylvia to go out to work, so that she could stay at home and help to look after me. Luckily for Sylvia my father thought otherwise and insisted that she get a job at the Crown Agents, where she was employed for the duration of her working life. She may have wanted to stay at home with Mum and me but then her life would have been even more limited than it already was by the family environment. She never has shared many of her feelings about having a baby sister come into her life, just when she was growing into the teenage years and needed support and encouragement herself. Surely she must have experienced some measure of jealousy. She has always been very kind to me, though, even if a little possessive at times. I can sympathise now: it must have been hard for her. She was born with a slight deformity, which today could have been treated much more effectively, but at the time I think it gave Mum a reason to over-protect her, as well as me, and in so doing, robbed my sister of self-confidence and kept her close to home all her life. She was always second in line to my brother, who commanded more attention when they were children, and then just as he was growing up and spreading his wings, I came along. She later shared with me that she had always longed for times when she could have Mum all to herself.

Perhaps in some way having me around was a distraction to the family dynamic, and at least gave my sister some form of companionship. We had to share a bedroom, and as I grew up I found this suffocating. I wanted my own space and privacy so badly, but there was only the small room next to our bedroom which was unoccupied, and this had to be kept for my grandfather when he was staying with us. This had a profound effect on me, and I still cannot bear to share my living space with anyone at all.

Sylvia used to take me out, play with me and buy me things, and I have happy memories of going with her to Gilbert and Sullivan operas at the Savoy Theatre, and sharing our pleasure of the music and seeing our favourite performers. However there was tension between us as I grew up and wanted to expand my self. We are very different people, my sister and I, in looks and in character, and our relationship has not always been easy. I do not know fully what effect my anorexia had upon her life, but it must have caused difficulties and unhappiness for her. She is not one to share thoughts and feelings readily, and it is a difficult subject to broach. However, since our mum died, we have become closer and more understanding of each other, more able to accept each other as we are and support each other in our differing lives. I am so grateful for this flow of healing and creative energy into our troubled family, and I hope that it may continue for the rest of our lives.

* * * * *

As I grew up and entered puberty, the world became an even more frightening and confusing place. I could not relate to the world of pop music, discos and boyfriends in which my peers seemed so immersed. I was brought up on classical music, and Sunday afternoons were often spent listening to opera on the gramophone, a great big old thing which could be temperamental, with its playing arm and needles. I was afraid of boys and did not know how to behave with them, nor did I know what was expected of me. Somehow I felt I *ought* to know but was afraid to ask. My emerging sexuality seemed to be an embarrassment to everybody at home, most of all to myself. Seeing my breasts and pubic hair forming was a source of guilty fascination and alarm that my body was doing its own thing and I couldn't control it. My first menstrual period arrived at the age of eleven years and felt to me to be a surreptitious and dirty event. I absolutely hated periods, from the time they commenced until the time they ceased. The inconvenience, the smell, the embarrassment, and above all the agony, made me very angry. I resented having to go through this encumbrance of womanhood every month. We never talked about sex in our home, and there was never any sign of affection between Mum and Dad, other than the statutory kiss on the cheek.

Unsurprisingly, boys were not attracted to me, and even though I tried hard to connect with them, I found that I managed to put each one off after an initial meeting. Anyway, I didn't really much like the ones I met and neither did I like sexual experimenting, although I felt I ought to. It seemed to be something my body knew how to do, but my heart was not in it, and secretly I found it boring and dirty. Afterwards I felt disgusting and wanted to cleanse myself – as if sexual contact with the boy had been an intrusion, and had polluted me. My first kiss was on a holiday in the Isle of Man with my best friend from senior school. After the boy had gone, I swilled my mouth out with Dettol several times to try to get rid of the sense of shame and uncleanness.

With the development of my breasts and female figure, my

body certainly felt out of control. On one hand there was a sense of covert narcissism, but on the other there was a growing feeling of shame and alarm. It wasn't too long before I decided I was too fat and started dieting. I was about thirteen at the time. I was good at dieting – at last it felt that I had found something in which I could excel and achieve results. The feeling of elation and lightness as the pounds began to drop away from my body was unlike anything I have ever experienced, and that continues to the present day. It was really the only thing that 'turned me on'. The experience of sexual orgasm is pale and insignificant in comparison! Thus I began the long and gruelling torment of anorexia nervosa and had I known that it would continue until the present day, I would probably have ended my life at that time. Sometimes it is merciful that the future is not known to us.

I passed what was then known as the Eleven Plus Examination, and went to Rosebery County Grammar School for Girls. It was a lovely school, in beautiful grounds, and the headmistress was a kind but strict woman, whose parents had been missionaries. There were rigid rules about uniform, and everything had to be 'regulation' clothing, bought from certain shops – from the boater hats to the green knickers and the sensible shoes. I admired the older girls who looked so grown up and slim in their uniform with a belt drawn tight round a narrow waist. I was determined to get my waist that slim, so I could put a belt round it and show it off. My best friend from the junior school did not pass the Eleven Plus so she went to a different senior school, and I missed her.

I was very scared and lonely on my first day at Rosebery. All I could see when I went into the classroom were rows of desks with girls sitting at them, all talking to each other. I dived into the nearest desk and made it my little home, trying to manufacture a shred of security for myself. I was afraid of most of the teachers and most of the pupils. I certainly wasn't popular, and my strangeness and inability to compete in the hurly-burly of school relationships often made me an object of cruel jibes and derision. Groups of girls are frequently expert in such skills. Eventually I managed to make a few acquaintanceships, usually with girls who were a bit different and therefore not part of the in-crowd, but I never found it easy to get on with my peers.

I had one 'best friend' who was somewhat troubled and a bit overweight, but I think that I was too possessive in my friendships and just wanted the person all to myself. I didn't like my 'best friend' mixing in with others, especially not the in-crowd, as I was unable to do so myself and always felt left out. I think that my friend turned to me because I was sympathetic and understanding and tried to help her, but she frequently ditched me for others whom she found more interesting. I never felt wanted as a friend, unless it was to help someone with their homework. I was devoted to homework and to trying to be top of the class, always eager to please and to do well at whatever earned admiration and praise. However, I was useless at sports, partly because of my breathing difficulties and also because I was unable to assert myself sufficiently to be part of a team and compete with others. I was always the last choice, or reserve, when the captains chose their team for netball or lacrosse. It was very much a traditional sports-orientated school, and if you were good at sports you were popular. Everyone had crushes on the team captains. I am sorry now that I didn't take part in any extra-curricular activities as there were plenty of them, in a variety of areas of interest. I was always eager to get home and be with Mum, somehow drawn irresistibly into the vacuum that was at the centre of our domestic environment. At home I studied piano, clarinet and organ in my spare time, and had very little social life except for occasional activities at the church such as youth club, which I didn't like very much. I was a Girl Guide for a time but didn't like that either. It was too regimented and seemed like more of the same thing, working for badges and trying to please the guide captain or the patrol leader.

* * * * *

When I was fourteen, I had to have some complex orthodontic treatment. My teeth have always been problematic which perhaps bears a significant relationship to all the emotional trauma I have had that is connected with my mouth and food.

After my first experience of old-fashioned dental surgery at the age of eight, I had developed a strong phobia of dentists. Although I went regularly, I felt weak at the knees at the thought of an appointment and wept when it was time to go. However, the dentist who was treating me at the time was a pleasant and kind man who wanted me to have an appointment with a colleague of his, Mr Wilson, who was a consultant in Harley Street – well known at the time for high-class and fashionable treatment. I was intrigued by this and agreed to go. Amazingly, it was all paid for by the National Health Service!

I went up to Harley Street with my mother for the appointment. It seemed a funny old place to me. The waiting room had chintz hangings on the walls and you had to go up by lift to the dental surgery. When the nurse came to call me for the appointment, I went up with her alone, with much trepidation. However I was completely taken aback by my first meeting with the orthodontist. He was a charming, softly spoken, white haired man, with a gentle, teasing manner which initially unnerved me. I was unaccustomed to this kind of personal relating from a male, and was uncertain as how to respond. I was astonished that he seemed to regard me as a person in my own right, and it felt almost as if I had been 'seen' for the very first time. I was both terrified and eager for more. Mr Wilson must have perceived something of this, for after a while, having x-rayed and examined my teeth, he gave me a canny look and said 'You don't trust me and inch, do you?' I said 'no', and he laughed. This was the beginning of a six-year relationship with Mr Wilson, which, though it was based on dental treatment, helped me to see the possibility of something different in terms of who I perceived myself to be. It helped me to flower a little and to begin to interpret my female identity in a way that offered me something other than the family identity stamp.

I have no idea what sort of life Mr Wilson lived other than as a dentist, but in a sense that didn't matter at the time. He was real enough to be something other than just a fantasy. He was a real person – who was reaching out to me. As I was writing this account, I became fascinated by the memory, and rooted around in my large collection of diaries to see if I could find the entry relating to it. I did find it, and read it eagerly, as if it were a compelling novel. The experience was as fresh and wonderful in my heart and mind as if it had only happened yesterday. I remembered how, as an adolescent, I went over and over the component events of this meeting, as if to extract every drop of precious nourishment from it. I wished that I could see Mr Wilson again to thank him for what he did for me, not just for my teeth but for my hungry soul. Maybe he is not in this world any more, as our meetings took place over forty years ago, but I am eternally grateful to him.

As my school years progressed I became thinner and thinner, until at the time of my A-levels I was withdrawn, isolated and a miserable walking skeleton. My menstruation had stopped, and did not return for at least seven years. In the years that followed, it stopped and started several times, often ceasing for up to two years. There was no one whom I could trust, no one who could really help. I was sent along to my GP because my periods had stopped, but she only dosed me with hormones, which made me feel bloated and fat, so I didn't continue taking them. At some point in this era of my illness, family therapy was suggested by the GP. My mother was keen to try this, but my father refused to co-operate.

My family were understandably anxious about my weight loss, but they also seemed embarrassed by it. 'What will people think' and 'you're worrying us', were the kind of comments that I received. It was only that, comments, not real questioning about what was going on inside me. Even that dreaded proclamation of 'we like you with a bit of weight on you', which is horror to an anorexic's ears, came my way now and then. Of course none of this kind of approach did anything to convince me that anyone wished to reach out to me or understand the emotional and physical agony that racked my whole being. It only served to emphasise that I was supposed to exist simply as what they wanted me to be, and as long as I weighed a certain number of pounds, they felt comfortable. Nothing else mattered to them. Needless to say, I dieted even more rigorously and was secretly proud of my triumph over my body. At least it proved that my body was mine, and I could do what I liked with it. This was my last-ditch stand.

* * * * *

During the years at Rosebery Grammar School, I met another girl who seemed to be something of misfit. She, too, was not part of the in-crowd and her ways seemed different from most of the other girls. I liked her, and we gradually became friends. She had a shock of red hair that always looked untidy, and her uniform often did not conform to the required smart appearance. This wasn't in deliberate defiance, but was just the way she was, a natural, unconventional girl. Her home was in the country, and I think she lived with an aunt during term time. By and by she invited me to go to stay with her for a weekend at her family home in Pulborough. Although I was timid of doing new things, I accepted. It was a lovely place, right out in the countryside, and had the feel of a farmhouse about it. She had three brothers quite a bit older than herself, of whom two had left home. The remaining brother, Robert, was something of a drop-out. He had left university without finishing his studies, as he did not enjoy the course, and was living at home. He was interested in photography and gave me an old single-lens reflex camera to use, teaching me how it worked and how to take good photos. I really liked this personal attention. Robert was an unusual

27

young man, and I was fascinated by his controversial ideas and thoughts. He decided he wanted to take my photo, and set up his studio room with lights and camera, asking me to pose for him. Well, I was hooked from that time on! At other times we would all go for walks in the country. The family gave me huge old trousers to wear, which I tied on with a belt or two, feeling that I was like Cinderella, living a fairy tale with my prince, so lovely was the experience. Once on a steep incline, Robert took my hand to haul me up to the top. Oh, the magic of the touch! It was all so new to me – so different from the life I lived at home.

Robert became the object of my fantasies. Yet it was almost a foregone conclusion that sooner or later, reality would intrude upon this rosy world and send me crashing into depression. My anorexia and compulsive food behaviour were gripping tighter. Even at Pulborough I could not resist the urge to eat secretly and to steal food. Robert was a good baker and used to make the most delicious bread with a wonderful, compelling aroma, which he would leave in the kitchen to cool. I could not help but creep in there and steal crumbs, and even a slice or two if it had been already cut. The shame was unbearable. I said that I was ill, and had to be taken home. It was the beginning of the end with Robert, or rather with the imagined Robert, as he had never really returned my affections. He probably did not know how to handle the situation, as he was a confused person himself, ill at ease with his identity. I remember well the Christmas when I realised once and for all that there was no future in the relationship. He had been ignoring my letters, or just writing non-committal, non-personal half-pages of sentences devoid of deeper meaning.

Unable to bear the pain of the rejection of my first love, it was as if my whole personality turned inside out, and from anorexia I went into a cycle of compulsive eating and bulimia. I suppose it saved my life in one way, as at the time I was so thin that any more weight loss would have endangered my life, but in another way it was life-threatening in its own right, for I was so depressed, disgusted and horrified by the uncontrollable gain in weight that I started taking overdoses of medication.

The Edges of Insanity

The windows of my trembling mind
Closed tight
Against the outer darkness,
And cringed within
Self's twisted form
Lies bound and bleeding in the night.

The heavens are as gates of brass,
Shut against my cry.
Impervious on celestial throne
God reigns omnipotent, alone,
My punishment pronounced, to live,
Yet sentenced me to die.

To beg for mercy and entreat,
I plead without excuse;
No bail or bargain can I make,
For nothing do I own,
Not even me –
The court's decree
My petition to refuse.

And so within my cell I lie,
As one discarded from the race
Of beings who inhabit light
And still have means of grace.
Tormented to the edges
Where life and death converge,
And tear their victim soul from limb,
Until a spectre, foul and grim,
Shall gradually emerge.

Myself a horror to myself,
Now I have become,
The stench of my own vapours
Rise as dark perfume,
In never fading incense
To the one who, at my cry,
Upon me spoke this sentence,
'Condemned to live and die.'

Jacqueline Kemp

Chapter Two

University

It was such a lonely place. She gazed longingly at the lighted windows as she made her way back to the university halls of residence, searching for something that looked homely and comforting. She missed Mum so much. It was horrible having to leave her after going home for the weekend.

She went home every weekend, in her car, which had been bought for her specifically for that purpose. At home she slotted straight back into the family routines of helping with meals, helping Dad, going shopping, watching TV, and enduring the family Sunday tea to which her brother and his family also came. She tried to appear grown up and clever, working hard and studying, preparing for a career doing Something Important, but underneath, the emptiness was always there, alongside the gnawing agony of feeling so ugly, so fat, so stupid, and the non-stop craving that was tearing at her mind.

She made her way up to her study bedroom in St George's Hall. It was a nice room, so much better than the ghastly place she had been in before, sharing a room with a girl who had made fun of her and who stole her food. She had her own fridge in her room now. She had had to get special permission for it. In it she kept her food – food that was safe and wouldn't make her fat, not like those disgusting starchy meals served in the hall canteen. She passed the communal kitchen on her way to her room. Cold food was delivered there in the late afternoon at the weekend, in place of a canteen meal. What a mess the place was in, as usual. She stopped and tentatively looked in. She knew she shouldn't, as she might be tempted, but her eyes were pulled in the direction of the basket. Oh no! There was some food left, some bread and a few little butter pats, some individual jams, a piece of cheese and some biscuits. She fled down the corridor to her room, frantically unlocked the door, dived inside and slammed the door shut.

Trying to unpack her bag and get organised, all she could think of was that bread and butter in the kitchen. After an hour or so of struggling pathetically in the vice-like grip of the drive to go back there, she lost the fight and tiptoed down the corridor. No one about, so no one would see her taking it. Furtively she snatched the bread, the butter, the cheese, the remaining biscuits and whatever else was there and put it all in her bag, walking hastily back to her room, trying to look nonchalant, as if she were just coming back from the bathrooms – which were next door to the kitchen.

Safely inside her room, she locked the door and buttered the bread with shaking hands. Can't be bothered with a plate, takes too long. Smothering the bread with jam she sank her teeth into it and chewed ecstatically. Another piece and another, then the cheese, followed by the biscuits. Her panic was escalating and the craving was roaring inside her head, MORE MORE MOREMOREMOREMORE! I WANT MORE!

There was nothing left in the kitchen; she had scoured it even for crumbs. You've got to stop, she told herself over and over again. The craving would not take no for an answer. Desperately she threw on her coat, and grabbing her purse and a bag, went out into the darkness. Thank goodness it was getting dark early now. She hoped and prayed that no one would see her. She hurried down to the shops on the Green. 'I hope they aren't closed, please don't let them be closed,' she muttered to herself. Ah, one shop was still open. As casually as she could she sauntered in, choosing several bars of chocolate, a packet of biscuits and an individual cake. She didn't have money for any more, purposely not keeping much at university in case she spent it on food. She felt embarrassed when paying at the till, and hoped the shop assistant would think it was for friends, or a party.

As soon as she was out of the shop, she tore open a bar of

chocolate and stuffed it in her mouth, savouring the stunning sweetness. By the time she got back to her room in St Georges Hall she had eaten the whole lot and was feeling revoltingly sick. Despair was waiting for her as she entered her room, and falling on the floor she sobbed and rolled in agony, reviling everything about herself. On the phone again to Mum weeping and wailing, 'I've had another binge... I can't stay here... What am I going to do?... Mum had no idea how to help, and could only offer platitudes. 'Go and have a bath, darling, you'll feel better in the morning.'

University was the expected sequel to completing education at a school such as Rosebery County Grammar School for Girls. In spite of anorexia nervosa and chickenpox – which assailed me at the time of the A-level examinations – I managed to get the required results and was accepted for a degree in psychology at Reading University. Everyone had to have a medical before they were accepted, to certify that they were fit to attend. Amazingly the doctor to whom I went for this passed me as fit. 'You're a bit thin,' she said, and that was all. I had seen her before in conjunction with loss of periods, and as usual had broken down into tears. She was kind and I liked her. She was not like some of the doctors whom I had seen, who were totally uncomprehending as to the seriousness of my illness, and just told me not to be silly, or some other belittling equivalent. Maybe she realised that for anything to change I had to get out of the home environment. She opened a door for me to escape.

I did not really know what I wanted to do. Psychology sounded interesting, and at the time I was fascinated by books about extra-sensory perception, magic, ghosts, witchcraft, UFOs (Unidentified Flying Objects) and whatever other unexplained phenomena I could find. Perhaps I thought that I could find the answer to my anguished incarnation in another dimension, although I did not crystallise my thoughts in this way at the time. Naively I had the idea that the study of psychology would nurture my interest in this field, but the degree course turned out to be very self-consciously scientific. Psychology was at that time something of a newcomer to the arena of science, and its proponents were anxious to prove its credibility.

My first day at university was terrifying. Leaving home for the first time was a major wrench for both me and my family, all of whom needed me in their own way. It was hardest for my mother as she seemed to need the presence of my sister and myself to comfort her loneliness in her estrangement from Dad. We had differing relationships with her, but I think that Mum and I were more physically close, and we had a deep spiritual relationship as well, whereas my sister was a constant companion to Mum, and later on, a devoted carer. When Mum told me that she kissed my slippers at night, I wept buckets of tears, and felt terribly guilty. Carrying the burden of separation did not help me to contend with the new environment and all its social and intellectual requirements. I felt so gauche and ill at ease compared with the other students, who in my eyes were bursting with self-confidence and competence. As I arrived at the university registration hall, all I could see was a seething mass of bodies and excited faces.

My father had brought me to the university for this first day. I think that he was proud of me for gaining a place and really wanted me to succeed. If only he had given me in my upbringing the attention, affection and affirmation that I so desperately needed to build my identity so that I could make the most of the education he had worked hard to provide for me. Instead he had given me the goods to fail, undermining the very foundations of my selfhood and womanhood. Of course, it wasn't all his doing. He and Mum were like a pillar box through which society posted its powerful messages to me. Sadly, instead of nurturing in me a healthy self-respect that would enable me to sort through the 'mail' and make some kind of sense out of it, between them they did just the opposite, managing, without conscious intention, to shatter any possibility of my building a positive self-image, or any sense of self respect.

My first placement in a hall of residence was very uncomfortable for me. It was an old-fashioned building, cold and dreary, right on the main road, with the relentless noise of traffic as a daily accompaniment. The warden in charge of the hall was a strange woman, and seemed to me to be something between an upper class titled lady and a university don. She ran the hall on strict *in loco parentis* lines, and expected the inmates to behave with suitable decorum. I was obliged to share a room with a girl who was a very different sort of person from me. She and the two girls in the opposite room on the top floor were outgoing and confident, with a notable disrespect for rules and authority. They called me 'Flo' as a derogatory nickname and mocked my timid and retiring ways. I had come armed with food for the week, as I was terrified of eating hall meals, and for my breakfast, I boiled eggs surreptitiously in the electric kettle. This greatly amused my room mate, and she and the others got a good rise out of my anorexic strategies. Sometimes some of my food disappeared, and although my room mate never admitted taking it, I am sure that she did. Maybe she did it just for a joke.

I lasted out for just about a year of this horrible existence, and then at the end of the first year I decided that I could not endure it any more and told my parents that I didn't want to go back. Dad was very upset and angry, while Mum was just anxious and sympathetic. I daresay she would have liked me to give up and come to be at home again with her. After lots of tears and arguments, we decided that I would try to get a place in a different hall of residence where I could have my own room. Dad did most of the negotiations, and I think that I managed to get a letter from my doctor saying that I needed supplementary food, or something like that. It was an anxious wait while my 'case' was assessed by university officialdom, and an enormous relief when I was allotted a room in St George's Hall, which was a modern hall of residence with individual study bedrooms.

On my first day back after the summer break I arrived at St George's Hall with all my baggage plus my own little fridge for my special food. My new room was very nice and I felt much better there. I could maintain my privacy and carry out my food routines without being spied upon by mocking eyes. Dad, too, liked my new room, and often used to come up and visit me there. I am sure that he would have loved to have had the opportunity to go to university himself, but his parents did not have much money and he had had to go out to work at the age of eleven years. It seems amazing to reflect on that today, when in this country most eleven-year-olds are just starting senior school.

For the first two years at university I had no real friends. I made the acquaintance of another girl who also had a lot of problems, and we used to commiserate with each other and exchange stories about our visits to the university health centre and what we thought of the doctors there. I found little help for my anorexic despair at the health centre. The most that the doctors could offer was a kind of 'pep talk' approach, telling me that I had to put on weight and so on, or giving me antidepressants.

I continued to return home every weekend to slot into the home routine and was quite unable to make the most of university life. I still had the car, which my father had bought for me expressly for the purpose of coming home. First-year students were not allowed to park a car on the campus, so Dad rented a garage for me within walking distance of the university. I was always desperate to get away on a Friday afternoon, and often drove through inclement weather such as thick snow or heavy fog in order to fulfil my compulsion to return to the environment that was destroying me. Sometimes I would binge secretly at the weekend, or in desperation, stop off at a sweet shop on the way back and purchase a bagful of chocolate, biscuits, crisps and the like, which I ate while I was driving. It was surely divine providence that I never had an accident, as the all-consuming sensation of devouring the food interfered with my ability to concentrate on my driving. Only once did I come close to a serious collision. I was stuffing Mars bars frantically into my mouth, and was distracted from noticing a traffic jam ahead. I am thankful for whatever alerted me, just in time.

I was very anxious about my studies and spent a lot of time working, though I was greatly hampered by the debilitating effects of my constant starving, bingeing and purging, and the depression and despair that were the inevitable accompaniment. I was constantly phoning my mother and howling with loneliness and despair. It must have been awful for her. She was laden with guilt and caught up in her own unhappiness and limiting perceptions of life. How could she possibly help me? It was as if we had a pact, a pact of unconsciously pulling each other down, but this was masked in a guise of mother and daughter love. There was a truth of love present in our relationship, which since her death I can recognise more clearly, but until I managed to detach myself sufficiently from our combined identity, that love was strangled and twisted by the bonds of our entanglement.

My attraction to Robert, my school friend's brother, extended over from school to university. Sometimes I would visit the family straight from university, instead of going home. When it became apparent that Robert had no real feelings for me other than a passing fancy, a profound change happened in my psyche over which I felt I had no control. It must have been that the loss of my first beloved resonated with the feelings of loss related to my brother, and the apparent absence of my father's love, although those feelings were deeply buried at the time. It was one of the most devastating and appalling things that has ever happened to me, although in a mysterious and roundabout way, I suppose it saved my life. I can remember it well, but the memories are so painful that I can hardly bear to entertain them.

I was about nineteen years old and had returned home for the Christmas holidays. Christmas was awful enough as it was, with the heavy atmosphere devoid of any real joy or celebration, the obligatory family gatherings and all the terrifying, fabulous, mesmerising food there, in abundance. I was at home alone and a crack appeared somewhere inside my rigid controls. It was as if my whole personality turned inside out – a ghastly, unspeakable experience, as if I had been brainwashed. I lost control of my eating completely and began to eat compulsively, non-stop, and was unable to do anything about it. Up until then I had always managed somehow to bring a binge under control and get back to dieting, losing the temporary weight gain from the binge, but this time, there was no going back. From being a highly organised, ultra-disciplined, stick-thin automaton, almost overnight I became a disorganised, apathetic despairing lump of flesh, unable to motivate myself or take charge of my life. I perceived myself as a formless blob, my identity obliterated by the encroaching mass of blubber. I gained four stone in six months, and of course, everyone, without exception, said how much better I looked, how well I was, and so on. The nightmare of this experience I could never describe – no words could do it justice. How I lived through it, I will never know. The terror, isolation and utter revulsion towards my own flesh drove me to the edges of insanity and stripped me of every shred of self-recognition and self-respect. So many times the darkness closed over me, and I descended into a kind of mindless hell where I could not think, and where I saw and heard horrors. These were not just to do with myself, but were also as if I had opened a window into the suffering of all living things in the whole world – animals, humans, vegetation, earth, spirits, all screaming and writhing in agony. This state continued unabated for year after terrible year, and I had no defence against it, nor any means to explain or communicate it.

When I did make attempts to communicate it, I was met with a variety of pathetic, insensitive and even aggressive responses to my appalling suffering. I can now see that most of them were no doubt born of ignorance, and were perhaps a defence against confrontation with the pathos and depth of abject human suffering. My efforts to communicate were largely futile, and so lost was I that I will never really know what held me together. I clung blindly to some inner core of integrity of which I was not even aware. It was as if I were being tortured and brainwashed, year in and year out, to accept an identity that was untrue to my self, and which simply was not me. I could only perceive the world as trying to 'normalise' me.

* * * * *

I think that, because we live on a plane of existence where separateness is a reality to us, it was necessary for me to establish a sense of self, not just of ego or the smaller, everyday self, but of a more transcendental awareness of the life that expresses itself through the particular human organism that I inhabit in my incarnation. There are all sorts of differing beliefs, religions and metaphysical systems which attempt to define, describe, explain, direct, control and moralise this phenomenon which we call being human. I cannot pretend to have extensive knowledge of any of them, but after many years of reflection and questioning, my conclusion is this: a strong sense of the uniqueness of self, as a prerequisite to any kind of sacrifice or letting go of the self, is crucial to surviving the anorexic illness. Without this inner determination, the illness would have eaten me alive.

Now that I have developed a better idea of who I am, and feel confident that I am continuing to do so, I can turn my attention to more esoteric pursuits, such as becoming aware of my connectedness to all living creatures, learning to respect and balance my own needs with those of others, and to give unselfishly. With a well defined sense of self, such practices enlarge and strengthen me, whereas when I had no boundaries and no idea of my identity, they simply contributed to my fragmented experience of being. In a strange way the anorexic symptoms were for me, and I suspect are for many, a last-ditch stand at holding on to self. To lose one's anorexia is to die, whereas to die from a bony proclamation of self is to live. For me, I had to learn to hate those whom I felt were threatening the very core of my being, and to defend my right to be myself whatever that meant in terms of weight. Paradoxically it was the energy of hating that saved me, as it drove me away from my parents and the suffocating home life. I am not of course recommending hate as a way of life or something that should be acted out, but the recognition of the energy of hate and its appropriate release can be a life-saver. I have explored this concept in an early section of Chapter Nine.

As the separation from home gradually took effect, and I began to experience myself more as an individual, I began to form tentative relationships. I was so inexperienced and so inept at relating to people that I really had little idea about how to get along in a group. I have so many people to thank for those early years of my clumsy efforts to get to know real people in a real way! So many people reached out to me with kindness and support. I joined the Christian Union in my third year of university, and though in some ways its strong evangelical framework and charismatic idealism held confusion and anxiety for me, nevertheless it gave me a matrix in which to survive, a belief to hold on to for a time, and above all, friends who were warm-hearted and kind to me. In particular, the pastor of the Baptist Church that I attended spent hours listening to me, praying with me and comforting me, and drew me into his large family and helped me make friends with other students. I even studied at his house, and I am sure that it was largely due to his support that I managed to scrape through my degree with second class honours. I did come across some of the more extreme elements of evangelicalism, people who were convinced that I was possessed by various devils, but I suppose this was because of the obsessive and compulsive nature of my illness and the desperation that this provoked in me. I was exorcised many times! Unfortunately this only exacerbated my terrors of the malevolent forces with which I was instinctively acquainted, and for many years it prevented me from pursuing an intelligent enquiry into metaphysics – which was then labelled as occultism, witchcraft or black magic.

During the time that I attended the Baptist Church I was encouraged to undergo a baptism by full immersion. This was a kind of evangelical baptism, the purpose of which was to receive the Holy Spirit and thus demonstrate spiritual gifts such as speaking in tongues. I had already been baptised as an infant in the Anglican Church of which my mother and father were members, so I wasn't really sure that I needed another baptism. However, it was very much part of the tradition of this Baptist community, so I went along with it. I don't know what I really thought about it in my heart and mind. So much of my participation was trying to believe, feel and think what the significant people in my social milieu conveyed to be appropriate and desirable. This also became the pattern if I had a close relationship. I realise that it stems from my heroic efforts to please and to sustain my family environment, but I hated myself for it in the underlying levels of my consciousness, and this contributed powerfully to my sense of shapelessness and ugliness.

The day of the Baptism arrived, and I tried to convince myself that it would be wonderful and that I would be filled with joy and the Holy Spirit would descend upon me. Several of us were to be baptised that day and we had to be dressed only in a white garment that was provided by the church. It was weighted at the hem so that it didn't float upward in the water and show your knickers. You walked down into the little pool – like a mini swimming pool – and the pastor uttered certain sentences, finishing with 'I baptise you in the name of the Father, the Son and the Holy Ghost.' Immediately after this, two strong men standing in the pool whipped each of us in turn backwards, dunking us under the water. When each arose from the watery trough there was some singing: 'Be thou faithful unto death and I will give thee a crown of life.'

When it was my turn I felt apprehensive. At that time I could not swim and was afraid of going under water. I think they told me to take a deep breath and hold my nose – a little undignified perhaps. Anyway I survived the dunking. Unfortunately my preoccupations were more worldly than spiritual and I was worried that my eye makeup would have run and my hair would look awful. Predictably there was no rush of spiritual fire and I did not speak in tongues. I felt a failure again, as instead everything went on as usual – the despair, the starving and bingeing, the utter hatred and disgust of my body, and the inner bewilderment, doubt and fear. I do not mean to imply that this ceremony was in any way insincere. Indeed, I imagine that for some who underwent it, it was a most moving experience that may well have changed their lives. Everyone who was involved, ordained or lay, was totally devoted to the service of his or her beliefs. However, for me anorexia was the most powerful force in my life and nothing at all could impinge upon it. It swept everything away in its path.

* * * * *

While I was at university, the careers advisor, a vibrant and perceptive Jewish woman, took a special interest in me and went out of her way to help me. I looked forward to going to see her and talking to her about my problems, and even visited her in her home sometimes. It was people like her who gave me the essential recognition and interest that was as food to my starving soul. They were life-savers for me – angels in disguise, who reached out with a shaft of sacred light to penetrate the tormented gloom of my interior mind. It would be impossible to recount all the input from the multitude of people whose kindness, be it ever so small, was a transmitter of light and who were, probably unknowingly, agents of the divine who assisted me through those dangerous and troubled waters.

Towards the latter part of my university degree course, I met a woman whose love, caring and wisdom were to be a foundation of my sanity, a rock upon which I could gradually and painstakingly build my recovery. Dr Marion Ashton was a Christian counsellor who had been a missionary, and who herself had suffered a serious depressive illness. I came to her as a result of reading a very small book that she had written, entitled 'A Mind at Ease', given to me by the pastor of the Baptist Church.

There was a chapter at the end that was headed 'But if not', which meant a great deal to me. It outlined her belief in the goodness of God even if she did not recover, and her refusal to believe otherwise. It made me think of the Biblical Job, with whom I had always identified. I felt that I must see this woman. In fact I was desperate to meet her, and I wrote to her to ask for an appointment. She replied and invited me to come to her home in Surrey, where my first meeting with her was an experience of such relief that I wept and wept.

At last there was someone who listened to me, with such an exceptional quality of listening that I have rarely encountered again. There was no judgement, and no advice, only compassion, enquiry and a sense of being held. She had a remarkable devotion to prayer and it was like cooling waters to the fires of my anguish to listen to her praying with me. Just to go to her house gave me an immediate sense of relief and no matter where she was living, I would travel miles to see her. I went to see her every week for about seven years and she never once let me down, that is to say, she was always there for me, a stable, loving, praying presence. Also I wrote to her constantly – a multitude of long, desperate letters full of self-hatred and despair. I don't know how this wonderful lady managed to read such a deluge of negative thoughts and attitudes so relentlessly coming her way, year after year, but she did, and she always responded to me so graciously. When I stopped seeing her as a patient she asked me if I would like the letters back. She had carefully kept them all! I was amazed. I did take them back and still have them today, but I have never had the courage to re-read them. I continued to visit her and corresponded with her long after I finished seeing her for treatment. I was very sad when she stopped answering my letters, due I am sure to advancing age and poor health. I imagine she must be in the next world now but my gratitude to her is eternal.

I do not mean to say that I thought her to be some kind of perfected being, or that it would have been appropriate for me to continue to see her indefinitely, but for that time in my life, when the waves of despair had covered me and were threatening to snuff out my life, she was a life-line of Light to me. I used to be convinced that God wanted me to be fat, and like the rest of the world, HE was conspiring to coerce, trick, blackmail, brainwash and use whatever other means available to make me put on weight against my will. I should acknowledge here that the Christian doctrines of submission and martyrdom which I encountered at the time did nothing to allay my terror and hatred of that 'God'.

Once when I was praying with Dr Marion after a counselling session, she suddenly sat up and said with quiet authority that God wanted me to be free to choose a weight that I liked. That statement rang out like a great bell pealing through the chaos of my mind and spirit, and I clung to it with all my strength. Over the years my interpretation of it has changed, but the truth that I am entitled to choose what makes *me* feel comfortable, healthy and happy in my own body is still being revealed in ever deepening layers of my being.

As I reflect now on this moment in my life that was so significant in restoring my sanity, I feel an even greater respect for Dr Marion and her vocation as a channel of divine healing. The message that she transmitted to me was entirely suited to the person I was at that stage of my journey. I think that such a statement could be misinterpreted were it to be inappropriately offered, for the anorexic mind generally likes a weight that is always going down, or one that is so low that it cannot go any further without resulting in death. This is not a free choice made by the sufferer, for such a preference is driven by a powerful inner compulsion that is derived from complex forces. True freedom to choose one's weight comes from a loving acceptance of one's own body, and respect and understanding of its needs and processes. That kind of attitude leads to a desire to be whole, and thus be a weight that is both healthy and comfortable for one's own unique body. Since Dr Marion's statement was so precisely and perfectly applied by the divine force which inspired her, I did not interpret it as a divine licence to abuse and starve my body to death, but as a deep and healing understanding of my suffering and a divine affirmation of my longing to be whole.

I think that because of the demands of my anorexic illness, I did not really enjoy my time at university, nor did I make the most of it. Looking back on this, I feel sad, as it was such a privilege and such an opportunity to be there. I was conscientious, and the studies seemed arduous. It was a very different scene from the tightly programmed schedule of lessons, homework and exams at school, to which I was accustomed. University life should have been an opportunity for curiosity, investigation, expansion of horizons and development of thinking for oneself, but I was too locked into trying to please and to do what I thought was expected of me to be able to use the educational opportunity in that way.

There were no computers or access to an internet at that time. Everything was in books and libraries, and I spent so many miserable hours in the university library, anxiously looking for information, much of which had very little inner meaning for me. I hated that library, a looming presence, laden with vast tomes that made me feel panicky and so lonely. People were reading and studying, apparently absorbed in their work, whereas I could never really be absorbed in anything, but felt I was just trying to stuff my already overloaded and weary mind with facts that bore no relevance to my inner torment. Then they would head for the café to consume quantities of coffee, sweets and cake, while smoking cigarettes. I would follow on, pretending to join in and be one of the crowd, all the time agonising over trying not to buy a cake and eat it. I usually failed to resist and bought several, and went outside to gobble them secretly.

There were one or two aspects of my time at university that I enjoyed, as far as I was able. While studying for my degree I also took clarinet and organ lessons, and I liked both of the teachers. It seemed a welcome break from the relentless pressure of reading, studying, going to lectures and writing essays. I especially liked my organ teacher, who was organist and don of Christ's College in Oxford. He was a troubled man, friendly and approachable, and often had a bottle of whisky with him, placed strategically on the organ. We shared our problems from time to time, and I appreciated his confidence.

* * * * *

Once I had managed to separate myself from the home environment to some extent and make some friends in the Christian Union, I found it a welcome input into my life to be part of a group of friendly and warm-hearted people, even if I could not really align myself with all that they believed. It was good to be able to relate to young men in that kind of relatively safe situation, and some of them were really kind to me. This helped me to begin to develop a different perspective on my identity.

There was one boy whom I liked a lot. His name was Antony and he was half Polish – an attractive, outgoing, fun-loving boy who was studying electronics. I wished so much that he would be my boyfriend, but he was going out with someone else from the CU – a pretty, slim girl whom I envied fiercely. I hoped so much that they would break up, and when they eventually did, I was glad and hoped that Antony would ask me to go out with him, but he never did. He did not live far from me and occasionally we talked on the phone, and I think that I visited him once. At university we chatted and spent some time together, but we never developed the relationship for which I longed.

I met another boy through the CU who was quite a different character, fairly quiet, proper and reserved, nice looking but not attractive in the same way as Antony. Quentin had an unhappy background, and like me, had a deep sense of neediness, which he concealed. He was kind to me and sensitive to my problems, and somehow we became boyfriend and girlfriend. He was a good guy, did a lot for me and supported me in many ways, and our relationship persisted for quite some years after I left university, which is certainly a testament to his loyalty and commitment. We explored sexuality together and he was extremely considerate of my fears and inhibitions in that respect. We did not have intercourse, or even kissing as far as I can remember, and our body contact was fully clothed. With him, for the first time I learned what an orgasm felt like. I did not find it an experience of passion, more just another bodily reaction like sneezing or belching, from which I remained emotionally detached. I had never experienced it before, and it must have been quite a feat of self-restraint for him not to coerce me into intercourse. I think of him with respect and gratitude for that very gentle introduction to sex. After we both left university, he got a job for a while and then returned for a PhD. I went back home, and without the distance from the destructive atmosphere of my home situation and the support of being part of the CU, I began to deteriorate again. Quentin and I continued to meet while I was living at home, but we were very ill at ease in the heavy and uncomfortable atmosphere of my parents' house. I felt self-conscious, and that I was being watched all the time.

At home there was no room for my emerging womanhood, and I do not think that Dad ever really wanted me to have a boyfriend. He had been unhappy about Robert, and was never interested or supportive of any of the other fleeting relationships that I had. I remember when I was quite young and the novelty of television serials (in black and white!) had captivated my age group. We all had crushes on some TV personality or another. I was enthusing to Dad about my current beau and how handsome he was, and he said to me, in a harsh and irritated voice, 'You and your handsome men! Aren't I handsome enough for you?' I never spoke to him again about my inner fantasies.

I used to meet Quentin after his work, and we would wander round London, sitting on stations or sneaking back into the County Hall where he worked to find an empty room where we could cuddle. Many times I was lured by the Festival Hall restaurant, just a stone's throw away, and found myself dragged in there by some unseen force, to consume several cakes and deserts before meeting Quentin. Afterwards I would be in despair, feeling utterly disgusting and shameful, and he comforted me. How he could still love me in the midst of all this I will never know.

Eventually anorexia began to destroy my relationship with Quentin, and to save ourselves we had to split up. The illness that controlled me had reached out its tentacles to draw him into its web, and his love and devotion to me made him an easy prey. We were caught in a descending spiral of trying to make me better – a bottomless pit of failure and despair. I had seen this process happen before – between me and my mother – and it had been the initial separation of going to university that I believe prevented us from being completely ensnared together. I was aware of this unhealthy entanglement happening between Quentin and me, but I could not stop it. The unconscious processes were so strong, and so well camouflaged, that I did not have access to a way of changing myself. It seems as if anorexia has a life of its own, a voracious, devouring craving for people's bodies and souls. Quentin and I kept drifting back together again, drawn by an invisible magnet and only really separated finally much later, when I joined another community. He eventually married someone else and I lost touch with him, but I hope he is happy. I am still deeply grateful to him for loving me in those nightmare years.

After my initial soul-shattering inflation of body size, I used virtually all my available energy in trying to get control of my weight and reduce it again. I tried everything conceivable, every trick of the trade to stay on a strict diet, but defeated myself every time by throwing all restraint to the four winds and bingeing my heart out, over and over again. Looking back, I cannot count the years that I spent ricocheting between starvation and gross overeating, sliding up and down the weight scale like a yoyo. The feelings were always the same, going down the scale made me feel safer and happier, whereas going up the scale sent me into a frenzy of panic and made me feel suicidal. These elements are still present within my psyche to this day, and although I do have more control and understanding of many aspects of my relationship to food and eating, and the nature and nutritional substance of food itself, I cannot become complacent. That all-consuming, devouring loss of control and the attendant fierce desire to end my existence still sometimes seems only a breath away.

Towards the end of my time at university, I had somehow managed to get control of my weight and was beginning to descend the scale again, although it was not any kind of resolution to the anorexic conflict. I had more friends, was staying away from home for longer periods of time, and was beginning to feel that I had some sort of identity. I dieted as strictly as I could, and although this time was still punctuated with binges, I contrived by various means to minimise the effect enough to lose weight consistently. I kept a chart of my weight, and was so happy to see the line dipping steadily downwards.

This was probably the best of my time at university. I wasn't yet too thin to have become totally enslaved to my skeleton, and I was not what I considered to be grossly fat – a condition which everybody else called 'normal' – and I was learning how to make relationships. With Dr Marion's constant support and love I felt some kind of inner security, a platform from which I could make little expeditions into life. I wonder how it would have worked out if I could have continued in this pattern. Would I have relapsed again or would I have slowly made progress and eventually established a reasonably balanced lifestyle? I shall never know, and it is futile to speculate, although my regrets are so deep and painful.

In May 1970, just before finals, I had my 21st birthday. I remember it with mixed feelings. In some ways it was as if a window opened on the life I thought that I wanted to lead. My family hired the local church hall and held a big party for all our relations and all my university friends. A big crowd of us went down from Reading, with quite a few stuffed into my little car in a way which would now be considered entirely dangerous and illegal. It was fun then, though, with people sitting on laps, laughing and talking all the way. I had never had much fun in life and this was like a breath of warm, fragrant air into my generally sad and lonely life.

I had always hated weekends when I was at school, as I felt that I should be going out in the evenings, meeting boys, going to parties and discos and so on, but I rarely went anywhere. Mostly I stayed at home, helping Mum get the meals, going shopping, trying to keep Dad happy, and when Sunday evening came, I felt a sense of hopelessness. I was dressed up in my best clothes, but the only place to go was church, with the family.

On my 21st birthday I felt like a queen for a day. Everyone gave me such lovely presents, made a big fuss of me, and I was the centre of attention. Yet lying in wait was the old dragon. I had determined to 'be sensible' about the Birthday Cake, a glorious edifice laced with succulent dried fruit, encased in marzipan and decorated with beautiful icing. When the party was over and my friends had returned to the university, I was at home with the family and a few relations, and I fell prey to the spell of the cake. It was sitting there in the kitchen, innocently, so it seemed, and nobody really wanted anymore of it, except me. I thought that one more little slice wouldn't do any harm, but of course then the craving and compulsion had me in its grip. Another slice, another and another were bolted down secretly. I kept making excuses to go into the kitchen and sneak a bit more. I don't really think that anyone noticed, and if they had, they could never have known about the rising panic and despair inside me. I think that somehow I managed to cover up my distress – how could I make everyone unhappy on my 21st birthday?

The next day I went out with Antony, my Christian Union friend, in my car, as he had stayed on to visit his own family. It was lovely, or was it? I was suffering from the effects of the Birthday Cake binge, feeling fat, ugly and disgusting, planning frantically how to lose the excess weight that I surely must have gained. I did not tell Antony any of this of course. Finding that people never really understood my struggles, and that even the best-intentioned person was liable to come out with statements like 'but you need a bit more weight on you', I had learned to keep quiet and try to conceal my distress. I longed for Antony to say he loved me and make me his girlfriend, but he was just kind, pleasant and entertaining, as he always was, and I knew that there was nothing more.

When I returned to university after the party, Finals loomed inevitably on the horizon and I was in a desperate panic. I had studied conscientiously, as best I could, but really I had no idea how to organise information in a creative and useful way. It wasn't that I had a bad memory, but was more that my mind was so overloaded with obsessive thoughts and compulsive rituals that I had very little space left for academic work. I was so afraid of forgetting, so fearful of failing and not pleasing my father and my tutors that I could not let go of my anxieties and examine a subject with the best of my intelligence. The one task that I had quite enjoyed was the compulsory dissertation, prepared in the term before Finals. I chose 'animal behaviour related to tool using and human evolution', and became somewhat fascinated by the picture that built up under my pen. At that time the theory of evolution according to Charles Darwin was seen as heretical amongst some Christian believers, and I became curious as to the emergence of *Homo sapiens*, the form in which I find myself. I am still very interested in the ancient history of our species.

My studies for Finals continued to be fraught with panic. In between battling with the craving to eat and organising all sorts of ruses to stop myself, I tried desperately to force the necessary information into my mind. The degree course had not been especially well-organised, being in the midst of changing from one format to another. We had had first year exams, which I managed to pass. In some ways these exams were easier as I studied physiology, biochemistry and zoology as subsidiary subjects, and these were better organised – being officially recognised as sciences. I had hated having to read about experiments on animals, though, and found that I could not bear the thought of the poor suffering creatures, so I did not read the material. I thought, and still do believe wholeheartedly, that such experiments are entirely unethical and in the long run counterproductive to human development and survival. The end can never justify the means, and unless we learn to live with respect and compassion towards our fellow creatures, ultimately our own race is doomed. Given the incredible inventiveness of the human intellect and technological superlatives which are in evidence today, it must surely be possible – if it were thought to be necessary – to find effective alternatives to the abuse of animals for the purposes of testing substances that are intended to benefit humans, or performing experiments on animals that cause suffering, for any purpose. It is good to know of certain companies which now eschew animal testing and use other means to verify the safety of their products.

At some point after becoming involved with the Christian Union, a combination of factors caused me to 'backslide' and lose the faith that had always underpinned my existence. Partly it was that there did not seem to be any answer to my desperate prayers and the many prayers of others that I should be cured of anorexia nervosa. Many years on, and with much water under the bridge, I now see things quite differently, and I understand that there was no way that I could be 'cured' by having my anorexic illness whipped away from me, so to speak. I was terrified of that possibility, although I was not really fully aware of it at the time. Anorexia nervosa was my whole life, literally. To be stick thin was to live, whereas to be covered in flesh was to die. Anorexia gave me an identity. It was my driving force, and in a strange way my protection. To take it away in a flash – as I naively beseeched God to do – would have left me naked, trembling and unformed, a prey to all manner of other shaping forces of life. It took me about thirty years to accept that this illness was to be a companion and teacher on the road of life, a journey of transformation and transmutation of those elements of my being that were manifesting as anorexia nervosa. I am still on that journey.

Another factor in my lapse from grace was the singularly unenlightened instruction which fell from the lips of some of the psychology lecturers. Since the subject of psychology was supposed to be a science, some of them took this to a self-conscious extreme of promulgating a mechanistic view of human behaviour and of the universe itself. According to them, anything spiritual was definitely unscientific and factually unsound. I think of one lecturer in particular who taught social and clinical psychology who was sold on Behaviourism and exercised himself in remarkable displays of verbal gymnastics to explain every aspect of human and animal existence in terms of stimulus and response, with perhaps a bit in between. I was primed to be taken in by this, so disillusioned was I by the apparent futility of belief, prayer, devotions and practically everything to do with religion.

I tried to silence the agony of my heart, when I read about distressing things happening and being done to humans and animals, by telling myself it was only a stimulus-response phenomenon. Fortunately that did not last long as my heart refused to believe it. I became very depressed, stopped going to church, and tried to find answers to my questions by constantly asking my CU friends to explain. It's a wonder they put up with me! The pastor and several of the elders were concerned for me and often asked me round to their houses to talk. They could not answer my questions in a way which went deep enough to give me peace, and now I understand why, but their kindness was sincere and deeply comforting to me, and eventually I shelved the questions and went back into the fold. Times and knowledge and understanding have moved on in enormous leaps since those days, and the current rediscovery of ancient wisdom in the light of modern science has provided me with enormous relief.

As I have said earlier, the pastor of the Baptist church kindly invited me to study at his house, for emotional support and company, and I was so grateful. It made it bearable somehow. I found study very isolating, stuck in my room alone with piles of books and papers glaring at me. Often I would just collapse in despair. How sad it was that what could have been an exciting adventure of enquiry turned into a towering ogre of expectation looming over me. I will never know how I managed to pass the final examinations with second class honours and get the coveted certificate. I still have it, mounted in its frame sitting on the wall over my desk! I am proud of it in some way, not for my intellectual achievement – which wasn't very astonishing – but for the fact that somehow I had managed, in spite of the searing torment of anorexia nervosa, to stay the course and achieve a goal. It would not have been possible without the love, kindness and generosity which flowed out so copiously to meet and support me, from such a wide variety of sources. Dad was very proud of me, and for once I felt I had succeeded in my heroic efforts to please him and to gain his approval. He took me up to London to celebrate, and we went to his office where he showed me off to his colleagues and I felt like a million dollars. He bought me a gold watch to mark the occasion. This was one of the few presents he actually bought for me himself. Usually he just gave Mum the money and asked her to get something.

Sadly the euphoria did not last long as I had to decide what to do with this wonderful piece of paper and my life. I wanted very much to stay in Reading and to do a PhD, but in spite of a multitude of applications for jobs and PhDs, I was never accepted for anything. I had no self-confidence, no means to sell myself as a marketable commodity who could deliver the goods. Eventually I gave up, as I had nowhere to live nor means of self-support, and I went back to live at home. It was probably one of the worst decisions of my whole life.

Often I go back over things in my past with a vicious blast of self-recrimination and regret, and that is one of them. If only... Why didn't you...? Could I have done anything different? It is pointless to contemplate the issue. Somebody with more motivation (of the right kind), more confidence, less parental suffocation and cushioning, more self-awareness, more this, that and the other could have done, but then they would not be likely to be suffering from anorexia nervosa in that case. The upshot of the matter is that I went back to live at home, straight back into the cooking pot of my illness. Predictably, I began to relapse, quickly losing all the ground that I had gained at university.

To the God who is not there

My God I seek thee
Day and Night.
In the horror of my fleshly torment,
There no light
Penetrates the hollow caverns
Where I dwell alone,
Echoing the nightmare tombs
With shriek and tortured groan.

Images that haunt the shades
Cruelly play
Upon my ragged shreds of soul;
They lay
Waiting as I flee in fear
Or grasp
And fall upon the empty air.

Starving, ravenous I crave
Your life,
The sweetness of your touch,
But strife
And yawning emptiness are mine.
Despairing rage
Would flood my inner sanctuary,
And I
A desperate animal
In cage.

The edges of existence
I scrape
With bleeding hands;
My shape
From gross disfigurement
Defending,
While vultures wait, anticipate,
Attending.

O wretched self, afflicted
Beyond all recognition,
For thee in thy Gethsemane
Awaiting slow procession
That leads thee to thy dying place
Where human love runs dry,
By darkness rent asunder,
Alone, against the sky.

Jacqueline Kemp

Chapter Three

In between

She leaned her head against the side of the door, clutching at it, hardly able to stand up. The kitchen of her bedsit was strewn with wrappings. Chocolate bars, a WHOLE BOX of chocolates, a block of cheese, butter, jam, bread, a packet of biscuits and goodness knows what else had been devoured in one go. The tyranny of the scales compelled her to weigh herself. It can't be true! She had gained another half stone in only a week. What on earth was she going to do? The bingeing had got the better of her again – eating, trying to diet, purging, taking an overdose of antidepressants, bingeing again, all alone in her little torture chamber. Oblivion... She craved oblivion.

'I'll really do it this time... They'll miss me... What will they think... Poor Quentin... I'm going to DO IT.'

Emptying out all the pills in the bottles – antidepressants and major tranquillisers... Had she been given these because they thought she was schizophrenic? Maybe she was... Her brain just didn't work properly any more – she couldn't control herself, and didn't have a proper idea of who she was. Did it matter anyway? She gulped them all down.

Panic, panic, panic... What have I done? God help me. Flopping down on the bed she drifted into a distant land, an awful place where the Devil was coming up from behind to get her, to devour her.

Quentin was at the door. She managed to go and open it. 'I've taken an overdose,' she told him. He forced her to go to hospital, dragging her there somehow.

A nice foreign doctor attended to her eventually. 'That was a silly thing to do', he said.

She slept, on and on, occasionally being dimly aware of

nurses taking her blood pressure or doing something else to her. At length consciousness dawned and she was angry. 'Why am I still here? Why didn't they let me die?'

The psychiatrist called her in. 'What did you do that for?'

She couldn't really give much of a coherent answer. Anyway, who would understand if she said, 'I'm fat, and I can't stop eating'? From past experience she knew there was no point in trying to explain.

'Do you think you will do it again?' he asked.

'No, Doctor.'

'You can go home then, but go and see your GP.'

Oh dear, she didn't like her GP. Trying to communicate with him was like talking to a brick wall.

Well it's amazing that I am still here to tell the tale! I took many overdoses over a number of years, and yet there must have been a very strong will to survive somewhere hidden deep inside me.

After I had graduated, I came back to live at the family home for about eighteen months. In spite of completing a very large number of applications for jobs and further training I had not been accepted for anything, and I had begun to lose hope. I did not really want to return home, but I had no confidence in myself, and the shaky success story of my degree did not sustain me in the face of endless failures to find employment or post-graduate training.

I really feel for all the job-hunters nowadays – an excess of people in the work force and a diminishing job market can so easily lead to a sense of despair in those who are vulnerable.

I was afraid of stepping out into the world at large and the false 'safety' of home exerted its fatal pull on me. One of my friends got herself a job as a care assistant at some kind of residential home for children with special needs. The wages were low and the work tiring, but she held on to the job, refusing to go back to her home life, which she hated. I admired her determination. Why didn't I have the courage to do that? Why, why, why? I am always saying to myself 'Why don't you just...?' Those few words, which carry an implication of admonition and judgment, had often been thrown at me, when what I needed so badly was acceptance and understanding. Maybe it is easier, at times, to castigate ourselves – or others – rather than expend time and energy in gathering an understanding of the wider perspective of the issue in question.

During my time at university I had eventually managed to separate myself, to some measure, from my family, and carve out some sort of identity for myself. I had managed to get my weight under control again by extreme measures, and to my way of thinking, I was acceptably thin. However, back in the family environment again, it seemed that I lost all the ground that I had gained. I still kept trying for jobs, but was rejected, time and time again. Much of my life was spent in the same family routines as before, except for my relationship with Quentin, which he and I managed to maintain somehow. I began to binge and starve again, and to lose control so that I started to regain the weight that I had lost, and with this came the self-loathing, the apathy, the horror, and suicidal despair. It was a dreadful time for us all.

After some time I managed to get myself a small flat a couple of miles from home. It was a really nice little place, and had been a 'granny flat' before the old lady who inhabited it died. The couple who owned the house were kind and pleasant people, and I was very fortunate to get that flat. It had its own front door, and I loved having my own little home. However since I had no income, I could not afford the rent, so Dad paid it for me. Poor Mum, I don't think she really wanted me to go away again. I remember telling her not to come to see me, and she was weeping. I could not cope with the tangled confusion of emotions that I felt towards her. I felt guilty and desperate, full of hate for my poor mother, whom I blamed for my predicament. At times my hate was so violent that I didn't know

63

what to do with myself. I wrote vilifying diatribes on pieces of paper, stabbed them with a knife, tried to stuff down the hatred with more food, hated myself, punished myself, prayed, wept, and screamed. I loved her, needed her, hated her and all this tore me to pieces. I hated Dad too, but I was already used to hating him and his vile moods and temper. Somehow it had always made more sense than hating my poor, gentle, loving doormat of a mum. It was only after years of spiritual discipline and the development of psychological understanding that I even began to unravel the tangled threads of my psyche and establish a more mature relationship with my parents.

I had started going to an Evangelical Church fairly near to where I lived. I didn't like the church that my parents went to any more, with all the people who knew our family telling Mum and Dad, and me, how much better I looked. How futile and empty the boring rituals seemed, and how useless they were to meet me in my utter degradation and depravity. The Evangelical church was a lot more friendly, and the style of service was more like that which I had become used to at the Baptist church while I was at university. Several people tried to help me, praying over me and counselling me, and exhorting me to have faith, and I am truly grateful to them for their efforts. However their well-meaning attempts made no impression at all on the fierce tide of my anorexic illness, which swept everything away in its path.

I did make a few friends there, and one of them, Penny, offered to get me a job at the Christian publishing firm where she worked. I did not really want to take the job. I considered it to be somewhat beneath my exalted status as a university graduate, as I viewed it as a lowly clerical job. I worked in the packing department for most of the time, stamping mail and taking it to the Post Office in giant sacks at the end of the day. Sometimes I would be sent on an errand to deliver something and have to get the Underground train to Bank Station. On my way I had to go past a shop with gorgeous cakes and cookies. For me this was like running the gauntlet. I rarely managed to survive, and in spite of myself I was drawn in there to purchase as many goodies as I could afford, and I stuffed them down guiltily on the train back.

I started leaving all my money at my flat, just taking enough for the fares, but that didn't work either, as the petty cash tin was kept in the office and no one noticed when I helped myself to it for money to buy cakes. I felt unbearably guilty and disgusted with myself, but I was a slave to the compulsion: it had to be obeyed.

Sometimes I wrestled with it for a time, and at best lasted up to a week, but if I could feel it coming on, I knew that I would always succumb in the end. I always replaced the money in the tin, bringing just enough in my purse, but eventually I would always 'borrow' again. When I left the job I made sure that I had replaced every penny.

Everyone was so kind to me at that firm. The manager of the stock room where I worked was tolerant of my bungles on the franking machine. There was I flaunting my Degree and I couldn't even frank mail correctly. I just couldn't concentrate, and my mind was foggy with the effects of high doses of antidepressants and tranquillisers. The staff tolerated me falling asleep at my desk, rushing out when I had had a binge, bursting into tears, being absent for one reason or another, and so on. They never complained about me and I received no reproof. Bless them. The work gave me something to cling to, even though I hated it.

Dad was very keen for me to keep that post. In his mind any job was better than no job, and now I see something of the wisdom of that as it applied to me at the time, although I don't think it is an absolute truth that can be applied to all situations. Dad really wanted me to be independent, and although he had unknowingly undermined any ability I had to establish this, in his way he was trying to be helpful. He used to walk the two miles to my flat every day, and walk with me to the train station to see me off, trying to encourage me to stick at it. He had been an office boy for a firm of insurance brokers from the age of eleven, and had managed to work his way up to the level of senior accountant. Maybe he thought that I would be able to make similar progress. However times were changing, and people and jobs were becoming much more mobile. I wasn't content to be an office girl and started looking for other 'degree level' jobs.

To my great surprise, I was eventually offered a graduate post at the Road Research Laboratory. The salary was around £2000 per year and it seemed like a fortune! The Laboratory was in Bracknell, quite near to Reading, where I had been at university. It was a lovely place – a smart and imposing building, surrounded by countryside. I drove there and back every day, about eighty miles in a round trip. I felt very proud to be an employee and was determined to succeed. However, the experience turned out to be a very sad story, and remains forever etched in my mind as one of my life's most painful failures.

I was put to work in my own little office, all by myself, and my task was to code questionnaires about Tufty Clubs (road safety for children) for the computer. I did this all day, form after form after form, just reading the answers and coding them. Did I really need a degree in psychology for this, I wondered? Apart from this task being incredibly boring and meaningless to me, I was utterly lonely. I had no one to talk to, all day, except when I emerged for a tea break or to get some more forms. I suppose that had I been possessed of the necessary drive and vision, I could have made the job into something more interesting in due course, or got myself promoted to a more stimulating occupation, but I was too far gone to be able to survive the boredom and isolation. After about a month I broke down, weeping uncontrollably and hardly able to stand, and went on sick leave.

It is difficult to remember clearly the events over the next period of time. It seems like a haze of drugs, binges, overdoses and despair. I only once took enough to kill myself, at a time when I had no more strength left to bear the extreme torment in my mind. After surviving that episode, I still abused medication, but just took enough to knock myself out for hours at a time. My GP was not especially sympathetic, or possessed of any insight as to the suffering of an anorexic, and gave me a resounding telling off after I was hospitalised for an overdose. I never told him about an overdose again.

Throughout this time of my life I had the most terrifying dreams and experiences. The dreams were always variations on the theme of Someone (whom I called The Devil) coming up behind me, grasping me and trying to suffocate me. At times when I was lying on my bed in semiconscious stupor, I felt a pressure on my head – a tight band upon which Someone seemed to be pounding, trying to get in. I fought off these attempted invasions with all my strength, and would emerge from the struggle totally drained and exhausted. I do not try to postulate an explanation for what this experience could have been. There are so many ways of looking at it, and so many possible ideas, depending on one's particular interpretation of the nature of human life. At the time I regarded it as an attack from evil spirits, and so did those people in my immediate social matrix. Maybe it was. Who knows?

At some stage, my GP sent me to see a psychiatrist. I had to go to Westminster Hospital in London to see Dr Peter Davis, who was known as a consultant specialist in anorexia nervosa. I went on my own. The interview with this man was extremely unnerving for me, for he spoke to me in a probing and challenging way that I had rarely encountered before, questioning my religious beliefs and asking deep questions about my relationships with my family. He did not seem to approve of religion, and was cynical about the help that I was receiving from Dr Marion. He said that I had to come into hospital as an inpatient for treatment with the 'truth drug', which I believe was sodium pentothal. I had no idea what this meant, and it sounded very frightening. I left his office shaking.

While I was waiting for the summons to go into hospital, I

was told that I would be treated by one of Dr Davis's team of psychiatrists. Although I was fearful of the proposed inpatient treatment, I was so desperate that I waited with longing for the letter containing the appointment to arrive, perhaps seeing it as some kind of straw to clutch. My first outpatient visit was bewildering – an empty, depersonalising and isolating disappointment. The psychiatrist was a youngish woman. I had to lie on a cold and uncomfortable couch for one hour and say whatever came into my mind, while the psychiatrist sat silently, occasionally interjecting a monosyllable or two. I gazed at the holes in the ceiling in despair. What on earth was I supposed to say? After a few futile attempts at a monologue, I fell into silence and ever-deepening lonely anguish. This pattern went on for months, and I became more and more depressed and unable to cope with living.

The summons to Westminster Hospital for the 'truth drug' treatment seemed to have been lost in the hospital bureaucracy, and no one seemed to know anything about it. By now I was living in my own flat, and my poor body and my tortured mind and soul writhed daily in solitary agony. I wrestled with that which I called 'Christ' and also 'The Devil', and at times an unspeakable sense of evil nearly choked me. I hated and feared God as much as the Devil, and could not 'trust God' as I was perpetually instructed to do. I had an innate suspicion of what I perceived as a man-made concept called 'God', which conveyed to me cruelty and control – another someone who wanted me to be fat. Without Dr Marion and the spiritual Light that was sent to me I would have surely destroyed myself completely.

Eventually I rallied a little and decided to return to Reading to be closer to Quentin, who had faithfully stuck with me through all of this nightmare, and to return to my job at the Road Research Laboratory. My family did not encourage me to go. This seems amazing to me now, but there was such tightly-knit dysfunction amongst us that no one really wanted to change it. I think I knew somewhere deep inside that if I wanted to stay alive I had to break away from the hold that family relationships had over me. A strange wisdom this, when most of my conscious thought was of longing to die. Yet hidden in the labyrinths of my being, there must have been a vigorous determination to *live*, and not merely to stay alive. So I found a small bed-sit in Reading and moved in with help from Quentin and other people at the church.

Going back to my job was a heroic effort, but was sadly unsuccessful. When I returned to my office I found that I now had to share it, with two bright, ambitious girls who were determined to make careers for themselves. If only (again that thought...) I could have been like them. They had taken down my pictures and got rid of the personal touches I had made to the office. Beside them I felt gauche, stupid, inefficient, and still on substantial doses of tranquillisers and antidepressants, I hardly knew what I was doing. Within two weeks I had collapsed again – this time into the sympathetic arms of the personnel officer, who kindly took me home. After some months, upon the tactful suggestion of this same man, I resigned.

Investigations by my GP revealed that there had been a miscommunication with Westminster Hospital, and that it had never been intended for me to go as an inpatient for the 'truth drug' treatment. I felt devastated. The hope of a cure, however terrifying, had been snatched away. Looking back on this I can see now that a guiding hand had saved me from a treatment which would certainly not have cured me, and would very likely have done me a great deal of damage. Dr Davis informed my GP that the analytical treatment that I was receiving was not working, and recommended that I be transferred to the mental hospital in the Reading district. I was not to know at the time but this edict eventually led me to a life-saving relationship that helped me alter the desperate and downward spiral of my life. It is amazing how the seemingly meaningless and unconnected events of life can later reveal a purposeful pattern woven into the tapestry of one's existence upon earth.

*   *   *   *   *

Throughout this jumble of events that presented as my life at this time, I must have somehow clung to some sort of integrity which kept me alive. One saving grace was that I could still feel care and concern for others, both animals and people, and I think that this indeed was a true grace that brought the Light into my darkened mind and heart, over and over again. I continued to be prescribed high doses of tranquillisers and antidepressants, which, acting as a kind of chemical straightjacket, kept me in a deep state of apathy. Often, it was only the need of another person or creature that could penetrate this fog and motivate me to reach out, to offer help.

It was during this period that Quentin and I had started to attend the Anglican church. It was quieter and more sedate than the rousing evangelicalism of the Baptist church which we had attended throughout our time at university. There, the emotional hymns, long services, and lengthy, vigorous sermons had exhausted me, and although people were very friendly and helpful, I felt that there was a kind of expectation that I would be 'cured' by Jesus and by prayer. And of course I felt that I constantly failed in this.

The minister of the Anglican church was a kind-hearted, undemanding, intellectual man, and he spent many hours listening to me and trying to help. He introduced me to the writing of C S Lewis, including the tales of Narnia. In these simple but profound stories I found some images which communicated with my inner self and gave me a means of conceptualising my torment. In one tale there was a little devil that sat upon a man's shoulder and tormented him day and night with his suggestions. An angel approached and asked the man if he should kill the devil, but although the man longed to be rid of it, he was afraid of losing it. Capitalising on this, the devil fed him with all sorts of fears of what would happen if he let the angel kill him. Finally the man became so desperate that he shouted at the angel to go ahead and kill the devil. When he did

70

so, the devil turned into a magnificent horse, and the man changed into a prince. This story spoke deeply to me of my battle with anorexia nervosa, and I wept when I read it.

I made various friends at the church, some of whom were to be catalysts of a life-changing and life-saving decision on my part. One kind-hearted couple, Jasmine and Percy Hope, took my illness seriously and did not preach a quick religious panacea. What a relief this was! They became good friends, and I often visited their home just outside Reading, to talk, and sometimes to be a baby sitter for their young son. Their home became a little haven of comfort and understanding for me.

However, when they went out and I was left alone with their child and their food, I found the situation very difficult. I did not want to steal their food, and consequently try to deceive them to hide my guilt, but it was torture to know that all that lovely, enticing food was sitting in the fridge and the cupboards. I decided to confess to Jasmine and Percy about my torment, and their understanding and compassion really touched my heart. They agreed to remove all 'tempting' foods from their fridge and cupboards – locking it away or taking it with them, so that there were only 'safe' foods, such as fruit, in the house.

I used to spend many hours talking late into the evening with these friends. Although we never really came to any breakthrough which would bring about an obvious change in my condition, the fact that they were willing to listen, over and over again, and to be involved with me in my struggle, gave me another lifeline.

Like Jasmine and Percy, so many people have tried to help me, by all manner of means, and although at times it may well have seemed that they tried in vain, I was somehow able to incorporate all their kindness and positive energies into my being. This helped me to find the courage to go on living – searching, trying, hoping, longing and above all intending wholeness. The transformation of anorexia nervosa remains central to my life, and kindness in many diverse forms from others continues to sustain me.

71

Jasmine and Percy were sympathetic about my unhappy experiences with my GP. They told me that they had a friend who was a doctor, and recommended me to his practice. This was another important step. Dr Pearson was sensitive and compassionate, and treated me with respect. He never made light of my illness and suffering. His wife, Amanda, was also very kind, and the couple took me under their wing, often inviting me into their kitchen for a cup of tea and chat after my appointment, and sometimes I would sit with their four children while they went out. The children were old enough to stay up until their parents returned home, so I felt safe from the temptation of food. I loved going to the surgery, which was also the family's home. It seemed so much more personal than the large medical centres which are a feature of modern-day primary care.

I recently revisited Dr James and Amanda Pearson at their current home. It was about twenty years since I had last seen them, and perhaps about thirty-eight years since I was first a patient. Their children are now married with children of their own, and one of the daughters had come over specially to see me again. The youngest, Damien, who was just a little lad when I last saw him, collected me from the bus station in his car with his wife and son. We are all still the same people, but we have been changed by the progression of our experiences and the hidden inner journey of our souls. Although our lives had diverged, the love, affection and gratitude were unchanged, and for me had been refined by understanding and my own personal development. The memories of those days give me cause to reflect on the march of time and its unfathomable mystery.

* * * * *

During my time as Dr Pearson's patient, he arranged that my treatment as a psychiatric outpatient be transferred from Westminster Hospital to Greenways Hospital, which was near Reading. First of all I had to see the consultant psychiatrist in charge of the unit. He was a large, thickset man by the name of Dr Lumsden. I remember sitting miserably in his office and his saying what a whining voice I had. Probably I did have a whining voice – and maybe justifiably so. Doesn't a dog whine and cower when it is beaten and kicked? I had been beaten and kicked emotionally by many events in my life, and perhaps it was not surprising that I was whining. I hated him for what he had said, and those words are one of the few things I remember clearly about him. Words can be so powerful in how they shape a fragile identity. Surely it would have been more conducive to a useful therapeutic outcome if he had greeted me in a positive way – employing language that would help to build up my self respect and give me the opportunity to see myself in a different light? My other clear memory of him is his *telling* me how angry I was – not enquiring or asking – and that I needed to express that anger. Once again I felt invaded by his words.

In retrospect, I wonder how he would have responded if I had expressed my anger on the spot by offering an insult comparable to his description of my voice, and suggesting that he should try using a bit of courtesy for a change. I rather doubt that the response would have been particularly accepting and affirming of my anger. So often in therapy I have been told to express anger, but if I plucked up courage to venture an angry outburst, I have been put down and rejected for it. I don't think that anyone has ever congratulated me! I am sad to recall that I quailed before this onslaught and asked Dr Lumsden timidly what the point was of expressing my anger. I wondered if anyone would really be interested, or whether it would have any effect at all.

'What do you do if you are constipated?' he asked.

'Take a laxative,' I replied, not mentioning that I took several packets of laxative after each binge.

'Well you feel better for getting rid of a load of shit, don't you,' he stated, turning a question into a fact, as if he had researched and verified the matter. How enlightening... This was my introduction to therapy at Greenways Hospital.

Maybe I should add that although my experience of Dr Lumsden was consistently negative, I understand that in general he was respected by staff and by patients. I am sure that he took his work seriously, and no doubt had the intention of helping his patients. I learned later on that when I was a patient of his he had been going through personal difficulties. I have wondered if those difficulties had affected the way that he had related to me, or whether his approach was deliberately abrasive and was intended to be constructively challenging. If it were the former, this poses a question. If the psychiatrist is so affected by his own personal struggles that those issues which have arisen overflow into his relationship with a patient, should he be permitted to continue with his work at such times?

The original meaning of the word 'psychiatrist' is 'doctor of the soul'. I believe that, at the very least, such a person should demonstrate clearly the aim of enabling his patients to cope better with their own lives. This is work for which he is paid. Yet a psychiatrist is only a human being, and as such is bound to suffer something of the troubles that assail other members of the human race. If working through those troubles enlighten him (or her) with wisdom and compassion, which can subsequently be offered to patients, that is all to the good. However if such troubles are not fully faced and integrated, they could have a detrimental effect on the relationship between doctor and patient.

After this interview I was admitted as a day-patient for group psychotherapy, which I found to be a nightmare of interactions that felt threatening and invasive, insulting and diminishing, and with which I was totally unable to cope. The process began with a meeting of all the patients in psychotherapy – a large gathering of distressed and hungry souls, all craving the solace and restoration of true recognition and respect. I wonder if any of them found it. I certainly did not. After this we separated into smaller groups for various attempts at group therapy. The type that I disliked most was psychodrama. To me, it seemed akin to the party game of charades, and I was never any good at acting. I tried to enter into it, more for the sake of other patients than myself, but my input felt stilted and false.

Perhaps I am being over-critical of the efforts of the staff to help. I am sure that for many, the intent was laudable and sincere, and maybe for some patients, effective. To me the therapy in these smaller groups seemed like a circle of emptiness. There seemed to be nothing that would nourish my inner self or build me into someone whom I could accept as myself. I did make one or two friends, one of whom became a very long-term friend. We shared a lot of good times together in later years, often reminiscing about our time as patients. One therapist in particular convinced me that she cared, even if she could not penetrate my deep withdrawal and despair. I met other patients who suffered, and I tried to understand them and interact with them in ways which might help. Thus, although the psychotherapy itself did nothing to help me, the context in which it took place had some value, and the experience formed a stepping-stone to the next part of my journey.

After six months of group psychotherapy I was to be discharged, as according to the consultant, it had had no therapeutic effect. I agreed with him. There was apparently no concern for what would happen to me after discharge, and the only possibility offered was further medication. I wandered dejectedly through the labyrinth of corridors, all looking the same and smelling of disinfectant. A voice called my name from behind, and I turned round to see Max Jones, the clinical psychologist. We chatted for a while and I told him that I had been discharged and didn't know what to do next. He indicated that he would like to help me and suggested that perhaps we could try behaviour therapy. I was surprised, but grateful for any offer of help. This was the beginning of a relationship that marked a significant turning point in my life.

Max's suggestion of behaviour therapy was approved by the hospital, and I started seeing him once a week for the treatment.

However, behaviour therapy was not very well developed as a treatment for mental illness in those days. It was modeled on aversive conditioning, in which a certain action or behaviour becomes associated with a negative event or 'punishment'. It was based on the work of cruel and insensitive researchers who delivered unpleasant stimuli such as electric shocks to poor undeserving animals, to see how they would respond. I had hated having to read about this in my degree studies, and now I myself was to be a recipient of this barbaric procedure. By 'barbaric' I refer to the procedure as applied to animals in scientific research. I think that in the case of some consenting humans it could have a useful effect, perhaps as a simple kind of prompt to help to steer people away from habits which they wish to modify. There was a male patient who was given to exposing himself, who was also receiving this treatment. I couldn't help wondering what effect it would have on his future intimate relationships, if any.

I was so desperate that I would probably have submitted to almost any treatment if I thought that it would stop me bingeing and would cure me of the illness that was devouring my life. A forlorn hope indeed. I was attached to wires, and was given a painful shock every time I touched or took a mouthful of 'binge' food. I know Max really wanted to help me, but I can hardly believe such gross methods were officially approved as treatment for anorexia nervosa. The consultant had even suggested a leucotomy at one time! I am not sure if it was meant to be a joke, but if it were, it was entirely tasteless and cruel.

The memories of the agony of that time continue to help me attune to a universal experience of despair that can affect all living creatures. There are an infinite variety and number of expressions of despair, and one can perceive it everywhere, even in the earth itself. Human beings can go to great lengths to avoid acknowledging its existence; the entanglements of the mind dress it in fantastic forms, and the body may become an unfathomable dictionary of it. The web of life that is woven upon our earthly home has great pathos entwined amongst its threads. However it is important not to become overwhelmed by a sensitivity to despair, but to perceive it alongside the comparable infinity of expressions of joy, beauty, nobility, kindness, courage and other such principles that manifest amongst all life forms.

The behaviour therapy was not working. I think that Max hated doing it do me. I was a nervous wreck, and my anorexia continued unabated. One day, after I had taken a bite from a Mars Bar and shot out of the chair with a scream of pain from the electric shock, we both decided that neither of us could take any more of it. He decided that individual psychotherapy would be a better option, and so from then on, I went to him for these sessions. Max's room became a special place for me. It seemed more private and personal than the scrum of interactions in group psychotherapy. I easily become attached to places, and I have found that they can become repositories of meaning and significance for me. Max's office became another world for me, where another person cared enough about me to make a determined effort to get through to me and to require my response in a genuine and helpful way.

At first I was equally determined to evade the directness of his approach, attempting to avoid the pain of feeling the emotions that rose in me. I tried all the tricks of evasion that I had at my disposal. We were wily opponents! During this time my heart began to open and I felt love for Max. With it came great pain, of course, but I think that without that opening of my heart and loosening of my emotions I would surely have died.

Psychotherapy can be an intense and focused experience, in which one relates to the therapist in a situation which is removed from everyday life, and is therefore somewhat rarified in terms of interpersonal interactions. One usually knows the therapist only in the context of therapy, and because of this, it is possible to perceive the therapist in a range of ways that help in the task of externalising one's inner drama. I think that, for me, this particular therapeutic intervention provided the opportunity to feel love in relation to a man, without those feelings being abused. In part, it was a childlike love – the kind that my father was unable to accept and to nurture. While my adult self held a mature regard and affection for Max, the child self reached out in desperate longing for something she had never received. Those longings were held with respect and compassion, and this gave me a ray of hope.

Some of my memories of that time are amusing and some of them sad. I still miss Max. There has never been anyone like him in my life since. Recently we met again, after fifteen years or so, and for me it was a wonderful experience. On a subsequent occasion, my sister Sylvia accompanied me to meet Max and his wife, Adelaide. We had lunch together and enjoyed general conversation, exchanging anecdotes about our families, and things we had been doing. This was a very special privilege and provided me with an opportunity to engage in the experience of everyday life with someone who had been previously been so important to me as a therapist. Time had gone by and life had brought us differing experiences, all of which enriched our meeting.

At some point during my treatment at Greenways Hospital I found a feral kitten in the grounds. I had heard mewing during a group meeting and it had upset me terribly, and as soon as the meeting was over I went in search of the kitten. I found the poor little scrap hiding in the flowerbeds. I could not bear to leave him there, so I took him back to my flat. Keeping pets was forbidden, but I hoped that the landlords would not find out until I could find a good home for the kitten. I called him Freud.

Unfortunately the landlords did find out. They inspected the flats when the occupants were not there, coming in with their own keys. I explained my situation, but they were unsympathetic and gave me notice to move. I was desperate, as I had nowhere to go and did not want to give up on little Freud, whom I had grown to love. Quentin came to the rescue and took Freud to his tiny bed-sit, where he lived while he was doing his

PhD. We also rescued another kitten whom we called Princess.

Quentin looked after Freud and Princess until it became apparent that our little Freud was blind and had cat flu. The vet felt that it would be kinder to have him put to sleep, and as we did not have the resources to nurse him, we had to agree. We were both very upset. Princess lived with Quentin for quite some time, until he had to move, and then she was given a home by a kind friend of mine. The landlords let me stay a bit longer when I told them that the kitten had gone, but I think that they wanted to get rid of me anyway, so after a while I was given notice again – this time with no possibility of renewing the let.

After a desperate search for alternative accommodation, a woman from the church offered me a room in her house, and with the help of Quentin and another young man from the church, I moved in with her. Unfortunately this arrangement did not work out well. Mrs A was an extremely upright, uptight person with rather narrow religious views and was determined to *make* me 'better'. I felt very uncomfortable around her. She and some of her friends knew of a psychiatrist who specialised in exorcism, and being convinced that I was possessed of a malevolent spirit, she arranged for me to have an appointment with him. It was kind of her. I believe that she certainly meant well. She paid for the appointment and drove me to this psychiatrist with one of her friends.

Dr McKenzie lived in a beautiful old house in the New Forest, where he saw private patients. I had read his book, and had been impressed with the accounts of patients being delivered from oppressing spirits and cured from chronic psychiatric illnesses. I had to prepare for the appointment by drawing up a family tree and noting any mental or physical illnesses suffered by members of my immediate family and our ancestors. Dr McKenzie's theory was that a troubled spirit in one's family line could influence vulnerable members of that line and cause psychiatric symptoms. The interview with him was not unpleasant. In fact I found him kind and friendly, when compared with many psychiatrists I had encountered previously.

However I was alarmed by his diagnosis, which was that I was indeed oppressed or possessed by a troubled spirit which had probably got a foothold in my family tree in the long distant past and was now manifesting through me. He arranged to do a public exorcism in the church of which I was a member, in conjunction with the vicar. The vicar was, I think, a little sceptical, but he wanted to help me, so he agreed to participate and oversee the service. I was instructed to invite as many people as I could to come to pray and support me. I was so desperate that I would have done almost anything, and an exorcism seemed a small trial through which to go, if it would cure me of anorexia nervosa.

When the day arrived I was full of dread, wondering what would happen. Would there be puffs of smoke out of hell, or screeches from dispossessed demons? Would I fall to the ground and foam at the mouth like those delivered from demons in Jesus' day? My mind was taken over by a veritable cinema of fantasy. Kneeling at the altar as the service began, I was aware of a great yearning to be free of the terrible torment that had been labelled anorexia nervosa. I longed for my mind and body to be my own again, and to feel in control of myself.

As the service progressed I began to wail and howl. But this was not because a demon was issuing from my agonised being. It was because I knew that nothing was going to happen, and that I would get up from the altar with the same torment as when I had knelt down. Most people must have thought that a powerful deliverance was taking place, but I knew that there would be no instantaneous miracle. I wept so much that I was completely exhausted at the end of the service, and certainly not radiant and triumphant as Mrs A had expected. She had prepared a little tea party and had invited several of her clique to it, and I was expected to be the guest of honour. Oh, the shame and despair that I felt! I had failed again. My kind GP, Dr Pearson, who had attended the service, stepped in and said that I was overstressed and that he would take care of me. He packed me into his car, still weeping, and took me back to his comforting home. How very grateful I was. It was as if he was an angel in disguise.

Eventually I crawled back in disgrace to Mrs A, and things were very strained for a while. Dr McKenzie was not disconcerted, and said that everything had gone according to plan. Could he have said otherwise, I wonder? He said that I would gradually recover, and indeed I have, but there was no recovery subsequent to the exorcism and nothing that I could directly attribute to it. In fact I became more and more desperate.

It did not seem appropriate to stay with Mrs A any longer, as she could not handle my disintegration, and I was so unhappy there. After a while I managed to get a bed-sit through someone I knew at the hospital, and with the help of another kind person from the church, I moved in there. It was rather basic and not as comfortable as my last place, but the people were friendly and the landlord more lenient. It was relief to have my own place again, but I was well past the stage where I could maintain a viable life on my own.

Reflecting upon this experience now, I think that my mind and body had never felt like my own, and that I had always been at the mercy of all manner of forces which I did not recognise or understand. Somehow I had never felt 'solid'. Now, as I go about my daily life, although I can still feel very anxious and do not always cope very well, I generally feel that I am a person, and that my body belongs to me. This seems nothing short of miraculous, in comparison with those long years of disintegration. However the memory is but a breath away, and I can never take my sanity for granted.

I cannot judge the effect of the exorcism in spiritual terms. Maybe something *was* released, who knows? The miracle of my sanity was not brought about by a spectacular deliverance but by years and years of persistence and determination – living life day by day with the unshakable intent of becoming a whole person, seeking and absorbing healing and help from all manner of sources.

* * * * *

Sometime during those years I managed to get a job in a shoe firm. The managers were members of the church that I attended and were keen to help me, so I was given a job as a junior clerk in the accounts office. The man in charge of the office, Herbert, was a humorous and kindhearted person, patient with my dopey inefficiency and endlessly helpful with my confused bungling. The other people in the office, and the chief accountant, Mr Jay, were also very pleasant and kind, and somehow I limped along in the job for about a year. I was forever making mistakes, but no one ever made me feel bad about it. Even the blotches I made on the ledger were only met with a resigned 'Oh dear, it does look rather untidy' from Mr Jay.

There were no computers in offices at that time and most of the work had to be done by hand. The office did possess some adding machines, which some of the staff operated with remarkable skill and speed, but my efforts at using them usually resulted in a different total each time. I was tactfully moved onto the sales department, where I had to check the shoe sales at each branch. This kind of office would be unusual now, with computers as an essential part of business life, but for me at that time, it was a peaceful and protective environment in which to work.

The atmosphere was sedate and quiet, and there was plenty of room for chat and friendliness. I was allowed to leave a couple of hours early one day each week to go to my appointment with Max. I used to go and change my clothes in the toilets, thankfully slipping out of the obligatory skirt into my best trousers that still fitted me. I did not like wearing skirts, as I felt that my thighs and knees were such a disgusting shape.

Apart from rooting around in the shoes in the warehouse, I did not like the actual work, although I loved the people and was terribly grateful to them. I hated any kind of office work, and still do. All the frustrating bits of paper and sitting about all day made me feel bored, trapped and stagnant. There was too much space for my mind to continually return to its obsessive pursuits. I think that the accounting system of the shoe firm must have suffered from my efforts, but the job, while I was able to hold it down, did give a little structure to my life.

One of the managers was wealthy and had a beautiful country house a little way out of Reading. He had various evangelical gatherings there, to which I was invited, and the family also invited me to stay for the weekend whenever I liked. I loved going there, more for the company than for the evangelism, but the food was a problem. I had to force myself to stay away from the kitchen in case I stole any of the food. I felt uncomfortable and embarrassed sharing meals with them, as I felt sure that my guilty cravings must be obvious to all.

I have never liked eating with other people – the effect of the stressful mealtimes when I lived at home continued to affect me. As far back as I can remember, I have had a deep sense of shame about the actions of my physical body, in particular anything to do with eating. I think that my discomfort with food and my body must have been apparent early on, as I remember sitting in a school packed-lunch group and someone saying to me, 'Jennifer doesn't want to eat with you, she says you eat funny.' Jennifer had gone to another group and I had asked where she was. That remark was so painful that it has stuck with me all my life. Needless to say I never ate with the lunch group again, but went off on my own to devour my rations.

Dr Pearson and his wife had started attending a prayer and praise meeting run by a community which had come to live at Fairfield Manor, a large country house in the village of Davebury, about eight miles from Reading. They invited me to go along with them one evening. I was reluctant. I didn't want to go back to that kind of exhausting and energetic Christianity. However I was so grateful to Dr Pearson for the help he had given me that I would have done anything for him if I could, so I eventually agreed to go.

On my first visit, Fairfield Manor seemed a very strange

place – a large, beautiful and imposing old building, swarming with a sea of people, mostly American as far as I could tell. They all seemed to be hugging each other and saying 'Praise the Lord'. I didn't really like it at all. I felt rather frightened and ill at ease, and hid myself as best as I could on a hard uncomfortable chair, next to Dr Pearson.

When everyone was settled, the singing started. It was mostly gospel songs and choruses, performed with expertise and enthusiasm using a variety of musical instruments. Then it was time for prayer. People began to pray out loud in an informal way, addressing God and Jesus in simple everyday language, which seemed very odd to me. I was used to set liturgies and formal prayers, and even in the Baptist church which I had first attended when I was at university, there was a set service and set ways of saying and doing things. A young woman began to speak of a vision that she had received, and my attention became riveted. Without knowing anything about me or even that I was there at all, she was telling my story in pictorial language, portraying vividly the despair that I found so hard to communicate. I started to weep and then to howl uncontrollably throughout the rest of the service. Gentle singing covered my embarrassment, and when the service was over, the priest came over to see if he could help. This was the beginning of my involvement with the Community of Transformation.

Isolation

FEAR stalks through the labyrinths
Of my cringing mind,
Dark halls echoing
With memories that bind.

Hostile faces, cold blank stares,
Unfriendly faces, harsh words
Chase each other through doors
That open and shut.

Mocking laughter, children's taunts,
Raw humiliation haunts
The avenues down which I wander,
Wells of silence in which I ponder.

Tormented I turn
Seeking oblivion.
In unbearable pain I lash out
To destroy the nearest creation,
Myself, or something or someone I love.

Drifting voices persecute,
Clawing at my sleep,
Into the sinews of my thinking
Stealthily they creep.

Out of control
My mind grasps desperately
At the last dregs of sanity.
Rigid systems collapse around me,
My life crumbles in a heap of ashes.

'My God, why hast Thou forsaken me?'
I cry to the empty space.
Stooping down to the ground I see
The image of a face.

The eyes are compassionate,
The lips do not smile,
Grave with the sharing
Of my pain.

Out of the horror of doubt and darkness
The Son of God I recognize.
With infinite patience he draws me
Out of my prison,
To the place where I know
He is risen.

Jacqueline Kemp

Chapter Four

The Community of Transformation

i

Following my collapse at the community's prayer and praise meeting, I was invited to go out to Fairfield Manor and visit the community itself. I began to do this on a regular basis, joining in with work such as cleaning, gardening, dish-washing and so on, and staying for the services.

At first I was terrified of everybody, cringing from the hugs, unnerved by the directness of communication, and bemused by what seemed to me to be a vast number of people. On the whole I had lived a solitary life, and even as a child I had been very much a loner. I had few friends and my companions were mostly family members. I had very little in the way of social skills and found it very difficult to relate to people. The benefit of the brief period in my last year at university, when I had opened out a little, had become lost to me as my emotional and mental struggles escalated. This situation had been exacerbated by the stupor that was induced by the drugs I was taking. However, through the friendly welcome of the community folk, I began gradually to recognise faces and to make tentative connections.

Yet the life that I lived between my visits was becoming increasingly untenable and disordered. Thoughts of suicide and longing to die were at the forefront of my mind, and apart from my therapy with Max and my visits to Dr Marion and my GP, I hardly saw anybody. Every day I went out and bought a huge pile of sweets, cakes, biscuits, bread and other 'forbidden' foods, and ate until I could not force anything else down. I spent the rest of each day collapsed on my bed, overcome with revulsion, horror and self-hatred, and frequently took too much of my medication.

My metabolism was very disturbed and I was gaining about, half a stone every week. No one could really believe me when I spoke of my horror of being just a mountain of flesh, with no personality or identity left. An amorphous blob was how I envisioned myself. Even Dr Marion could not penetrate this area of my reality, nor discern from where this nightmare of annihilation was generated. This therefore was my solitary torture chamber. The fear of this kind of experience manifesting again remains to this day.

One day, after packing myself full of food for the umpteenth time, I stepped on to my ever watchful scales, which sat brooding like an eye in the bathroom, waiting to reflect to me the extent of my depravity. I had put on weight again! It was obvious that the needle was creeping up and up, faster and faster, day by day. It was as if a hammer of doom sounded inside me, and I knew that my whole being was cracking open under the pressure of my internal agony. I could bear no more, and felt certain that I would be dead in a week or two if something didn't save me. I fell on to the floor and cried out 'God you can do what you like with me.' I have no memory of how I pulled myself out of this state of disintegration.

It was not long afterwards that one the elders of the Community of Transformation invited me to go to live with them and to become a member. I accepted, unfortunately more out of desperation than of religious fervour, but this radical decision saved my life, and changed the whole course of my destiny. My fear of people and of making such a change was so great that it was probably only suffering and despair in its most extreme form which propelled me to step through that fear, and to make a choice which gradually began to lead me away from the brink of insanity and death.

I spent about nine years as a member of the Community of Transformation. My experience of that lifestyle was so varied and far-reaching that I can record here but a series of small windows into it. The tapestry of my life and relationships in that era of my life would fill a book in itself. I shall recount just a selection of those events, the ones which seem most relevant to my journey with anorexia nervosa.

ii

When I first moved into Fairfield Manor, I had someone with me day and night – twenty-four-hour supervision. I shared a room with a gentle young English woman who had joined the community some months earlier. She was very kind and supportive to me. Looking back I often wonder how she is getting on, and wish that I could express the depth of my gratitude to her. It can't have been easy, having to share a space with someone as desperate as I was.

One of the community elders was appointed to look after me, and I was with her most of the day, working in the office with her. When I wanted to go anywhere else I had to ask her permission, and tell her where I was going to be, even if it was just to use the toilet. I hated and resented this restriction, but with the fear of death at my heels, I accepted it – with some muttering – and in fact, it began to stabilise me.

It is strange how that fear, and an awareness of the lack of viable alternatives, kept me sticking to a lifestyle that was demanding, confronting and exhausting. However, despite the drawbacks of that system, I believe that it led me gradually towards greater maturity and health. Reflecting upon this I see more clearly now how light and darkness are inseparable, and that darkness is not intrinsically evil or dangerous. The term 'darkness' has acquired negative semantic space, especially in spiritual parlance. Maybe this could have something to do with an inbuilt evolutionary fear, of a time of day when it is more difficult to see and therefore to detect danger. I prefer the oriental idea of yin and yang, where both polarities are part of each other and of equal value. The Light and Darkness in our western religions are all part of the same process of journeying towards wholeness.

Although we can rarely exert complete control over the experiences that come to us in life, it is a matter of our choice how we respond to them, and whether we can use each one as a creative learning experience. This is easy to say, and unbelievably difficult and challenging to put into practice. By some means that I do not completely understand, I was able to respond to the opportunity offered to me by the Community of Transformation and use it creatively in my process of growth towards wholeness.

It was fortunate for me that amongst the members of the Community of Transformation there were three doctors. My own GP and his wife and family had joined the community shortly after me, and there was another English couple already living there who were both doctors. The elders of the community felt that I should give up taking my drugs, but I was fearful about this, as they had become far more than a prop and provided a strange kind of solace.

One of the doctors was asked to oversee this process and I made a giant 'leap of faith' by getting rid of them all at once. I flushed all of them down the toilet and have never taken another one since. However I am not recommending this as a suitable method to follow when coming off drugs, as for some people, it could be very unwise, and even dangerous.

I spent two weeks with severe withdrawal symptoms, my body reeling from the shock of the sudden change. After a time, my system began to clear, and with lots of support and prayers, I started to stabilise. This was a major turning point in my life, as it was not just a matter of stopping medication, but the beginning of a clearing out process of my whole being.

The community lived a kind of early church lifestyle, and shared everything. In theory everything was common property, so my possessions were no longer my own, although I was allowed to keep some of them around me. In practice however, things did seem to work out a bit differently. I found this incredibly hard. I have always respected and valued material things, and have been strongly attached to what I considered to be mine. They seemed to provide some kind of clothing and shape for my amorphous concept of self.

My beloved car had to go into the common pool of transport, and this was tremendously painful as it was the one that my father had bought for me. It was one of the few gifts that he had actually chosen for me himself and which we went to purchase together. It was a symbol to me of the love and recognition that I craved from him, and also a symbol of my independence.

However, I had to let go of all the structures of my identity when I entered the community life. I found it heartbreaking that I was not allowed to continue my therapy with Dr Marion or with Max. It was explained to me that the community was the expression of Christ on Earth, and therefore in itself was sufficient, and that all needs could be met within the Body of Christ. At the time I didn't really understand this, and it did nothing to assuage my pain at being prevented from seeing the two people who had sustained me through desperate times and whom I had grown to love dearly. It was one of those doctrinal constructions of the community that seemed to me to be illogical. Other practical needs were met from outside sources – why was *my* need singled out for the application of a theoretical interpretation of Biblical text, whereas in other circumstances it was applied more loosely?

I felt that it was a convenient myth to protect the community power lines from outside influences which might challenge the set up, but of course I did not dare to say this at the time. Perhaps I could not formulate this perception clearly when I was suffering from the apparent injustice of the edict. I just felt that something wasn't right, and didn't hold water. However there was nothing I could do about it if I wanted to stay, so I had to accept the prohibition and suffer the pain.

In a sense I lost myself to the community for a time, but in spite of the inner pressure from my illness and the rigid requirement to conform to the way of life of the community with its particular system of ideas, somehow I never allowed it to have the last word on my identity, and never allowed it to define me. The context of the community's lifestyle allowed me to develop considerably in my personality and life skills, and later I felt the need to move on. I have a great deal of gratitude for all that I gained from the experience of living there, and to the people through whom that experience was mediated.

I found the discipline of the community to be strict and severe – not so much in the monastic sense, but according to its own code of behaviour. There were no rules, or so I was told, but there were plenty of unwritten ones which masqueraded in various guises – and woe betide you if you broke them! One of these rules was 'Commitment' and another was 'Responsibility' – words whose frequent use sounded like meaningless jargon to my uncomprehending ears. They seemed to me to mean putting the interests of the community before one's own, even to the extent of violating individual convictions and intuitions. Responsibility seemed to be a matter of being responsible to the life of the community, and perhaps therefore not being one hundred percent responsible for your own thoughts and actions. It was a difficult matter to interpret, and I pondered endlessly, trying to make sense of it all.

I later thought that such principles might actually foster a lack of personal responsibility, in the sense of doing what one was told rather than fully taking on whatever came by way of one's choices in life. Generally speaking though, in my first few months at Fairfield Manor I received a great deal of kindness, and even the severity of the elders was tempered in my direction. I gradually began to respond to people, and to my surprise, found them responding to me in return. My battered personality began to take on a new form. In my efforts to relate to people as I was required to do, I found my heart expanding and my love beginning to grow.

For a time, life seemed comparatively easy and sane when compared with the way I had been living before. Fairfield Manor was a truly beautiful place, set in the heart of the Berkshire countryside, and this itself had a healing effect on me. During my years with the community there were so many people who touched my life, in a variety of ways. Each touch was meaningful and precious, even if I did not like the person concerned, for those touches brought me back to life, and nourished me as I lived through each day.

My little tasks within the community lifestyle gave me some kind of identity, even though I resented some of them. One that I did like was working with the head gardener, who was not a member of the community but who had taken care of the grounds for many years. Mr Thornton radiated a kind and steady presence and was a man who was accustomed to working with the land. He would send me off into the bamboo bushes to cut canes, or into the greenhouses to water the plants, and I loved the opportunity to disappear like this for a short while. I also worked in the community office and later on the telephone exchange when it was put in. I don't think that I was very good at the latter, and found all the plugs and switches rather confusing. Important conversations were at risk of being cut off, when I was on duty! However I found the work took my mind away from its habitual short circuits of thinking endlessly about food and my weight, and this gave me a measure of relief.

A breath of blessed freedom came when at last I was trusted enough to go out alone to drive one of the old bangers belonging to the community down to Davebury village post office to post the mail. One of the women in our office often gave me money to buy some fruit or other treats for us, and that was a real honour for me. I found that to be trusted with the money gave me a sense of dignity, and I had no inclination to spend it on 'binge food', as I loved bringing back the treats to share around.

At that time Davebury was a lovely little picturesque English village with a quaint air of benign gentility, which soothed and comforted me, and gave me a sense of stability.

On Saturday evenings the community held 'celebrations', which were compulsory whether one felt like celebrating or not. These consisted of some sort of entertainment provided by members of the community for each other. The community was divided into households, and each household took a turn. Many people were very talented, and celebrations could turn out to be elaborate and sometimes hilarious affairs. I began to discover that I had a wry sense of humour, and enjoyed contributing ideas for celebrations. This sense of humour emerged increasingly as I became more myself and was to save me time and time again from the grip of suicidal despair. Sometimes, in the last moments of endurance and without any premeditation or conscious decision on my part, it was as if a window opened and I would suddenly find myself able to write a penetrating satire on community life, or produce a revealing cartoon. At that point I seemed be in touch with an ability to look through and beyond all the complicated dramas of our lives and see the point of simply being human. I learned that sometimes my perception could be too sharp and my pen too caustic, and that humour, like every other gift, can be a double-edged sword. It can be used either with compassion and sensitivity, to lift people's spirits and to help them on their way, or to expose pain, and to humiliate, thus destroying dignity and self-respect. I had to learn this lesson and I am grateful for that.

I once wrote the following songs for a community celebration, adapting some Gilbert and Sullivan opera 'patter' songs, which I remembered so well from the days when I used to go to these operas with my sister. I had quite a bit of fun devising these, and even more performing them for the rest of the community with Lola singing the verses and me playing the piano. Lola had trained as an opera singer before joining the community and was extremely good at anything musical, especially singing. We had the pleasure of making everyone laugh, and receiving an ovation for our performance.

The Little List Song

As some day it may happen that a victim must be found,
I've got a little list, I've got a little list
Of community offenders who might well be underground,
But who never should be missed, who never should be missed.
There's the pestilential nuisance who never is on time,
And all people who take lengthy baths and leave them caked with grime,
All children who are sassy and can floor you with their flak,
All people who 'just borrow things' and never give them back,
And all those persons who on leaving junk around perennially insist,
They'd none of them be missed, they'd none of them be missed.

Chorus:

For she's got them on the list, she's got them on the list,
And they'll none of them be missed, they'll none of them be missed.

There's the drivers who on driving cars forget to bring back keys,
They never will be missed, they never will be missed,
The people who leave dirty cups wherever they may please,
I'm sure they won't be missed, I'm sure they won't be missed.
The person in the choir who is singing out of tune
And who gets his music muddled up and leaves it in the room,
Persistent guys with cameras who take awkward photographs,
All people who have cheesy grins and irritating laughs,
And people who don't understand and get things in a twist,
They'd none of them be missed, they'd none of them be missed.

Chorus:

There's the genius in the kitchen making endless oatmeal bread,
I've put her on the list, I've put <u>her</u> on the list,
The guy who wants to talk to you just as you're going to bed,
I know he won't be missed, I know he won't be missed.
The people who write memos and who pop them in your tray,
And hand you lots of paper stuff for <u>you</u> to put away,
The person in the room above who bangs around at night,
The laundry lady washing clothes who shrinks them till they're tight,
And all those persons who on shouting 'Praise the Lord!' persist,
They'd none of them be missed, they'd none of them be missed.

Chorus:
For we've got them on the list, we've got them on the list
And they'll none of them be missed, they'll none of them be missed.

Adapted from The Mikado by W S Gilbert and Sir Arthur Sullivan
by Jacqueline Kemp

The Christian in Community

I am the very model of a Christian in community,
I dwell with all my fellows in harmonious fecundity,
I've changed my life of luxury to living impecuniously,
And to pastoral confrontations I've developed an immunity!
I've given up my image of success and worldly vanity
And in the midst of doing it have held on to my sanity,
You'll never hear me uttering a swear word or profanity,
I smile and say 'We'll praise the Lord!' in every calamity.

My speech and conversation are the height of all piosity,
I never show upon my face a trace of animosity,
In services my bearing has an air of great pomposity,
I never tell the preacher that his sermon's a monstrosity!
My conduct is exemplary, distinguished by sobriety,
I never join in foolishness or giggling or riotry.
I manage my affairs with individual propriety
And make myself aware of the dynamics of society.

If anyone has troubles that to him seem problematical,
I offer him advice that is discreet and diplomatical,
I tell him that he'll be all right if he is charismatical,
Or maybe that he needs to take a very long sabbatical!
If anyone has questions I have arguments immutable,
I know my Bible back to front, my doctrine is inscrutable.
In short I always make the best of every opportunity
To prove that I'm the model of a Christian in community.

Adapted from The Pirates of Penzance by W S Gilbert and Sir
Arthur Sullivan
by Jacqueline Kemp

I had two animal friends at Fairfield Manor. They were Bizzie and Whiskers, the cats who belonged to the doctor couple who took care of me in the early months there. The cats had to live in the cellar and I felt sorry for them. It seemed rough justice to relegate them there, after they had been used to a comfortable suburban life. I asked if I could take their food down to them and the owners were perhaps relieved to be saved the bother. I used to love going down there, into the subterranean privacy of the cellar, with plates of cat food and whatever titbits I could find for them. We became fond of each other, and sometimes Bizzie would wander into the office to see me, and go to sleep in my 'In' tray. Whiskers preferred to find a warm seat in the corridors, where he was allowed to doze for a while. Other small creatures inhabited the cellar, and I was thrilled if I found a frog or a toad. A particularly large toad used to sit on the cellar steps, and I loved meeting him on my way to see the cats. These meetings with living creatures were always so personal and so precious, for I shared with them an intimacy and a knowing that I could rarely share with people.

I did develop a certain camaraderie with some of the members of the community. For a long time I had to share a room with various women, and though I hated this enforced lack of privacy, some kind of bonding did grow between me and my room mates – with some more than others. Certain incidents could be the trigger for a lot of girlish giggling between us – something that I had not enjoyed for years. For example, when one room-mate and I were attending a very solemn and formal Eucharist held by the community at a nearby church, the woman pronouncing the blessing made a slip of the tongue. It was either that or she had a very broad American accent. Instead of saying 'The grace of the Lord be always with you' she said 'The grease of the Lord be always with you'. My pal caught my eye and whispered, and we spluttered into our handkerchiefs, contemplating the delightful image of a greasy Christian slipping into salvation through the gates of heaven. Irreverent perhaps, but it brought a touch of innocent relief.

Another incident sticks in my memory, an amusing snippet of 'lavatory humour' that brought us all back to basics. The drainage systems of the old manor house were ancient and in need of repair, and did not cope well with the influx of energetic and hungry religious folk, when for years they had had to serve only a few ageing nuns. Toilets were frequently blocking up and sewers overflowing. The toilet just opposite my room developed a problem. Someone had deposited an enormous pooh in it, and it just would not flush away! We did not know who the culprit was, but Someone In Charge was called to examine the situation. There was a great deal of flushing, exclaiming, and finally in sheer desperation, chopping up the excrement! Meanwhile my room-mate and I were hiding behind the door splitting our sides with laughter. I am not sure whether the offending item was ever flushed completely or not, but sewage repair was very soon on the agenda. I could fill several pages with examples of the lighter side of life in a religious community. It was those touches of human fallibility that helped me to see right through to the core of existence, and not get caught up with identifying myself too closely with the constructs and systems that we have created.

On the other side of the coin were various nightmares of community life that had to be endured. 'Sharing' was one of them. This was the time when the whole community got together in groups to share what they had been reading in the Bible and what the Lord had been saying to them through it. It would be the worse for you if you had nothing suitable to share! One of the elders could be particularly cruel and scathing, and I dreaded being in his group. However I soon discovered that I had a knack of finding a passage of scripture and relating it very pertinently to my life and thoughts. Whether this was born out of a terror of getting a roasting in the sharing group, or from a spiritual hunger, I cannot really tell, but probably it was a bit of both. At that time I believed sincerely that it was the Lord speaking to me through the words of the Bible, and I found that my researches into the Holy Book did penetrate my character and spirit in a remarkable way. What was relevant and helpful at that stage of my journey would not necessarily have the same meaning and significance now, but I think that integrity and a profound desire to change were the elements that sharpened a gift I already had and turned it into something which contributed to my growth and healing.

Mealtimes were another occasion which I dreaded. The whole community ate together in the large hall of the manor house, gathered round tables and generally in household groups. I hated communal eating. Food was prepared communally in the adjacent kitchen and everybody had to eat the same foods. Diets were not allowed unless approved by the elders, and you had to have a portion of every food item that was served whether or not you liked it, and eat everything on your plate. Consequences for not doing so were dire. The uneaten food would be presented again at the next meal, and no other would be allowed until it was eaten. Meanwhile you came under fire about various violations of commitment and responsibility, setting a bad example and so on. I found this oppressive regulation very threatening, as I had to eat foods that I perceived as 'dangerous'. I felt that my individual relationship with food, which was such a fundamental factor of my identity, was being obliterated, and that my right to choose my weight was being taken away.

I could understand the community's stance against waste of food – in itself a crime against those who go hungry. Yet it took no account of individual metabolism and differing nutritional needs that exist across a spectrum of people. Often the meals were not nourishing or appetising, and of course I was always terrified of 'calories' and 'getting fat'. However in comparison with the extremes of dieting, starving and bingeing that I had been going through for years, even this was preferable. It definitely provided a more stable eating pattern for me. Many of my comrades were very sympathetic to my eating difficulties at these meals, and would encourage and help me in many ways. Sometimes one would surreptitiously eat a bit of the food on my plate that I didn't want, or hold my hand under the table, or the boys might give me a sly poke in the ribs to make me laugh.

Eventually I did manage to get permission to 'go on a diet'. I managed this feat by means of a duodenal ulcer and several visits to the local doctor's surgery. One of the doctors there was an ex-army doctor, renowned for being somewhat tough and unsympathetic with his patients. One of his favourite prescriptions was 'open a window and take some exercise' – which does now seem to be a sensible piece of advice in view of today's focus on pharmaceutical drugs as a cure for illness. One always had to see whichever of the two doctors was on duty, as there was no appointment system, and my heart sank when I realised that he was in attendance. To my astonishment he showed understanding of my dilemma and was unusually sympathetic. He gave me permission to lose weight, but said that I should not go below a certain level of pounds, and advised me to avoid foods which were liable to be difficult to digest. Another angel in disguise! I was so grateful to him, and over the years that I was there, built up a measure of relationship with him.

There were rotas posted each week for duties – washing up, serving, putting food away and clearing tables. I hated the latter as I could never resist eating leftovers from the serving dishes, surreptitiously stuffing them into my mouth as I hastened out with a dish. Washing up took ages but it could be fun, with opportunities for banter and a bit of slapstick comedy. You always had to do it someone else's way though – wash the cutlery with a dishcloth, rinse the dishes like this, use a pan scrubber like that. There did not seem to be much room for creative initiative even in the scullery.

As I mentioned before, the community had a considerable number of very talented people amongst its members. An aspect of its *raison d'être* was to stimulate and promote renewal of the Church, particularly in the area of worship, and the skills of the members were applied very effectively in this direction, in the form of music, dance and drama.

Part of the community's living was earned by making professional tapes and records of music for worship, and I was thrilled to be invited to join both the regular choir and the recording choir. I had never done anything like this before and it was a new and exciting experience. Elspeth and Lola were both gifted professional musicians who organised and directed the musical activities of the community. They were the driving force behind the community's musical expertise, and it was through them that my own musical skills began to expand and develop. They were both highly creative in their use of the varying talents and abilities available, together with the diverse collection of musical instruments that many of the members had brought with them. Somehow they blended us all into a harmonious whole to produce a new and vital sound. I felt honoured to be asked to play my tenor recorder on one of the first recordings. It was a mark of recognition and opportunity that my soul and personality craved. It was fun and also interesting, directing my mind away from its treadmill of obsessions towards other horizons.

iv

After about a year at Fairfield Manor, rumours of a Great Change began to spread through the community. I was terrified, feeling that I had no control over decisions that might be made, which would affect me profoundly. The only choices that I could see were of remaining with the community and submitting to what was asked of me, or returning to my life of self-destructive hell. Maybe there were other options, but in the grip of anorexia nervosa, with my back against a wall, it was not within my capability at that time to consider them.

It was finally announced that the accommodation at Fairfield Manor was not suitable long-term, as it was too expensive to run. The community was to be divided into three parts, each part moving to a separate location. Locations were chosen on the basis of there being an existing religious community or a chance to build up a community within a church congregation from which some of the members had come. I looked with trepidation at the three places on the map – Barrowgate in the south, Peel House Community in Dorset, and the Isle of Drumduish off the west coast of Scotland. I thought that if I had to go anywhere, I would rather go to Drumduish, where it was likely that most of the people I had got to know would go, too. The Bishop of Argyll had offered the lease of the Cathedral on the Isle and its properties in turn for the community being responsible for the upkeep of those premises and serving the needs of the parishioners, including conducting services at the Cathedral. Gregory Mickleham, one of the founders of the community, was to be the Provost, and the other priests in the community would take responsibility for the small congregation.

Shortly after the announcement, each of us was called before the elders and told where they would like us to go and asked if we had any objections, although I am not sure if these would have been taken into account. I was told that they would like me to go to Drumduish, and I agreed, with a sense of relief and confirmation in my heart. It was a long way from my family and initially they were very upset about it, but it was to prove to be a healing separation. The increased geographical distance from them and the radically different lifestyle that I was leading began to break the damaging psychic and emotional ties that had bound me so tightly to the dysfunctional family dynamics that had contributed to my mental illness. The break was not easy for any of us, and it was not until after the death of both my parents that I could make visits to the family home, and know with certainty that the bondage had been broken. Yet we are never free from the influence of our parents and family until we can love and forgive them fully, and understand with compassion the threads that have been woven into each of our lives and personalities. That process is still ongoing in my life.

I was sent up to the Isle of Drumduish with Todd Harris, his wife, Christine, and their baby daughter, as a kind of advance party in order to start getting the buildings habitable and to take over the services. Todd was a young American priest who was a member of the community. The elders had decreed that the community should use public transport whenever possible, so we had to make this rather incredible journey by train. I had been to Scotland before as a child, on holiday with my family, but as the miles went by and I gazed disconsolately out of the train window, it felt like I was coming to quite a different land.

I was astonished to find that some Scots, albeit a minority, could be hostile and unfriendly, simply because I was English.

However that was in 1975, and since then I have met and made friends with many wonderful Scottish people. I think that, wherever you are, you will encounter a range of experiences of human nature, and that there is something to learn from all those with whom one comes into contact. From those who have been hostile, I have learned to look at my own prejudices, and from those who have shown friendship and kindness, I have learned more about how to offer the same.

Todd, Christine, baby Marie and I finally arrived at Lenzie station, clutching numerous bags and baggage. The ferry was about to leave, and as we ran to catch it, my bag full of clothes hangers broke, scattering them all over the quay. What a peculiar sight we must have presented to the curious onlookers!

When the ferry docked in at Drumduish slip, we had to heave all our stuff into the waiting bus, which took us into Fionport – the only small town on the Isle of Drumduish. Reaching the promenade and piling off the bus, we stood in a pathetic huddle in the freezing March wind, wondering where the Cathedral was and how to get to it. We had not been given a detailed itinerary! A kindly telephone engineer took pity on us and loaded us all into the back of his van, amongst a tangle of telephones and cables, and took us to the door of our new home, the North College at the Cathedral on the Isle. It was locked and we had to stand shivering in the cold wind while we waited for the factor to come and open it.

Although in lovely surroundings, this was the most unwelcoming and inhospitable place I had ever been to – cold and gloomy with long dark corridors and Spartan bedrooms each having the name of a certain virtue on the door. My virtue was 'patience' but I didn't think much of it and resented having it plastered on the entry to my dwelling place. The College had previously been inhabited by the organist of the Cathedral and his cats, and there was a prominent odour of cat urine in the sitting room. I love cats, but not that smell!

We soon discovered that the North College seemed to have other inhabitants – or was it just our imagination? The toilet opposite my room was flushed in the night and none of us claimed to have visited it. Sometimes I thought I heard footsteps in the top corridor when there was nobody up there, and Todd and Christine woke in the night from terrifying nightmares. I dreaded having to go up to the top corridor alone to the bathroom, which was unfortunately right at the other end. There was a sense of a presence there, which gave me a creeping sensation on the back of my neck. In spite of admonitions about saving electricity, I left all the lights on and ran helter skelter, as fast as I could, to and from the bathroom. In my perception it was yet another encounter with the menacing unknown that had followed me all my life.

Todd was in charge, and directed operations, giving me various tasks to carry out. One of these was to help with the endless cleaning that was necessary to prepare the buildings for the arrival of the rest of the community. Sometimes it could be satisfying, working together for a common objective, but Todd was meticulous and often critical of my work. I found this very difficult to accept and felt at times that he was being unfair. Other tensions arose over various matters. One of these was the purchase of food, for which I was responsible. A meeting was called and I was told that I was spending too much on items which were considered a luxury. Such terms are relative – what serves as a luxury for one may be considered very simple fare by another, and vice versa. I felt incredibly guilty and ashamed, as if I had committed a sin, but at the time I was only doing what I felt was expected of me – my habitual stance in those days. Discussions concerning difficulties or tensions could often be accusatory in the earlier days of community life, and it was only as the lifestyle matured that a more flexible approach was adopted.

One of my principal duties was to play the organ for services in the Cathedral. Ironically, I became a cathedral organist, something about which I had always fantasised. However, it was certainly not as glamorous as my fantasies!

Not having practised for several years, I had almost forgotten how to play, and I had never played for services before. Consequently I had to practise for at least three hours every day in the freezing cold cathedral, wrapped up in many layers, with a hot water bottle and a tiny fan heater. I wore fingerless gloves to warm my icy fingers and big thick bedsocks on my feet for playing the pedals.

I well remember our first service, which was on Good Friday. It involved a three-hour vigil in that refrigerator of a cathedral, followed by the Good Friday Liturgy. In addition we were expected to fast. My first hymn was 'Forty Days and Forty Nights', and I was so nervous that my fingers kept slipping off the keys as I struggled through this sorrowful dirge. Nevertheless this ignominious beginning eventually led to considerable development as an organist over the years, though I suffered many humiliations and nerve wracking incidents in the process. Although I never became the accomplished organist of my dreams, it was a valuable musical experience and I gained much from it. The organ was, and still is, my favourite instrument, and its sounds stirred within me a yearning for the ineffable which has never died.

In the many hours that I spent practising the organ, alone in the cathedral, I encountered a profound sense of menacing presence. The freezing temperatures, the sombre quality of the building, my frustration and struggles with my inadequate musicianship and the deep loneliness repeatedly brought me face to face with utter despair. I preferred playing for funerals – they were much easier and more predictable than services and weddings, and the sense of sorrow and finality resonated with my inner torment. Often the coffin would be brought into the cathedral and left overnight until the funeral the next day, and as I practised for the service, I felt close to dying and death, and felt an affinity with the body lying in the coffin.

One time while I was having an organ lesson with Lola on the day before a funeral, there was a loud crash near the coffin standing in the chancel. We both leapt up in surprise. I felt sure that the body had come to life and the coffin had opened, and I was trembling with fear. I am not sure why I was fearful. I had seen dead people before and thought that they looked peaceful. Maybe it had something to do with the oppressive atmosphere of the cathedral that made me afraid of what might have happened. Lola was made of sterner stuff and went to look, and I followed her with trepidation. We saw that a large candle had fallen out of its holder! Maybe the spirit had come back and knocked it over. I hope that the deceased on the other side of life, whoever it was, had a good laugh anyway.

In addition to these confrontations with my inner self, there was a more sinister form of darkness in the cathedral. I never liked the atmosphere in there, and hated having to cross the nave in pitch darkness all by myself to get to the lights behind the organ. Often the atmosphere would be so heavy that I dared not go in alone and had to persuade someone to go with me. While practising, there were times when I felt hostile presences and heard mocking laughter. It sent me rushing out in terror, and I began to dread going in there. At first no one believed me and it seemed to be viewed as part of my illness, but at last one of the elders who had become a good friend to me began to take me seriously. One or two other people also began to have uncomfortable experiences.

Eventually it was decided that there were two demons that were residing in the cathedral, and an exorcism service was held. The atmosphere did gradually improve, but there were still times when I was not happy in there on my own. Who or what were these demons? The word is often used to describe something with which one is not comfortable or which one does not understand. Were they ghosts of people who had once worshiped there, or denizens of another realm, or was it a corporate projection of unconscious hostility (there was plenty around) sparked off by my fears? I don't know the answer, but I cannot deny my experience.

Other members of the community arrived gradually until there were about a hundred of us living on the Isle of Drumduish when the numbers were at their highest. There was a big turnover of people who came to try out community life with us, and I brushed shoulders with a great variety of folk, of several nationalities and from different walks of life. Although this was difficult for me, it certainly broadened my mind and enlarged my heart. Whether I liked the people or not, I was always able to find a way to get a glimpse of their essential humanness and to respect that. For someone like me, who had been so isolated and terrified and so unable to relate to people, this was a healing experience in itself. I was learning that healing is not always an easy road by any means, and that great courage is required to pursue it.

v

Over the years that I spent on Drumduish my personality began to change more and more. I discovered surprising gifts and abilities that I did not know I had. Often these were brought to light by sheer necessity. For example, having never before lit a fire, I soon became a dab hand at lighting coke fires and keeping them going. The collegiate buildings were antiquated and open fires were the main source of heating, until central heating was later installed. For the sake of economy the community used coke as fuel, which was not the easiest method for the tiny grates and old flues. I hated the cold so much that I applied myself diligently to the science of coke fires, and also developed a knack of managing the one and only aged boiler. One of the priests was Boiler Man in Charge, and I was the assistant. This latter skill was developed largely through self-interest as I cherished the prospect of a hot bath at the end of a tiring day. My little successes as a pyrotechnician did not go unnoticed, and other busy folk who had no time to tend fires would sometimes ask me to look after theirs. I began to get a different perspective of myself and gain a little confidence in my practical abilities.

I rather enjoyed the so-called 'masculine' tasks to which I was allotted. For a while I worked on the grounds with Steve, who was in charge of them, and helped with renovation, maintenance and other such jobs. One of these was 'doing the trash'. I had to take all the big bins with burnable rubbish in them out to the bonfire area and burn the rubbish. There didn't seem to be any regulations about smoke and pollution at the time. Unfortunately people were not always careful about separating burnable and non-burnable rubbish, and sometimes a pressurised container would get into the wrong bin without being noticed. After being startled out of my wits one time by a loud bang from my bonfire, I got into the habit of setting light to it and then making a dash for safety. These tasks could be boring and irksome, but I found that a balance was beginning to emerge in me, as my crushed and repressed masculine energies found a little more scope for creative expression.

Some time after coming to live on the island, I asked if I could join the bagpipe band. The pipe major came to some of the informal services held by the community, and had invited any of us to join the band if we wished. I had always liked the sound of the pipes – in some ways loud and ungainly instruments, but capable of producing both stirring and haunting music.

Together with a young man, I duly joined up, and proceeded to attempt to master the bagpipes. It took me a while to get the hang of things, and at first I used to almost pass out with the effort of inflating the bag. I did my practice in the cathedral, hoping that it would drive out the demons. The pipe music itself did not give me much trouble as I was accustomed to reading music, but what did give me trouble was the teasing I received from the men in the band. At that time I was the only female piper, and some of the men were very traditional in their attitude to women! Most of them were ordinary straightforward people, but I was unused to mixing with men of that ilk, and found it hard to deal with some of their comments. One of them even picked me up, threw me over his shoulder, and ran out into the yard. I gave him a hearty thump on his backside and yelled 'put me down' – much to the amusement of the watchers.

Eventually I earned the respect of the men, and was surprised to find that underneath the teasing, there was gentleness and simple acceptance. This was a healing experience for me, as I had had such a rarified upbringing, which had given me little experience of relating to real men.

The pipe band added experience and humour to my life, sometimes in such unexpected ways. Once, after a band practice, I was walking past a field of cows and decided to do a bit of practice in the open air. I have always preferred to hear the bagpipes out of doors rather than in an enclosed space. When the band entertained the locals in the pub with a few rousing favourites, my poor ear drums used to suffer from the excess of decibels. I took to putting cotton wool in my ears when we had to play inside. It was a warm and pleasant summer evening as I headed home from band practice – just right for the sound of the pipes echoing across the countryside, I thought. So I tuned up my pipes and launched vigorously into 'Scotland the Brave'. After a few moments I noticed that all the cows in the field were running towards me, and very soon were lined up behind the hedge, curiously watching me play. Suddenly I spotted a large bull in their midst. I had heard him roaring earlier on in the week and had assumed that he was there to do his duty with the cows that were in season. There was only the flimsy looking hedge between us. I didn't want him to think that I represented competition, thus exciting his aggressive instincts, so I stopped playing abruptly and hastened away, the row of bovine faces still staring after me. When I got home I thought how funny I must have looked, and had a good laugh.

vi

On the Isle of Drumduish I became more aware of the natural world, and of the healing power of the Earth and her creatures.

Drumduish was so beautiful – a small island only about ten miles in circumference and a ten-minute ferry trip away from the mainland. Coming across to the island on the ferry, it felt as if you were entering a different world.

The sea and the countryside were my constant companions throughout my stay on Drumduish, and through that proximity I began to sense the rhythms of nature and absorb their stabilising influence. The sea and the weather were an integral part of every islander's life, and frequently formed a useful basis to start a conversation. 'What an awful day, the ferry is off again' or 'Lovely day isn't it, hope it lasts' and so on. I liked these comforting basics of communication that helped me to chat to ordinary folk, when otherwise I would probably have been silent, not knowing what to say.

The squealing, squawking gulls were part of the island's music and I grew to love them. However they could be a nuisance – sometimes stealing food out of an unwary day-tripper's hand, or depositing an unwelcome gift on top of an unsuspecting head. I envied their amazing aerodynamic skill and laughed at their clownish ways. Always hungry, they would wait on the roof of the community's bakery buildings and swoop down to make off with stale pies, rolls and cakes that the bakers threw out for them. They eyed the trays of freshly baked goods that the bakers were carrying on their heads from the bakery to the shop. Sometimes I hoped that an audacious gull would have the nerve to do a sky dive and steal one, but I never saw it happen. When I lived in the bakery flats, one fearless and determined gull developed a habit of landing precariously on my window sill and hammering on the window with its powerful beak. It carried on persistently until I threw some bread or cake out for it, which it was able to catch skillfully in the air. I had to admire that bird, and it was both healing and a pleasure to share food with it.

An owl inhabited the park in the centre of Fionport, and it was one which seemed to take devilish delight in frightening unsuspecting people who were crossing the park when dusk had fallen. It would swoop suddenly across their path with an unearthly screech. One day when I was in a particularly desperate state, I was walking through the park on my way to the bakery, and looking up I saw the owl barely three feet away from me, perched in a tree. It stared at me unblinkingly and I stared back. We must have looked at each other for several minutes – much longer than I could bear to look into human eyes. Something indescribable seemed to happen to me. The owl and I were one; we knew each other and we knew life. A sense of deep awe came over me, and looking into the eyes of that owl I came closer to worship than I have ever done in a church.

There was very little crime on the island when I first arrived there. Although the level did increase over the years, I was never afraid to go out alone, even at night. At least, I was not afraid of people. I was more afraid of the ghosts and spirits I thought I might meet. The only danger from humans was perhaps meeting a drunkard, rolling home after the pubs had closed. The worst sort of crime was something like a person pinching a homemade pie left cooling on a windowsill.

After a very late meeting with someone one evening, I walked home in the early hours of the morning. It was blissfully quiet and peaceful, and the only creatures I met were the enormous slugs – hundreds of them – that came out on to the paths when the weather was wet.

I loved to watch the lighthouse flashing, and the ships and fishing boats coming and going from the harbour. A special joy touched my heart when the moon rose on a clear night and spread a silvery pathway across the water. It looked like a pathway to heaven. I loved to see the fields and trees changing colour as the seasons spun out their rhythm, and I am sure that I spent more time gazing out of my office window at the surrounding countryside than I did doing office work, which I hated.

It was wonderful to walk on the beach on those surprising

days in winter when it was as mild and calm as in spring, and there was no one about – with only the sea and the gulls for my companions. The transitory affairs of human life seemed to lack substance beside the vast and ancient presence of the sea. The elements could be hostile though, and the wind was always a trial, testing me sorely with its constant buffeting.

For some years the community ran a small farm on the Cathedral estate. My love of animals and their messages to me became all the more poignant during this time. I realised that animals are great teachers, and that one of the remits of their manifestation on earth is to reflect us humans back to ourselves. They show us unflinchingly our weakness, our cruelty, our ignorance and arrogance, and our love, devotion and service. The mirror that they hold up to us is so clear, so penetrating, and so uncompromising. There is much about the attitude of humans towards animals that reveals an inability to bear the reflection that they offer us. What an enormous debt we owe to our fellow creatures, travelers on Earth's surface, just like ourselves. We have the impertinence and stupidity to say that they have no soul and that they are inferior to humans – that they are 'just animals'. What fools we can be. This attitude allows a convenient loophole for the exploitation and abuse of animals, to serve the purposes of humankind.

I cannot believe that there will ever be peace on earth until we can treat all beings with respect and compassion, even those that appear to be the least significant. If we wish to live in a world of harmonious relationships, mutual support and mutual endeavour, with abundance for all, this must necessarily include the animal and vegetable kingdoms. This can of course present difficult dilemmas – many questions, to which there are no unequivocal answers. While one may not be able to find ready answers to such questions, it is crucially important for our ultimate survival to think about them.

The first venture of the community into farming was a small herd of goats. I loved going down to their pen to help to feed them or to help with the milking, which was all done by hand. The goats were generally very friendly, especially the old Billy goat. He loved having his head rubbed, and would eat anything, munching away at my pockets even before I had brought out the treats that I had saved for him. He had a very pungent goaty odour, and I could not emerge from his pen without reeking of Billy goat. The females could be unpredictable, especially one of them who could deliver a hefty butt if she felt like it – just when you were not expecting it.

The little farm expanded to include a couple of pigs, three cows, some hens and a few geese. I had great respect for the geese, as they were like guard dogs and approached with necks stretched out, hissing like steam engines, when anyone approached their pen. One day, their carer went down to the pen to find that they were all dead. We never found out what had happened – if it was a sickness or if someone killed them out of spite – but it was a great loss.

It was a wonderful escape for me to go down to the pig pen and talk to the two pigs. I didn't go in, for if you did, they thought it was feeding time and rushed towards you, maybe delivering a vigorous shove in the knees and leaving the unfortunate person sprawling in the mud. I felt great empathy for them in their enthusiasm for food, and admired the unashamed gusto with which they devoured it. I often leaned over the side of the pen to scratch their backs, and they loved this so much that they would sink lower and lower towards the ground, and would finally roll over with grunts of pleasure. The humility and dignity of these creatures opened my heart and touched me deeply. I cannot find words to express my sorrow when they were taken to be slaughtered. Their nakedness was terrifying – no pretence, no masks – reared only to be eaten, with no way to protect themselves from their fate. They were 'just pigs'… When they came back as pork as few days later I could not bear it, but unlike the pigs, I hid behind a mask and said nothing. After that I made my decision to become a vegetarian.

The issue of eating animals is a very complex one, and I do not wish to make any pronouncements about what one should or should not do. It is up to each person to examine the matter for themselves and make their own decision.

vii

While I was a member of the community, another unexpected creative development arose in my life – in the form of hairdressing. I became the community hairdresser! I had always liked hair. Before I joined the community I used to go to Vidal Sassoon, in the era when geometric cuts were first becoming fashionable and the salon was still affordable! I was impressed with the precision of the cutting and the innovative styles. My hair was particularly important to me. As my body felt so hideous and disgusting, it seemed that one thing I could to do to attempt to look attractive was to have my hair cut and styled by the experts. I liked the feel of the scissors and comb on my head, too. For me, it felt like a safe and acceptable form of being touched, and I found it really soothing.

One of my fears about being sent to Drumduish was that there would be no good hairdressers in the vicinity, and I prayed fervently to God to provide us with someone who could give us beautiful haircuts. Some weeks after arriving on Drumduish, Christine and I felt that we needed to get our hair cut, and decided to go to a hairdressers in Lenzie. The experience was disastrous! I have rarely seen a more clumsy job of haircutting than the one we received at that particular hairdressers. We both looked as if we had had a 'bowl cut' – i.e. our hair was shaped like an inverted pudding basin with jagged edges.

Poor Christine fared worse than I, as her hair was completely straight and showed every scissor mark. I was furious with God, and thought it was typical of the punitive male tyrant who still haunted my belief system. After a week or so of invectives directed towards heaven, I decided that I could do a better job of hair cutting myself, and after my hair had grown again, I trimmed it and repaired the damage – with the aid of a pair of ancient dissecting scissors that I had kept from my days as a student in the zoological laboratory. The result wasn't at all bad, and was certainly much better than the butchering job done by the Lenzie hairdresser.

I continued to cut my own hair whenever it needed doing, and as I became a bit more adept with the scissors, community friends started asking me to cut theirs. I was afraid to, and refused, on the grounds that I might make a mess of it, but one person was particularly persistent, and badgered me until I gave in. She was pleased with the result, and from then onwards I got more and more requests for haircuts, until hairdressing became one of my main tasks in the community. I was amazed at the trust that people had in my very basic skills – far more trust than I did.

Slowly I became more and more proficient, and eventually I took a two-year City and Guilds course in hairdressing, at what was then Glasgow College of Commerce and Technology. It is now a university. The course was quite a major undertaking for me, as I felt constantly exhausted and had not studied anything since my degree. I had completely lost confidence in my ability to absorb and understand information and to discipline myself to study.

Although the course itself was not very taxing intellectually, I still felt intimidated by the prospect of it. I had to get up at 5.30 a.m. to travel to Glasgow on the train in order to arrive at 9.00 a.m., and I did not get back until 7.00 p.m. It was a long day, but I travelled up with three other community members, who were studying bakery at the same college, and the companionship made the journey easier. In the summer months it was lovely to wait at the pier for the first bus to take us to the ferry terminal. It was so divinely quiet and beautiful. In contrast, the freezing cold wind and the rough seas of the winter months were a challenge. Occasionally the ferry could not run because of a high sea, and then we were late. In later years, when a new slip was constructed and a larger ferry was used, this did not happen so often, but in the early days of the tiny slip and the chugging little boat, one was very aware of the power of the elements and our vulnerability in the face of them.

At college I was plunged into the Glasgow teenage scene, with all the other students being about half my age, most of them hailing from the suburbs of Glasgow. They regarded me as a very odd fish indeed – with my English accent, strange life style and what they considered to be an advanced age! However in spite of my fear of people and awkwardness, I managed to get along with most of them, and even made a few pleasant acquaintances. I found the theoretical work easy, and was a little flattered by the attention of the staff, who took an interest in me and considered me to be a very diligent pupil in comparison with the rumbustious Glasgow girls!

I was so gratified when I completed the course and passed with distinction. It helped to dispel at least a little bit the persistent image of myself as stupid and useless. I was both amused and delighted when a few weeks later I learned that I had won the Barber's Prize for the highest marks in the school. In some ways I felt that it was perhaps not fair on the other girls, as I had spent a large section of my life doing exams and was used to the process. On the other hand I was very grateful for the award, which had helped to restore a little of my shattered confidence. The prize was twenty pounds, and I bought a pair of hairdressing scissors!

Hairdressing was a gift that brought deep healing into my life, as well as being a valued service to those whose hair I tended. This way of touching people felt safe, and I found that I was not the 'terrified untouchable' that I thought I was, but someone with a caring and sensitive nature and a deep need to express it in creative ways of touch that were both communicative and non-invasive. I found that I had a natural sympathy for people's bodies – the feel of them, their appearance and their vibrations. I think that the agony in my own body was so great that it sensitised me to the language of the human body, and enabled me to attune to my clients.

I realised that in my anguish of being incarnate I had a choice – either to help people love and accept themselves, in whatever ways I could, or to erect barriers of hate and hostility and to try to undermine people. The recognition and acceptance of our own wounds makes us more able to accept people as they are, with their own kind of wounding. Denial will have the effect of keeping others at a certain distance, which is not life affirming. It was not an easy choice, neither was it a once and for all choice, for it is something that has to be chosen moment by moment, in each situation and encounter that arises. However I noticed that once I had set my intent toward the positive choice, the more I chose the positive alternative, and the more I would be likely to choose it at the next opportunity. There were, and still are, times when I wrestle with hate and hostility, but perhaps it is the wrestling itself which stimulates the formation of strength and character.

I found that through my hairdressing I drew near to people in unexpected ways. It brought me into contact with people in all the different strata of the community – from the spiritual leaders and elders to the children and some of our visitors. It was a way for me to relate to people, in situations where I would otherwise not have been able. The children were a prime example of this. I had always been afraid of children, and had no natural ability to relate to them, but with the focus on cutting their hair, I found many little ways of getting through to them, and was very much gratified by their responses. As a result of this my relationship to the community children gradually improved in a more general way, too. I found that they often came to talk to me, sometimes coming on their own initiative to ask for a haircut. This change was a great blessing, and I found that children often brought unexpected wisdom and healing into my life.

People coming to my room for a hair-cut often confided in me, and I felt that this was a great honour. I was amazed that anyone would trust me with their hair, let alone their confidence. Sometimes someone would drop off to sleep as I was snipping away, relaxed by the movement of my hands and the scissors. A kind of spaciousness began to grow inside me, as I made room in my heart for these many folk whose physical bodies I served and loved. This became a sacred task, and gave me an identity – a respected place in the community.

As I became more skillful, I took a few clients from Fionport. This was like a breath of fresh air in a way, as I gained insight into the lives of the island folk and a way to share in their thoughts, opinions and feelings. This served as a balancing factor in my life and it was in fact very valuable to my personal development, although I did not fully realise it at the time. Community life tended to be all encompassing, and one could easily forget that it was but one of many life styles, and that other people's ways of going about their lives were just as valid. My contacts outwith the jurisdiction of the community precepts helped me to resist total absorption into a life style and belief system that later became restrictive to my growth – a situation from which I had to break free.

I found the relative freedom of touch which existed amongst the community people to be very refreshing and healing. Although difficult sexual dynamics and repression did develop from time to time, there was also a sense of kinship which made affectionate and communicative touch seem natural and wholesome. I grew to like the way that a hug was a familiar form of daily greeting, even amongst the men, which was a bit unusual in the rather stereotyped traditions of the island. It was a subject of gossip amongst some of the islanders and a few rumours were spread!

The community tradition of 'back rubs' was one that I particularly liked. Often at a meeting, people would sit in pairs, one on the floor and the other on a chair, to exchange back rubs while important agendas were discussed. It certainly alleviated the boredom and tension of these everlasting meetings which were a feature of the community's very commendable efforts to live in harmony and fellowship with each other. At first I had regarded back rubs with suspicion, and felt that they were a bit risky – a bit too close and personal for me perhaps – but the pleasure of receiving these wonderful relaxing interludes soon overcame my fear.

For a while I did not pluck up courage to give a back rub, until one of the elders, a man whom I especially loved, asked me one day if I would do his back. I hesitated and then said yes, probably because I was afraid to say no. He invited me to his room and I felt even more hesitant, and when he lay down on his bed I felt even more dubious. Supposing his wife came in? What would I say? 'Er – I'm just giving your husband a massage...' The husbands and wives seemed a lot less possessive than in 'normal' life, but surely this was asking too much. Having said yes to his request, I did not want to disappoint him, so I rolled up my sleeves and got stuck into a massage on his back. To my surprise he fell asleep! When he woke up he said he felt much better, and I was surprised that my humble efforts were so much appreciated.

This experience gave me increased confidence to explore touch as a healing medium within community life. I had more time available than most of the members, as being constantly ill and exhausted I avoided getting involved in activities unless I was obliged to do so. I preferred silence and aloneness, and although this was not something that was generally approved of within community precepts, I managed to carve out a niche for myself in that respect. My space and gifts gradually came to be respected and valued, and I massaged many sore backs, feet, legs, hands, even faces and tummies sometimes, and held many exhausted and sorrowful folk in my arms and in my heart. I had a small office where I did my hairdressing and other work, and I made it into an attractive and comforting room, using all sorts of bits and pieces that I found to decorate it. It is amazing what you can find when you have no money to buy anything. The skill of creating beauty out of whatever might be available could be called 'the art of poverty'.

My room became a little haven of treatments for body and soul to which many people came, but it was also the place where I fought and wrestled in prayer, in my own silent agony.

viii

My physical health continued to be fragile, and a few years after coming to Drumduish, a duodenal ulcer had been diagnosed. In some way I was relieved – at least it was considered something real and verifiable, and not just some freaky attitude to eating. In those days anorexia nervosa was much less well identified and recognised than it is today, and was often thought to be only a silly dieting fad. The ulcer gave me an excuse not to eat the foods that I thought were fattening, and I felt that the pain in my abdomen was a kind of manifestation of the nameless, faceless inner torment that raged ceaselessly inside me. I have always found certain kinds of physical pain and illness to be a safety valve, letting off some of the pressure of the inner horror when it was dangerously high. For me, pain and illness have been at times a way to stay sane.

I accepted the medication that I was given and took it meekly for years, not realising that it contained aluminium – not a desirable substance to be ingesting. If I had known then what I know now, I would have sought a safer, more holistic treatment. However, financing such treatment might have been a problem as the community purse-holders were not keen to release funds for that kind of thing. In fact at a later date I did ask for money to pay for homeopathic treatment for the huge itchy weals that developed on my back and hips, but it was not granted. Instead a very kindly household gave me a portion of their meager resources to help me to buy the homeopathic prescription which I had obtained by writing to a well known practitioner. I see no virtue in poverty *per se*.

Along with the ulcer I developed a useful ability to belch

loudly at inopportune moments. My nickname became Sforzando – the musical term for 'suddenly loud'. I loved having nicknames. It was the only time I have had that kind of affectionate familiarity. I had several of them – Jackson, JK, Jack, Sforzando – depending on the user and the situation. I used my burps as a communication – a way of announcing my presence, voicing my complaint against life, and drawing attention to myself. Gregory, our Provost and spiritual leader, was amused by this characteristic of mine, and he was quite a good belcher himself. We used to have sly burping matches. I observed him to be a curious mixture of gentleness, humour and deep understanding on the one hand, and a highly complex power-manipulator on the other. He could at times be really cruel with his extremely effective verbal skills and could slay people with his onslaught. I generally managed to avoid this side of him, probably because I did not challenge him on anything, and satisfied myself by trying to score burping points against him by sitting in the front row, burping surreptitiously while he was delivering an address. I was gratified when I saw him trying to suppress his amusement.

ix

After some years, the community bought the bakery on the Isle of Drumduish. This decision struck fear into my heart, as the thought of working there was like a death sentence. In community life everyone was expected to work wherever they were needed, and not to have any objections or preference. There was reason for this, in that work needed to be done, and it would not do to have endless arguments over who did what. However the expectation of willing service did not always work out fairly, for those who made the decisions looked more at what required to be done, rather than at an individual's skills and needs. It seemed to me that people with influence usually managed to avoid a lot of the unattractive menial tasks by having too many important meetings to attend!

Leadership was considered a task and not an identity, but however hard an individual leader may have tried to live according to this precept, leadership conferred an identity even if the person did not desire it. The community professed equality of all persons, but in practice it was obvious that this was a theoretical ideal and that human nature inevitably established hierarchies, albeit hidden ones or those which masqueraded as something else. For example, in meetings, those people who had a way with words, and who could think quickly on the spot and were not afraid to express themselves, were those whose opinions carried weight. These were the kind of people who were chosen to be leaders, whereas people who were shy and who thought slowly and perhaps more deeply got left behind. I was one of the latter and always felt myself to be at the mercy of those fast efficient talkers. However, as the community began to give credence to the importance of solitude and time for reflection, more respect was accorded to certain people who professed a vocation in this aspect of spiritual life. Although I never felt called to a full hermetic lifestyle, stillness and solitude are an essential need of my being, and it was a great relief when that became more acceptable.

The power structure in the community was very strong, and it dawned upon me that perhaps those who held the reins did not want to let them go. There was no doubt a sense of responsibility for the community welfare behind this. Things are never black and white. Although I could not crystallise my perceptions at the time, I sensed the dynamics instinctively, and used to dread any meetings that were announced. I felt myself being crushed by forces that I could not name. As I became stronger in myself, I felt these forces more intensely as I began to challenge them and interact with them. While I was sick and mentally disabled, they served to uphold and stabilise me, but as I gradually sought to get in touch with my own power, they served to confine and crush me. There came a point when I knew instinctively that the structure had become too tight for me, and that if I wanted to expand any further, I would have to leave. This recognition did not come all at once, but was more part of a growing unease and restlessness – seeking after something that I could not yet define. It was only many years after I had left the community that I understood more clearly the process of my development there.

My fears of working in the bakery met with little sensitivity – certainly from the decision-makers. Friends were more sympathetic, but I doubt if anyone, other than another anorexic, would have understood the pure terror I felt when I was told that I was to work full-time in the bakery as a cashier. In addition, it would have meant sacrificing everything else that I was doing, including my hairdressing and organist work, which were the main creative avenues for me.

It was one of the rare moments in my life when I was overcome by uncontrollable rage. I felt totally betrayed and annihilated – sentenced to a torture of sitting at a till surrounded by food and people, becoming fatter and fatter through despair, boredom, inactivity, and the endless availability of bread, cakes, biscuits, buns, pancakes, muffins, and many other 'dangerous' bakery items. I shouted at the person who announced to me this desperate fate, punched him, and ran out weeping into the pouring rain. I stayed out for several hours, my mind full of panic and despair. I wanted to run away, to leave this oppressive and crushing regime, but I had nowhere to go and no means of survival, and the ogre of starving and bingeing was waiting for me wherever I turned. I felt trapped, and once again drew very near to suicide. Fortunately there were one or two people who were really concerned for me whom I could talk to, although they could not do anything about the decision.

The planned cash desk for the bakery had yet to be constructed, and meanwhile I was sent to work behind the counter for three-and-a-half days per week, to get used to the routine. Amazingly, although for that time only, the compulsion to eat disappeared, and I worked alongside the other bakery staff quite easily, with no interest in the bread and cakes. Only the numerous wasps that frequented the shop bothered me. When I spoke of my distress to the elder who had informed me of the decision, the response was to advise me to 'ask what the Lord wanted' regarding my work in the bakery.

It is only now, so many years later, that I can reflect upon that event with equanimity, and look the cruelty of it full in the face. At the time I had duly engaged myself avidly in prayer and soul-searching to find out what the Lord wanted. I never did feel convinced that He wanted me to work there full-time, and to have my creative gifts of music and hairdressing completely devalued, but I did finally come to a place of accepting what seemed like an inevitable death warrant.

As it turned out, plans were changed and the dreaded cash desk was never built. It was decided that I was needed in Administration and I was recalled from the bakery. I wondered what forces behind the scenes had brought this about. Was it the entity that I called 'The Lord'? Was it the way I wove my own web in the inner world, or was it the prayers of my friends? Whatever had happened, I felt that I had been given a reprieve, and was profoundly grateful. The lesson learned from this has remained with me ever since. Although it may look as if the systems of this world and people in authority are all-powerful, they never have the last word about what happens to us. That which comes to us is hidden in the mysteries of the soul's choices and in the intricacies of the web of life. We are all weavers of the web, on this side of life and in other realms, and somewhere along the shimmering threads, our pathway is worked out.

X

Not long after the community had become established at the Cathedral on the Isle, there was a serious fire in the North College, which is where I was living. Most members of the community were at the South College, taking part in a sharing and worship meeting, when it started. There was just one of the elders, Wayne, who was unwell, and a baby and two children who were asleep in the North College. The flames spread very quickly due to a high wind and the large amounts of inflammable material in the attic, but mercifully Wayne woke up and managed to rescue the baby, and the two children were rescued by members of the community. A bucket line was formed to try to halt the flames, but the fire had got a hold, and by the time the fire-engine arrived, the college was burning fiercely.

Unfortunately the fire service on the island was ill equipped to deal with such a blaze – the worst the island had seen in years. The hose was first of all laid out the wrong way round, so there was a delay in joining it to the mains. Then it was discovered that the there were holes in the hose and the water pressure was too low. It soon became obvious that the building was going to burn to the ground. The Ardgarry fire service was called in to help, but by then the North College was an inferno, and it took until nightfall before the flames began to die down.

I stood there with the community folk, watching our treasured belongings go up in flames. Many people, including me, lost everything that they owned. Although at that time I had few possessions, what I had was precious to me – especially certain sentimental items such as photo albums, letters and diaries, favourite clothes and so on. I have always had a respect for material things, and an attachment to those which formed part of my larger identity. As I watched them burning, I felt that a part of me was burning away too. Curiously, this brought a certain kind of peace, a kind of death. I knew that the essence of me was still strong and clear, while that to which I had such attachment changed form, from solid objects into smoke, vapour and ashes. I wondered if when I die I would feel something similar. All I had left were the clothes that I was wearing.

After the flames had died down, many of us had to live in temporary accommodation. The local council allowed us to use the Gate House, which was a fairly large building that was normally used for offices and summer holiday rooms. It had no heating or cooking facilities, and those of us living there had to cram several people into each of the small rooms, even sharing beds. It was so cold, damp and miserable that I wondered how we would ever survive. The woman with whom I shared a bed did not seem to like me very much, and complained about me snoring or pulling the bedclothes off. I was afraid of her and feared her temper, but eventually, perhaps through needing to survive the stress and difficulties, we formed some kind of understanding between us.

In some ways the disaster brought out the best in people. So many shared what they had and gave away treasured items to those of us who had lost everything. Friends and supporters of the community sent many gifts and items of clothing, and along with the others I began to piece together a new set of belongings. When the North College was safe to approach, some of us went in to rake around in the rubble, and found that a few items had come through the fire undamaged or only slightly charred. I discovered one or two bits and pieces of my former life, and I treasure these as a reminder of the transitory nature of the material world. Since then, I have known that when the time comes, I will detach from the apparently solid objects over which I expend so much energy and emotion, and I will change form and rise from them as if I were smoke.

xi

Throughout my life in the community I had a number of difficult relationships. I was always afraid of people, and found getting along with them difficult in itself, but certain relationships stirred up a whole lot of strong emotions in me. One of the unwritten rules of the community lifestyle was that you always had to be 'in fellowship' with everybody, and not harbour grudges, anger, resentment, jealousy, hostility and the like. This aspiration had much to commend it, and no doubt our society would be so much more healthy and pleasant to live in if we were all to observe such an aim. However, in the practice of our community life, it meant that there were endless harangues and examinations about who felt what about whom, and why. This sorting out of fellowship could actually be distressing and damaging in itself, with unfair judgments and accusations made. Sometimes households would have 'carpet sessions', where one or another person got a hammering for the way they were behaving and were made to feel guilty, unfaithful, selfish, and all the rest of it.

No one seemed to notice that the constant disagreements and fracas that arose between people stemmed, at least in some measure, from the hidden hierarchy and power structure of the community itself. Rather than being given space for personal differences, conformity to the unspoken group norm was inexorably and subtly enforced. Many people who joined with the hope of sharing in the community lifestyle left because they were unwilling to knuckle under. Those of us who stayed survived somehow, in spite of the pressures involved in such a complex structure of relationships. And as the community evolved, its corporate identity became more flexible and strong, and thus more able to give space for personal identity as a part of the whole. This was a very welcome development for me, as right from the start, I never really felt that I fitted in to the overall community structure. With a more expansive interpretation of 'community', I did gain some sense of belonging. However I never did feel that I was at the hub of community life, and to this day I still have uneasy dreams of going back to the community, and feeling that I am out of place, and that there is some sort of invisible divide between me and the people that I am with in my dream.

Whatever the flaws in the operation of the lifestyle, there was a great deal that was positive and life-giving about it, and I developed many close friendships and bonds of love with people whom ordinarily I would have feared, disliked and avoided. I learned to respect people, even if I did not like them, and in so doing gained more respect for myself. I came to understand that I myself was the person I disliked the most. Being around folk was obligatory, but I could always find something to admire and respect about each one, even if I had a general antipathy towards some of them. This extended across all age groups – babies, children, peers, and older folk – and served me very well as a valuable lesson for later life.

There was one man with whom I struggled the whole time that I was a member of the community. He was one of the principal elders, the Provost's right-hand man. Soon after I joined the community he noticed me and made some kind of perceptive and friendly gesture towards me – probably something completely normal and natural. I doubt if he would remember it, but I can still picture the look in his eyes, which captivated me at the time. I was so unused to this kind of attention from men, and so totally nonplussed by any kind of penetrating recognition, that I immediately fell in love with him. Wayne already had a secure relationship with his wife Lola, so my love was doomed to remain a hopeless yearning, which I carried clumsily for eight years or so. I catapulted between a loving and longing feeling for him, and a furious hatred. It was a matter of extremes – a bit like my starving and bingeing. Probably the manifestations of my unrequited love did not affect him very much, although I am sure that he cared about me. I was the Problem and he was the Pastor, so anything which he may have felt – positive or negative – could be conveniently obscured by the roles we occupied. In conversations that were presumably designed to help me deal with my conflict concerning him, I felt that I was obliged to disclose my secrets, whereas he could remain understanding but aloof – as I had typically encountered in the psychiatric profession. I lost count of the number of humiliating interviews and pastoral sessions that I endured on account of my feelings for him. I believe that it was due to the imbalance of openness that such sessions did nothing to help me resolve my feelings. The resolution had to come from within, at a deeper level of my understanding and spiritual experience.

The pain and grief of this situation was not without its lessons and strengthening qualities. I had to accept that I was full of hate and anger and not try to dress it up as something more acceptable. I was often instructed to repent and pray about it, but what I really wanted was a safe, accepting, understanding heart, to which I could pour it all out. That to me was what repentance was about. Trying to feel sorry about it and seek forgiveness got me nowhere – it just made me more angry than ever.

It almost seemed as if people were afraid of the violence in me – the erupting volcano of destructive rage that drove my anorexia and sucked me into despair. I found solace by emptying floods of fury, hatred, violence and despair upon the image of the Christ that was constructed in my mind and heart. From where I am now, this is a difficult experience on which to reflect. Yet at that time, the experience was entirely authentic according to my beliefs and concepts, and probably helped to save my sanity. It was perhaps the beginning of my mystical development, for as I continued in my outpourings of negativity to this inner being, a kind of inexplicable compassion began to creep through me, in the form of visions, voices and sensations. I think that to try to explain this experience and dissect it into various psychological, sociological and spiritual components would not be especially useful to me. In any case, there would not be a definitive explanation. I prefer to retain an attitude of contemplation and open-mindedness towards what was essentially a mystery.

The relationship with Wayne stirred up some of my fighting spirit. He seemed to take pleasure in provoking me to anger with sly pokes in the ribs, carefully chosen inflammatory comments, or by pinning my arms behind my back. I retaliated with whatever means I could find – a hefty bite, a wallop with a handy utensil, or an elbow in the stomach perhaps. Of course, this was in play, and my real violence had to be restrained. Wayne was often away on ministries and at such times, if I was desperate to talk to him I had to learn to contain my thoughts. He was very much in demand, and when he came back, many other people required his attention. Eventually I learned to listen to myself and watch for the working of my thoughts and prayers. Slowly I realised that I did not have to tell him everything, for the unseen watchers knew my heart and I could tell them anything without fear of condemnation.

A particular painful betrayal gave me further strength. I had shared a great deal with Wayne about the agony of my body, my terror of food and horror of flesh. One day as I was sharing something with him along these lines, he said to me, 'I like you fat. You need a bit of weight on you.' I froze inside... I couldn't believe what I was hearing. I didn't say much, but I never again trusted anybody with my inner suffering. It was not that I stopped talking about my anorexia and compulsions, but I closed over the place of terror and despair, and vowed never to let anyone in again. I never have done so, since this incident. In a way this was a positive step, as I took full responsibility for my own body, and never again allowed anyone to tell me how it should be or what I should do with it. This has served me very well in my journey towards health and wholeness, and it also serves to illuminate how a seemingly destructive event in one's life can be redeemed, and become strength. However, this was a fairly minor incident, and I would never pretend that such redemption would necessarily be an easy, or even a feasible, task for every situation.

In addition to this incident, I frequently reached an impasse in my effort to relate to Wayne. Each one of these times helped me to see that my whole emotional existence did not depend solely on one person. Though the relationship provoked immense pain for me, and I frequently descended into a numbing darkness of mind and soul over it, I came through stronger in the end. I became aware of a central core of myself that was not dependent on anyone for its existence. I learned that a relationship did not *have* to be 'worked out'. One could consign the problematical elements of the relationship to a a metaphorical 'bag' to be attended to at a later date, and still continue on with life. The opportunity or the ability to resolve the contents of the 'bag' may come very much later, or even in another lifetime, according to my belief. However as long as one has the intention of resolution to a relationship of harmony and understanding, I believe that temporarily unresolved personal dynamics and tensions need not be damaging.

I began to be able to back off and give the other person space, rather than constantly hammering at the entanglement, trying to make everything 'all right'. I realised that sometimes it was better not to wear my heart on my sleeve, and instead to contain my feelings. This was not necessarily 'repression' – a term which had been repeatedly flung at me when I was in the mental hospital. I felt that it was more like having a wardrobe full of clothes and choosing what outfit to wear for a particular occasion. In this material world we cannot be entirely naked to each other, and although honesty is desirable in relationships of all kinds, it is my view that complete self-exposure is not workable or appropriate to our stage of development as a species. We are always dressed in some sort of clothing. Maybe in the next worlds, the worlds of thought and mind, we will learn a different and more direct way of expressing ourselves.

My relationship with Wayne was only one of many difficulties in getting along with my fellow humans, but it was a central learning task, and I am grateful to him for engaging in relationship with me. It taught me to rely on the flow of visions and voices which came to guide me as I struggled through an inner ocean of dangerous currents, storms and collisions. Without these inner guides I would have been adrift, and at the mercy of the obsessive thoughts that travelled relentlessly through my mind. Advice, therapy, exchanges with friends and so on were mostly helpful, but words alone could not reach my inner being. The daily effort of simply being human caused me to search diligently for an inner spiritual pathway to give me form and steadiness as I wrestled with incarnation.

Community life involved many disciplines and commitments. One of these was regular attendance at all services and other religious meetings held by the community. My work as the regular organist was dictated by the church calendar, and this formed a certain musical rhythm to life, which became a stabilising factor for me. Though I suffered many a nightmare of playing wrong notes, or losing my place in the middle of a hymn or anthem, there was a great deal of healing in preparing and sharing music with other people. I was also in the choir, and played the clarinet and recorder, so I had a good variety of musical involvement.

Lola, Wayne's wife, was a very fine musician and gave me organ lessons. She was a wonderful teacher, though I found her somewhat stern and forbidding. She could deliver a swashbuckling blow with just a few words. I was afraid of her, and felt my musical abilities were very inferior to her talent. In spite of this uncomfortable relationship she taught me invaluable precision in music, and I learned a great deal from her. It was not only through music that I learned to love and respect her, but also through her example in everyday life, in which she practised the same kind of discipline.

In contrast I found Elspeth, who was the Provost's wife, to be easier to approach. She had six children, and I found her affectionate, with a comforting motherly presence. At the same time she was always busy and in demand, being a highly creative and talented musician at the hub of the community's musical activities. I often wished that I could have a little time with her by myself, but such privileges were necessarily very rare.

Services were often lively affairs. There were often dances, dramas, mimes and a great variety of music other than traditional church music. At that time such an innovative approach to worship could be controversial. Some of the local people voiced disapproval at all the song and dance in what to them should have been formal occasions of devotion. For me, these colourful services were an interesting spectacle, but I could never join wholeheartedly in them. Although I enjoyed participating in the music, the actual worship felt like a play in which I was obliged to be an actor. I tried my best, but all the while there was that yawning abyss of despair waiting for me, only a breath away from my annihilating plunge into it. No Light shone there, and this secret torment sapped my ability to perceive any meaning and purpose in my life.

For all their ceremony, services often held amusing moments, where the clumsiness and unpredictability of human existence peeped through with a clownish grin. In a solemn moment of Holy Eucharist, the priest, holding the host aloft dramatically and breaking it, dropped a piece which hit the chalice with a loud 'ping'. There was a hush, then the priest let out a guffaw and a ripple of laughter ran round the room. Another time, a lady waiting in the line for communion received an unexpected gift from heaven when a chandelier candle dripped a blob of wax right on her head. Then there was the time when the old bishop, a kindly gentleman of advanced years, stumbled a little at the altar steps, and almost lost his hat in the process. I loved these hiccups in the procedure. For me, it broke the tension. I was right after all – thank goodness it was only a drama, and ordinary life would still have its way underneath it.

There was one aspect of the community worship which I found really puzzling, and I still mull over it with questions in my mind. This was the phenomenon called 'speaking in tongues' or 'glossolalia' to give it a more technical name. This was something that the Bible says occurred when the disciples of Jesus received the Holy Spirit, some time after his crucifixion. They were purported to have spoken in other languages (which they themselves did not know), so that everyone who was listening could understand, each in their own language. Speaking in tongues was very much a part of the Evangelical and Pentecostal movement at that time, and while the community did not go overboard with this practice, it did make a fairly regular appearance in times of worship, especially in the more informal community gatherings.

At first, I simply observed these spontaneous expressions, which were often in the form of singing – the community being such a musical bunch of people. The sounds, though unintelligible (to me at least) could be quite beautiful and moving. I remember speaking to one of the pastoral elders about this, and saying to her that I felt that I did not have 'the gift', and her response was that I needed to believe that I had been given it, and like any gift it had to be practised. I decided therefore to give it a go, since I felt it was something that everybody else was doing and so I ought to be doing it, too. There was something of the mass mind and peer pressure going on here, I think, although in this case it did not have any detrimental effect.

After a few warbles, singing a flow of apparently meaningless sounds came quite easily to me. I can still do it if I want to, but perhaps anyone could. I did not feel that I was speaking a real language, in the sense of grammar, syntax, recognisable words and so on, but that it was more a preverbal expression of emotion and spiritual feelings.

Sometimes someone would claim to be given the gift of interpretation of these corporate offerings of sound. There was no way of verifying the accuracy of the interpretation – one just had to take it on trust. In the absence of some kind of linguistic analysis, my guess would be that speaking or singing in tongues is a kind of self-expression in sound, which when blended with others in a group becomes an expression of the group mind or soul in an act of worship. I think that the sound created is a valid expression – just like creating a wash of colour with paints or a symphony with a range of instruments – but to identify it as an authentic verbal language constitutes too much of a stretch of the imagination for me.

However, I do remember an occasion when in deep distress I found myself singing sounds which seemed to come from the pit of my soul. A little later, when I had regained a measure of composure, I wrote a poem – straight off and with no premeditation – and I had the feeling that it was some kind of translation of what I had been singing.

As I improved my skills as an organist and gained more confidence, I was asked to play for one service a month at the local parish church, so that their regular organist could have a break. I was very apprehensive about this, as it involved taking the choir practice before the service as well. The choir had their own ideas of how hymns and anthems should be sung, so it was something of a battle of wills when trying to introduce the Cathedral precision and spirit into the music. I did my best, and the interaction turned out to be quite affirming, as the choir and congregation were appreciative of my efforts. The organist was required to wear a long black robe, in which I must have looked rather comical, with my thick fisherman's socks and fingerless gloves that I used to keep warm while playing in chilly churches.

The minister was a rather dour sort of fellow, although well meaning I am sure, and used to come flailing into the church in his black attire as I was playing the introit, looking for all the world like Batman. The sermons were long and wearisome, but I liked the children's address, which always seemed much more digestible and to the point. The last hymn was usually a rousing rendition of one of the old favourites, such as 'Guide me O Thou Great Jehovah', and everyone appeared to enjoy letting rip and singing for all they were worth. I pulled out all the organ stops to try to keep the rhythm under control, but I wonder if their enthusiasm was not a measure of relief that the dutiful rites of the service and the heavy laden sermon were over! It certainly was in my case.

All in all, however much I was fraught with despair over my inadequacies as a musician, my work as an organist was a deeply healing part of my journey – building my character and spirituality as well as my musicianship. I feel a great sense of gratitude to all those who taught, played and sang with me in the music life of the community and the island.

The community was dedicated to the teaching of spirituality and Christian doctrine, and we were all obliged to go to various forms of teaching service, as well as the Sunday services with their long sermons. I dreaded those teaching services, for deep inside myself I was riddled with a profound sense of fear, shame and guilt for which there was no rational explanation in my mind. I pinned it on any little sin I could find, and was in constant terror of punishment from the heavy hand of God – that punitive father figure that I hated and feared but was supposed to love. The 'Love of God' had no positive inner meaning for me. For me, these teachings created a nightmare of anxiety. They were full of things that I ought to be doing and wasn't doing, and of things that I was doing that I ought not to be doing. My mind probed deeply with questions that no one seemed to be able to answer satisfactorily, and I left each session with gnawing anxiety still chewing at my soul, and doubt and confusion playing hide-and-seek in my mind. I was always metaphorically looking over my shoulder, terrified that someone would find out what I was really like. Looking back now, I can see that I was entirely justified in my questioning and doubt, and that matters presented as facts which I felt required to believe were not necessarily facts at all.

It was partly through these experiences that I learned more about inner listening. Leaving a teaching one day in my usual writhing anxiety, I told Jesus my thoughts. So clearly, a lovely voice rang out within my soul and formed itself thus, 'Well Jackie, let's sit down and talk it over then, shall we?' Such an immense relief came over me. It was what I wanted more than anything – to sit down with this kind, accepting and wise presence and pour out all my turmoil. Within the context of my beliefs at the time, I had touched the eternal wisdom and acceptance in which all the convolutions of my mind melted away. This powerful event gave me an unshakeable anchor for my growing ability to be honest with myself – a tool for self-development that I could use for the rest of my life. At last there was one place where I could be absolutely real, without fear of exposure, judgment, humiliation, condemnation and abuse – and that place was within myself, my own inner sanctuary. This place lies beneath all the self-critical voices in my head, and the descriptions, rules, judgments and so on that I have heard and learned right from the cradle. However this place has no easy access – the route to it is a secret way within my inner self, and must be pursued with firm intent, discipline and determination.

After this realisation, I did not fear the teachings any more, for I knew that they were not the last word or the ultimate truth, but were simply words that were reaching for the understanding of reality as we experience it in human form. The experience of reality is shaped and interpreted by our concepts, values and attitudes. It flows through them and evolves and changes along with the development of the individual and the species. Thus no one can make claim to any final and all-encompassing definition.

xiii

My battle with anorexia nervosa continued unabated throughout my life in the community. I felt that I received little recognition for the fact that I was suffering from a severe and life-threatening mental illness. If it had been something like cancer, perhaps my extreme suffering would have been given more credence. However, at that time anorexia nervosa still attracted bad press, and was often looked upon as something that one could choose not to have, or that it could be prayed away, or that one's will power could be used to control it, or something like that. I am not saying here that choice, prayer and will power are irrelevant to the condition, but it is not a simple matter of 'getting better' by applying these efforts to the illness itself.

For example, the place in which one is able to make a

choice may lie very deep down in the soul or the mind, and it may be a question of bringing that choice gradually to the surface of consciousness before it can be made. Such a process can take years of arduous toil and terrible suffering. There can be elements of great ignorance and cruelty applied to anorexics by people, including some professionals, who assume that a sufferer of anorexia nervosa can change their illness in fundamental respects simply by the application of his or her own volition.

The community refused my requests for outside help for my illness for several years, even though it was taking such a toll on my physical body and mental stamina. I mentioned before that in the early years at least, the community's stance was that the Body of Christ was sufficient, with all the gifts necessary for healing present within it. This was represented strongly to me by people in authority and caused me untold suffering, driving me deeper and deeper into the aloneness of my despair. No one seemed to be able to hear properly what I was saying or understand what I was talking about in terms of my anorexic feelings and associations about food and my body. And much group pressure was brought to bear on me – perhaps not intentionally but by inference – to give up the validity of my thoughts, perceptions and feelings. I often felt that I was being brainwashed and that I was going insane. Cracks appeared in my mind, and bizarre thoughts and sensations went in and out of them. I clung to the shreds of my integrity like a drowning person clinging to a straw. But yet, each time the dark waters of torment closed over my mind, some shaft of clarity penetrated, like a great horn sounding out over the clamouring confusion, and brought me back, enabling me to bring order to my thoughts.

I am sure that the pressure and suffering that I experienced in this respect was not in any way intentional on the part of any member of the community. I do not doubt that those who made the decisions which directly affected my life felt that they had my best interests at heart. However, I think that it does go to show how complex group dynamics really can be, and that beliefs, power structures, personal agendas of individuals, and the unconscious mind of the group can exert a devastating effect on a vulnerable person.

It was fortunate for me that there were some people in the community who possessed a great deal of wisdom and insight. These dear people spent many hours listening to me, praying with me, and offering me the benefit of their understanding. Sometimes it was a word or an image, or simply their kindness, which helped me to reclaim another tiny part of myself and toil onwards with the strength that I gained from this. Many friends gave up their time to help and comfort me, each one offering me something of their own unique gift of healing. We can all be healers, in all manner of ways, if we open to that great healing force of the universe, by whatever name we call it.

I will always remember one woman speaking to me of the 'treasures of darkness' – those priceless gems of character and understanding that are forged in the deepest of suffering. That has remained with me ever since, as a beacon to sustain me in the many dark times on my journey. To those dear people I offer my undying gratitude.

xiv

Another community in England – the Peel House Community – was associated with the Community of Transformation, and there were various exchanges of personnel between the two communities. One of the principal leaders, Lady Simone Peel, made regular visits to Drumduish to help with the pastoral work in our community. She was a very special person in my life. She was the only woman for whom I have felt such a deep emotion of love that I thought I was in love with her.

Simone had a great gift of getting through to people with her love, compassion and penetrating insight, and she helped a great many folk through all kinds of difficulties and troubles.

She was also a very determined and perceptive woman, and it was not easy to evade her if she was homing in on some painful area of one's psyche. I found this combination of qualities irresistible, and quickly developed a great longing to be around her and to talk to her. From time to time she would 'take someone on' in an intense and concentrated relationship, with the purpose of bringing that person through personal difficulties and helping them to become a pastoral leader in their own right. I longed to be chosen for this privilege, and asked Simone to help me with my struggles with anorexia. She agreed to this, but the prize of becoming one of her special protégées went to someone else. I was insanely jealous and hurt. Why was I passed over?

Why had this happened yet again? I had never been singled out for anything that I longed for – never felt wanted by anyone or never felt special. On the surface of things, this assessment was unrealistic, as I had good friends in the community, and had had relationships with other people who had really appreciated me, such as Max, Dr Marion, Quentin and a whole host of others.

On closer inspection, these feelings of never being chosen and of being unwanted became active in relation to people who managed to get through my considerable defences and touch a core of desperate need in my heart. This was the place where I had never been recognised and affirmed as a separate and worthwhile person in my family. My mother's own needs and emotional trauma caused her to project excessive need on to me, and unintentionally reward and identify me as sick and dependent person. My father did not affirm or accept me at all as an independent personality. It was only later in my adult life that I had the insight and strength to force him to do so. As a child, these relationships created a deeply embedded self image of myself as an amorphous, shapeless being, giving rise to a craving for the kind of love and recognition that would give my identity a form and shape. At the same time I was in abject terror of this blob-like self being seen, especially by the people upon whom I projected my craving for love, since I dreaded further rejection and humiliation. I felt that should I encounter such, it would be like a death sentence. Fortunately, in spite of this profound source of my self-hatred, I had managed to build up reserves of strength and integrity alongside of it. These reserves were the foundation of my ability to face up to myself and set about the incredibly demanding task of transforming the violent emotions that arose from the inner conflict.

In respect of relationship to Simone, I had to watch someone else getting what I wanted and what I thought I needed so much. It was an enormous dilemma because the woman in question was also a dear friend of mine – someone with whom I had shared a room for a short while, whose hair I tended, and who had been very kind to me. I could not possibly hate her with unbounded venom, as I wished to do, because I also loved her. This abominable conflict tore me apart for years, and I was very ashamed of it, finding it difficult to talk it through with anyone. Simone did spend time with me, but I could not open up my heart to her completely, as I was constantly wrestling with jealousy and resentment.

I had asked if I could spend some time at Peel House Community on a kind of retreat, and Simone had said that she would come down and that we would spend some concentrated time together. I envisaged this to be the kind of intimate involvement that I assumed was being developed with the chosen one, and I was thrilled and full of expectancy and longing. I was to go down and begin my two-week retreat, and then Simone would come later.

I travelled down to Peel House and enjoyed getting to know people there and joining in with the work. Somehow it seemed a softer, kinder atmosphere than the rigours of Community life on Drumduish. While I waited for Simone to arrive, I passed the time with reading and long walks, praying that the time we were to spend together would set me free. While I was there I also decided that I wanted to write a book on anorexia nervosa, and that I would make a start when I returned to Drumduish.

Time went on and Simone did not appear. I began to get anxious, and a little core of fear began to eat away inside me. Supposing she doesn't come? Maybe it's not going to happen after all. I tried to silence the fears, but they would not go away. I confided in one or two people at Peel House about the situation. They reassured me that she would not let me down, and that it was a great privilege to be with Simone, as she was so busy and had so many people needing her. Well, my fears proved to be correct, and she did not come until it was almost time for me to return to Drumduish.

I think that we spent only a couple of hours together. I hardly dared to say, 'Where have you been? Why didn't you come to be with me as you said you would?' Eventually I managed to ask and say tentatively that I thought she had said she would spend time with me. She seemed a little put out, and said that we *were* spending time together. I felt too crushed to pursue the matter further. I returned to Drumduish feeling scourged, and an inner rift appeared in my relationship with Simone. There was some comfort in telling myself that I had been right all the time and that my doubts had been entirely validated.

I wonder what would have happened if she *had* come, and had delved into my psyche as I had hoped. However, it was not to be, and never has been with anyone. Perhaps that place is too wounded. Maybe it is a sacred place, where only angels can enter.

XV

After I had been with the community on Drumduish for some years, Peel House Community forged an association with Dr Frank Lake, a psychiatrist who had founded the Clinical Theology Association and was one of the pioneers of Pastoral Counselling in the UK. This was a compassionate approach to mental suffering and mental illness which involved regressing in order to relive pre-natal or peri-natal traumas, bringing them into consciousness and into the Light of the Christian faith. Some of the pastoral leaders in the community on Drumduish had been reading his first book, 'Clinical Theology' and were interested in his methods.

I found the book lying around and had started reading it, and I was desperately eager to meet Dr Lake. I asked if I could see him, but was told by a certain pastoral leader that I should not be reading the book! Looking back on that event it seems preposterous. I was a psychology graduate with a keen intelligence and deep desire to understand – why on earth should I not be reading it?

For some time, the connection with Dr Lake was kept within the confines of elders' meetings. Once again, frustration, helplessness and fury rose in me, as I felt that I was being denied something that would alleviate my agony of suffering with anorexia nervosa. Once again, I experienced the cruelty of the power dynamics of the group process, but as had happened at the bakery, those processes did not have the last word, for somehow or other I met Dr Lake and he offered me a week at his Centre for Clinical Theology. This was an unforgettable time for me. The respect and acceptance that I received there made a deep impression on me, and I found tremendous relief in Dr Lake's recognition of my illness and pain.

Participating in primal regression was not easy for me. I was so afraid of making any noise at all that I found it hard to let go and experience my anguish. Most of the other people were making lots of noise – yelling and screaming in chorus during the regressions such that it made shudders go down me. Surely I must be in a torture chamber… Eventually, through the support and kindness of the group, the facilitators and Dr Lake himself, I managed to contact the enormous distress surrounding my conception and birth, and with spiritual counselling I was able to offer this suffering to Christ. While this was not a cure in itself, it did give a sense of authenticity to my journey with anorexia nervosa, and thus strengthened me and gave me further insight.

146

Dr Lake's influence spread throughout the community, and paved the way for a greater acceptance and understanding of psychological processes. Some of the community pastoral leaders began to facilitate primal regression, and a church minister also became involved with this aspect. I continued to have regression therapy for about two years with him, at the church where he worked, and I sometimes stayed overnight with him and his wife and family. It was a privilege and a welcome break from the community life, but unfortunately, and perhaps predictably, this involvement developed sexual overtones, and once again I was in love with someone unattainable – yet another busy person who could only spare me a few precious drops of time.

But I was not the only one! I learned that someone else who was going to him for primal regression had fallen into the same trap, and had fallen harder than I! Oh the weakness of human nature... And what about his poor wife? What a quandary it was. I liked her and felt sorry for her, as it was obvious that their marriage was having problems, yet I was so desperate for the attention and affection of the Reverend, I could not draw away. The situation was that someone who was supposed to be helping vulnerable people on to the road of healing had turned into a predator, and was seeking the gratification of his own needs. I cannot say that I was blameless. One can be so adept at justifying oneself and making such plausible excuses.

Since then, I have found myself in a number of situations of the same kind. Each time, when eventually, after a great deal of pain, I saw each for what it was, I thought 'Will I never learn?' I hope that now I am in my sixties I have learned that lesson. But one can never be complacent! I spot the warning signs very early these days.

I think that the experience with the minister did help me to open up in some ways, and a lot more buried material came to the surface. As it came through, it troubled the waters of my soul deeply, and many times I sunk into deep depression and my problems with food intensified. Many a night-time trip to the deserted kitchen resulted in the disappearance of a large slab of cheese, or the bucket of muesli being half empty the next day. No one ever accused or blamed me for this, but instead there was a gentle buffering of my extremes.

Dr Lake continued to visit the community from time to time, to help us and to talk to those of us doing primal regressions. I really looked forward to seeing him, and I had a special affectionate and uncomplicated bond with him. It was like a breath of fresh air when he came. On his last visit I was ill with flu and unable to go the general meeting at which he was speaking. I hoped that he would come to see me, but he did not come and I was very sad. Later on I found out that he had sent a message via someone to say that he would come if I wanted him to, and I had not been given the message. I was so angry about that, and later, when news came that he had died of cancer, the pain of loss was heightened. I think he must have known, for one day while I was alone in the cathedral practising the organ, I saw Dr Lake momentarily with my inner eyes. He was standing at the side of the organ and smiling in his wonderful accepting way. This was quite an amazing experience – not one that I often had. I could not say that I had seen a ghost, for it was Dr Lake, very much himself and very present to me. Death is but a doorway into another form of life. I hope very much that I will meet him again when it is my turn to go through it.

xvi

As time went on and the community matured, there was less insistence on family households and togetherness, and more recognition of the needs of single people to have a sense of authenticity. A 'singles household' was created, of which I was invited to be a part. In some ways it was a bit frightening to leave the larger arena of the household in which I had been living, but on the other hand I welcomed the chance to have more space to myself and more of a say in what happened in a household. There were just a few of us to start with – two men and two women – and we were given the flat over the bakery in which to live. It worked quite well for a while, although I missed the stability of the larger group and found myself getting very lonely and depressed.

The singles household eventually disbanded for various reasons, and I went to live in a small caravan adjoining another household which was a little distance from the main community site. Apart from the lack of a bathroom and kitchen in the caravan, I loved having my own little home. I was associated with the other household, but not fully part of it, and this served to strengthen my sense of identity. But it also meant that I was more on my own with my anorexia, and at times it was hard to stay on an even keel with food. One of the women who was a leader of the household was especially kind to me, and her wisdom, insight and patient listening to my outpourings was such a source of comfort and strength to me. Even when we moved to separate community houses, I used to trek back to her household to talk to her, often when I was doing her hair.

When the winter came, the caravan became unsuitable for a regular living place and I moved again, this time to the upper bakery flat, which I shared with another dear friend. We each had our own room, and this was really the best dwelling place that I had during my stay in the community. I loved my room and made it as beautiful as I could on very limited resources, with the help of my friend who was an artist and was a very practical person. This was my last home in the community and the one that I loved best.

The bakery was on the sea front and my room looked out over the sea. It gave me the most wonderful experience of being in touch with the moods of the sea and all its traffic, both human and animal. I could see Fionport harbour and also over to the mainland, and the flashing lighthouse and the coming and going of boats calmed my agitated spirit. The squealing gulls were so beautiful with their grey bodies creating ever-changing patterns against the sky, their wings catching the light as they dipped and dived. I laughed at their audacious courage in snatching whatever morsels of food they could find. On a clear moonlit night a magical silvery pathway was cast over the water, reaching right up to the shore sometimes, and I fancied that I could walk on it away to heaven, to a place free from fear and torment. In my subsequent life, in far from uplifting surroundings, I never forgot the wonder and beauty of my little island home.

As my independence developed, I was also starting to get another kind of experience – one that was much less welcome. I began to sense 'visitors' from the unseen world making their presence very apparent in my awareness, and this felt uncomfortable. To this day I have no watertight explanation for what was happening to me. Throughout my life I had been sensitive to invisible presences of one kind or another, and although I never saw a form, I knew that there was someone or something there. I often perceived these presences as menacing – like the ones in the Cathedral – and now this sensation began to intensify, so that there was a more tangible sense of an entity impinging upon my perception. Perhaps being alone more made me more vulnerable to this experience, or maybe it gave space for my inner fears to develop into thought forms that had their own energy. When there was a 'visitor' present, the atmosphere was as different as night from day. There was no mistaking it.

These developments in my life were, I feel, the beginning of changes that eventually led to my leaving the community.

xvii

In the Cathedral grounds were a small number of monks' huts, which had been used as a retreat centre by an order based near Edinburgh. I loved these huts, which were situated in a dell on the edge of the small wood in the cathedral grounds, secluded from the machinery of daily life by a surrounding hedge. Many birds came there, and in the spring the area was carpeted with bluebells and snowdrops. In the midst of the pressures of community life, it was a little haven of silence and solitude for me. The monks also had a cottage in the village and Father Edmund used to come there quite frequently.

Father Edmund became acquainted with the community through negotiations over the huts, and in time, his influence had a marked effect on the community's concepts. There was a greater respect for the value of solitude and silence, and 'quiet days' were instituted, when a person could take a mini-retreat. This was such a relief for me, for though I feared isolation, I felt suffocated and exhausted by the continual whirl of services, work, family groups, meetings and so on. I needed solitude and quietness in which to make contact with the centre of my being.

I got to know Father Edmund quite well and loved to go to his cottage for a chat, which I excused to the community as being spiritual direction. In fact, Father Edmund was well able to disseminate spiritual guidance in the form of a chat, and I found him a great source of wisdom, understanding and gentle humour. He had a knack of being able to convey profound truths in everyday language. He reached beyond the perspectives of the community's tradition, and had a kind of empathy for my terror that I had only experienced before with Dr Lake. Without knowing exactly what it was like, he sensed that my illness was not something to be 'cured', but that it was the driving force of my spiritual pathway and a transformational spark at every level of my being. When talking with him, I never had to make any pretence about my suffering with anorexia nervosa. I always remember Father Edmund in his inimitable way, taking his pipe out of his mouth and gesturing as if about to deliver an earth-shattering sermon. 'Jackie,' he said, 'when you come to death's doorway you won't be afraid. You'll say "gosh, here we are again, I've been doing this all my life!" ' I felt a sense of relief. Life and death are inseparable companions.

It was partly through Father Edmund that my life in the community began to change, and led to a door opening for me. As I gained increasing confidence in my individuality, I began to emerge from the group identity of the community. There were many aspects of the life that puzzled and troubled me, but it was not until I had been away for several years that I began to understand the less visible dynamics that I had sensed intuitively, and the personal and doctrinal elements that underpinned them.

My perspective is still changing. As I constantly seek wisdom and understanding to interpret my own journey, I see the events of my life in a different light. In my community experience I found that the more I emerged into my real self, the tighter the group boundaries began to feel. I was becoming larger and stronger in personality and spirit, and while at first the group had protected and nurtured me, now it began to constrain me.

There came a point where I felt that I could not develop any further within the confines of that lifestyle, but this perception was not fully crystallised in my thinking. It manifested as a feeling of being trapped. I wanted more freedom and independence but I had nowhere to go, and without resources or money, I was afraid of being alone in the outside world.

Spring

Out of the silence of brown-grey winter
Stirs a breath of life.
The cold earth remembers its treasures of seeds,
Hidden.
Their dormant lives change to growth,
By mysterious voice
Bidden.

For a caress of warmth
They put forth
Golden flowers.

Hushed creation waits for the miracle of life
The circle of seasons
Transforms death into bursting energy.

Rains blowing,
Plants growing,
Trees showing
Miniature leaves.

Dawn chorus, birds with young,
To unwritten music the song is sung,
Gulls squealing, grey wings wheeling
On the winds of spring.
Sea bright
With dazzling light;
Now calm as glass,
Now in uproarious dance.

No turning back!
Exquisite forms lying stored
In the blueprint of life held by God,
Brought to birth
Upon the earth
As spring gathers strength.

Jacqueline Kemp

My Love

My love is like a butterfly
Which upward danced toward the sun,
Lured from its chrysalis by golden warmth
To a new life just begun.
Sucking sweet nectar from petal cups
And beating its gossamer wings
Alighting on dewy grasses
In a world of sparkling things.
But the sun withdrew his shining
And the warmth became a cloud;
A chilly air that heralded
A rude wind, cold and proud.
The wings of fragile fluttering
Closed to the wind as it sighed;
The creature born of chrysalis
Fell to the earth and died.

My love is like a river
That springing from its source,
Carves its bed in the rocks of the earth
As it follows its twisting course.
A bubbling brook of laughter
Splashing the stones with glee,
Impatient torrent hastening
To reach its destiny.
A subterranean cavern-
There, waters hid from sight
Flow into mysterious depths
Where all is dark and night.
Now crossing life's panorama
And cold with deepest woe,
The river of love flows onward
With waters full and slow.
Soon to reach the surging sea,
The river, spreading wide
Swell and sinks in harmony
With the ebb and flow of tide.
Moving now to lose itself
At its mouth in the ocean frame,
Surrendering its substance
To the source from which it came.

Jacqueline Kemp

Chapter Five

Changes afoot

My relationship with Father Edmund proved to be the matrix within which a chance meeting led to the initiation of a life-changing drama for me. I say 'chance', but that word is a paradox in itself. One can look back down the road of life that one has travelled and see how apparently chance occurrences have shaped one's destiny. This is easier to see when it is something that has had an observable, major effect, but in fact every moment shapes our destiny. The past is gathered into the present, and out of the present the future is born.

On the quantum level it does begin to look as if chance is the foundation of our experience, and that by participating in this great vibrating web of energies we trap the chances, as it were, and form our own destiny. On the other hand, as we are all intricately woven into the universal web, we cannot dance entirely to our own tune. If everything is connected in some way to everything else, then nothing can be due to chance, everything has a meaning and purpose, and cause and effect chase each other around the manifest universe.

This is the subject of much New Age parlance, but I would venture to say that since we, as a human race, are only just beginning to understand the picture as the marriage of modern science and ancient wisdom proceeds, it is a bit soon to make pronouncements that may sound like facts, to the unwary ear. Of course we cannot resist theorising and hypothesising and surmising, and that is good, for it will lead to greater understanding of universal processes and the meaning of life. However, I have learned to be cautious of presentations that convey the message 'This Is How It Is'. To claim that each one of us is the master of our own universe, and the creator of our individual destiny, can lead to a lack of compassion and social conscience if we are not very careful. Oversimplified metaphysics can, for some, be the architecture of confusion and despair.

Being an incurable worrier, my efforts to understand the underlying processes of manifestation, by which one's thoughts and actions shape the outworking of one's life, made it very hard for me to make decisions. Every thought and every breath seemed loaded with a ponderous weight of possible outcomes, many of which, in the contemplations of my anxious mind, could be disastrous. I think that it was only upon reflection, sometimes after many years, upon the major events of my life and the minutia from which they emerged, that I began to realise that through the faithful steps of my everyday existence I was being guided by my intent. The agenda of my intent is laid out at many levels of my being, the higher aspirations changing little, while the daily focus changes rapidly and frequently. I have come to learn that even my apparently clumsy blunders and mistakes are woven into the unique pathway that I am treading, bringing me ever closer to my true reality, and that nothing is neither too small nor too great to be of concern to my unseen guides and helpers.

I found that the teaching of Christian doctrine concerning unselfishness caused me some problems, especially in the way that it was propounded by the community, where the life of the group and service to the wider populace apparently took precedence over the needs of the individual. Since I wrestled with a deeply embedded sense of worthlessness, I felt a sense of guilt concerning recognising and expressing my own needs and wishes. Despite this I was beginning to see that my service in this life was to seek to manifest my true self in its divine and human aspects ever more authentically, and that by doing so I was therefore serving the rest of creation in the highest possible way. I saw that to lose touch with my self and my own personal direction led me to spread hindrance and destructiveness, both consciously and unconsciously, by my thought vibrations and

160

my actions. I think that the general view, at least in the earlier years of community life, was that active serving of others by whatever means was more demanding and more sacrificial, and therefore of greater value than the work of self knowledge. In my own experience I could not accept this. I found that facing up to myself with the intention of complete honesty and commitment to change was the most taxing, exhausting, terrifying and challenging thing that I had ever attempted.

However, humans are social animals, and it is important for us to understand how to live harmoniously in groups, from the small, localised group to the concept of the global village. It is not always simple to see how to balance the needs of the group with the needs of the individual, and even in one-to-one relationships there is still the necessity for balance of personal interest and the needs of the other person.

It is my unshakeable belief that true unselfishness springs naturally from the recognition and acceptance of one's whole self. In an atmosphere of love and total absence of judgement, relaxation and relief can permeate the whole being and bring deep healing, setting one free to love oneself in a way which automatically radiates out to others.

The elders of the Community allowed me to go on a short retreat with Father Edmund, at the home of his Order in Edinburgh. It was such a special and unusual experience, which later proved to have been a key factor in steering my life in a different direction.

The monks lived a very simple existence, and their huts, which they used as monastic cells were basic to say the least! Fortunately mine had a little heater as a special dispensation of comfort. The bath, which was only used infrequently, was outside! I loved my baths, so faced this prospect with dismay – especially the thought of undressing with monks around! The fact that my undressing would not be of interest to them did not remove my anxieties.

It was my good fortune that a friend of mine from university lived just down the road, so I made a quick escape from monastic life now and then to take a bath in her home, and share news with her. It felt like a blissful taste of freedom!

Meals were very simple, too, taken in the communal house, but I struggled with the large amounts of bread and cheese, for which I had a particular craving. However, amongst the huts in the grounds behind their communal house the atmosphere was peaceful and soothing and I had unaccustomed time and space to myself to reflect on my life.

As always, my thoughts were dominated by the demands of anorexia nervosa, with its endless ramifications, and the relentless driving of its force showed no mercy. Like an insoluble riddle, the question of how to get well twisted my mind into knots, and when I tried to unpick them, I was trapped in an impasse of fear. Doors were closed in the corridors of my thoughts, and try as I might, I could not open them by any ordinary means.

While I was staying with Father Edmund, I met another priest who had come over to talk to him and share a meal. Both priests were university lecturers in theology, and over lunch they were discussing matters of angels and demons in church history. My ears pricked up! I was still deeply troubled and terrified by the presences that I sensed – not only in the cathedral but also round about me, sometimes manifesting in my room, unseen but with a terrifying intensity. Father Patrick seemed to have a certain authority when he spoke, and I felt that he could help me. We got on well, and there was an instant attraction between us. I had a strong inner conviction that if I had further contact with Father Patrick, it would bring about momentous happenings in my life. Later events revealed that I was right. An initial step was made when he invited me to visit him at his home in Edinburgh.

When I returned to the Community of Transformation I said little about my experience, but I had a strong pull in my heart towards Father Patrick and felt that I had to go and visit him. What is it, I wonder, that draws us irresistibly towards people and situations that bring about major events in our lives, either dramatic, traumatic, wonderful, helpful or whatever? Perhaps it is a mechanism no different from that which underlies all the minor events of our lives – those things that we hardly notice – but because major events impinge forcefully upon our awareness, it could be that we usually see them in a different light.

Eventually I managed to get permission to go to visit Father Patrick, although I am not sure how I convinced the community elders that it was necessary. It was quite a long trip to Edinburgh from Drumduish, on ferry, train and buses. All the way there I had a sense of anticipation – that Something was going to happen.

When I arrived, I found the surroundings very uncongenial and somewhat menacing. Father Patrick lived in a council flat on the second (top) floor of a long block of flats that had a communal staircase up the middle of each section, known as a 'stair' in that particular district. The council estate was huge and very run down, with lots of boarded up flats, and gardens left to run wild. There was a substantial area of rough ground in the middle of the large circle of almost identical flats, and the whole place had an air of dereliction. I felt very nervous as I entered the stair and made my way up to Father Patrick's flat.

The door was answered by a woman who was living with him, and I was quite taken aback by this. He had not mentioned her before. She welcomed me in and said that she was going out, and had left supper for us. She did not seem at all surprised to see me and did not ask my reason for visiting, and later on I learned why. The flow of events seemed to take on a mesmerising quality, as if it had all been set in motion aeons ago. As I talked with Patrick, I quickly realised that there was something about him that stirred hidden depths in me, depths of which I was very much afraid.

I had arranged to stay overnight at the flat, and after we had been talking for a while, Patrick asked me if I would like a bath.

163

I accepted, and he said that I could get undressed in his room, which was nice and warm. He left me alone, but I felt a bit uneasy, especially as I put on his enormous dressing gown which he had lent me.

Just as I was about to head for the bathroom, he appeared and put his arms round me. I stiffened in alarm, my mind full of fears. He reassured me, or tried to, but then I had a kind of déjà-vu. It was as if something had been set in motion, and I could either go with it and allow it to happen, or step out of the process and stop it.

While I was in the bath I received an impression that I could trust Patrick, and somewhere inside myself I decided to go ahead with the process. I think that this is a very important point. Although feelings of helplessness came over me, I was *not* helpless; I could have changed the flow of events at several points. I wondered, later on, did I *need* to feel helpless, and if so, why? Was it certain preconceived notions of feminine sexuality, so typically and insidiously disseminated throughout our society, or some need to hand over responsibility for my own sexual needs so that I did not have to identify myself with them? Maybe it could even have been the replay of an ancient drama in a past-life encounter, or perhaps the enactment of an archetypal master and slave collusion. I don't really know the answer, and at the time, I did not reflect upon these ponderous questions. I just 'went with the flow'.

When I emerged from the bath and went back to Patrick's room to get dressed, he was waiting for me, dressed only in underpants. I froze in horror, convinced that I was about to be raped. Again, from the distance of many years, I can see that even had that been his intention, I could have done something about it. It is impossible to say *what* I could have done, as such decisions and reactions depend upon the moment-by-moment flow of events, but various alternatives come to mind – racing for the front door and screaming in the stair, trying to talk my way out of the situation, or even attacking him. I may not have been successful in protecting myself, but the frozen horror was what kept me from trying, or even thinking of ways to escape. This must surely be the fate of many a female, when confronted by a rapist. Fortunately this was not Patrick's intention at all, and instead he put his arms round me and tried to comfort me. I remained terrified and frozen to the spot, whereupon he pulled off the huge dressing gown underneath which I cowered, and removed his underpants. At this point I fell to the floor and screamed, pleading with him to leave me alone.

Why was I so submissive? I feel angry about that now. I could have put up a reasonable fight if I had wanted to – especially now that certain sensitive parts of the male anatomy were available for attack. The overwhelming terror of being naked, and of naked male bodies, was probably what inactivated my considerable ingenuity in terms of delivering an effective blow. Maybe a deep-seated 'need' for this drama to be played out also contributed to my inertia.

The upshot of the scene was that Patrick picked me off the floor like a limp rag, and held me gently close to him on his bed, chatting conversationally about the spiritual dynamics of male and female, until the fear began to subside. I think that his approach could be given the name 'implosion therapy', or something like that, for a dragon of my deeps had emerged and been recognised.

There is a tremendous shame connected with my experience of anorexia. It could almost be called a shame of being alive, in a human body. Anything that initiates recognition of me in my body is a trigger for terror and panic. Under such circumstances I feel that I have been caught out and exposed, and that terrible consequences will follow. Although to a certain extent I have learned to conceal this shame, it is still a crippling secret held within my heart, which if uncovered, paralyses my thoughts and actions. For me, nakedness is a supreme exposure without escape, and therefore accrues the most violent of overwhelming shameful feelings.

Predictably, after this drama I fell deeply in love with Patrick. I was to discover later on that many other women had done so already, and others would follow! This was an era of my life in which I experienced some of the most powerful interweaving of light and darkness. I encountered a certain amount of opposition and disapproval from some community elders concerning my contact with Patrick, but others were more understanding. I continued to visit him approximately every month, spending a week with him each time.

During this period, I began to recognise a presence of Light that seemed to accompany and speak to me in a very definite way. I felt that this presence had been with me throughout my life, though I had only noticed it in moments of great despair. Life with the community had taught me to listen inwardly and attend to voices and promptings from other realms, and this acquired discipline gave me a way to make further acquaintance with the presence.

Walking along the shore one day, I felt two presences with me, one on either side. One seemed to be introducing the other, and at the time I assumed that one of them must be Jesus. Maybe it was. It was a comforting feeling, and I talked with these two companions as if they were old friends. I sat down with them to watch the beautiful dusk creep over the gentle lapping sea, and I was transported into another realm, where I was bathed in peace and understanding. All questions and striving melted away into the wonderful vast spacious awareness, and I could have sat there forever, heedless of the passage of earthly events.

I imagine that this kind of state is that which many people access from meditation. However, I have never been able to find this kind of awareness through any of my efforts with traditional meditation, or with modern methods using audio-technology. It was only mediated to me through the natural world and my unseen companions. To this day I still find that nature is my best teacher of meditation and contemplation.

After a while I felt a nudge, and I realised that I must come back to everyday life, albeit reluctantly, and pursue the pathway of my earthly existence.

Some weeks later, after a bout of flu, I was gazing mournfully in the bathroom mirror, searching the reflected image for someone I could recognise. Suddenly I knew the name of the presence who had always been my companion – 'One Who Comes'. I felt that it was my name, too – a script for the essence of my incarnation. One Who Comes is still with me, although our relationship has changed a great deal over the years. However, at that time, with the imminent changes in my life, and unexplored dark waters of anorexia ahead, One Who Comes was a life-saver.

Eventually, trying to combine my visits to Patrick and my life in the community became unworkable, and Patrick invited me to go to live with him, to continue my 'treatment'. I think that although he related to me very much as a lover, he kept me at a distance by seeing me as a 'case' – someone whom he was helping to get well. I sought to take temporary leave of absence from the community, but this was refused, on the grounds that the elders would have no control over what might happen in my life with Patrick. This did not seem fair to me, as I was not asking for licence to have some sort of affair, but to pursue something that I sincerely believed would help me to get well. There may have been other reasons behind the decision, or an unseen wisdom operating on my behalf, but whatever the case, I made the decision to leave permanently.

At that time, the prospect of leaving the relative security of community life was devastating and full of threatening unknowns, but looking back I am infinitely glad that I left. Whatever else transpired, I remain grateful to Patrick for being the catalyst for my breaking away from a lifestyle and belief system that were no longer suitable for me. The community gave me many gifts, and for these I feel profound gratitude, most especially for the gift of the friendships that I made there. However, if I had clung on to the apparent security and shelter of that structure, it would have stifled me.

I am not good at making changes, either small or great, and often need a very forceful impetus to effect a necessary change in my life. Anorexia nervosa, as it manifested in my life, was very much akin to an obsessive-compulsive disorder, and the attendant inner terror and disorientation made me cling desperately to outward routines and rituals, thought patterns and physical objects, to try to find some kind of structure to support my crumbling sense of self.

Going to live with Patrick was something of a culture shock, as well as a shattering and deeply traumatising emotional experience. I had become used to the gentle ways of life on Drumduish – the friendliness of the people, the openness of the children, the beautiful views and the nurturing sea, and an everyday structure to my life. In contrast, West Hapton, which was the part of Edinburgh where Patrick lived, seemed like a terrifying concrete jungle full of danger and threat. The ugliness of the surroundings, the harsh sounds, the wild and unruly children and the unfriendly glares or averted eyes of passers-by made it a truly soul-destroying environment in which to live. The aggression and anger of the atmosphere all around were palpable, the tension ready to erupt like an exploding bomb.

For about six months, I was secluded with Patrick in a theatre of our own making, and could only look out upon the devastation with wild imagination. Once I began to know real people, I found that there were many ordinary folk there, and often kindness and help would come my way from the most unexpected sources.

For a while, life with Patrick was so compelling that it masked the inhospitable nature of my new surroundings. I was so in love with him that I was blind to the trials and discomforts of living in that devastated place. In retrospect, I wonder to myself who it was that I thought I loved, and what it was I so adored about him. Certainly he was a fairly likeable human being, and like us all, deserving of love, but the amount of devotion and prostrate subservience that flooded my senses and motivated my behaviour towards him was out of all proportion –

almost obliterating reason.

I am so very grateful to the training that my life in the community had given me, and indeed also to the disciplines that anorexia nervosa forced upon me, as these two combined structural forces of my personality prevented me from falling entirely under his sway. I always kept a corner of myself to myself, and thus, I venture to conclude, was prevented and protected from complete disintegration – which I think would have led to my demise. In my view, Patrick had no malevolent intentions. I am sure that he sincerely wished and tried to help me, believing implicitly that he could. Yet the combination of the powerful undercurrents of unconscious forces from both of us, together with spiritual energies that were attracted to us and social structures that shaped us, came together to weave the most violent and dramatic epoch of my life.

I think that Patrick was drawn to women with complex emotional needs, and such women were also drawn to him. I was certainly one of these needy persons. After our initial meeting, it did not take long for me to start spilling the beans of my story to him. I was so desperate that I was always on the lookout for someone who could help me, and save me from the monster that was devouring my life. Patrick claimed that he could heal me, and I was only too ready to believe him, but during the sixteen months that I lived with him, I went through more traumas than I can begin to describe, and found myself in a very dangerous emotional and psychic situation. The pain of it was so intense that at times I thought it would burn me alive.

That which I thought was love led me to endure all manner of sexual and emotional humiliation and betrayal with that man. I will spare the reader the unedifying details, since they are events on the surface of this episode of my life, and would perhaps detract from the understanding of the deeper significance of it. The potentially creative possibilities of our first meeting became swamped by a convoluted sexual and religious dramatisation, underneath which lay a struggle for ascendancy, and a frantic, entangled search on the part of both of us for the disintegrated parts of ourselves.

When I left Patrick, I was utterly broken. I had left him on all levels, not just the physical. My heart had been shattered to smithereens and my being seared to the core. Even if I manage to forgive both him and myself completely, I will never forget that wound. Amazingly, through that very negative disillusionment and betrayal, I became stronger. Metaphorically speaking, I fought him to the death – the death of the illusion and the death of the relationship and the hold that it had over me – and in so doing, another part of me came to life.

Gradually, from needing to adore a man in order to feel that I had life and identity, I found a reverence growing in me for all life forms, for Life itself and for that which could be called divine. Old dogmas and preconceptions began to wither and die away, seemingly of their own accord. This process goes on, and no doubt it will continue, until through the progress of my incarnations, I become a transparent vessel of the divine truth. This will probably take aeons, but as far as I can tell I am at least going in the right direction. It is food for the deepest thought that this process was accelerated by an experience that could only be described as a living hell.

The ancient Norse goddess, Hel – from which the word 'hell' is derived – was queen of the underworld, and was associated with a uterine shrine or sacred cave of rebirth. Consequently, the origin of the word contains nothing of the everlasting torture concocted by Christian doctrine. In the hidden underworld of chaos which we fear so deeply, the healing fire is kindled and rises to eternity.

The hell that I experienced while living with Patrick was certainly of the torturous kind, in the inner realms where soul and body work out their incarnation. At the same time, I was being recreated by the forces operating within that experience, so that I emerged from it 'reborn' – the same person, but with a different understanding and outlook on life, and with a different vibration to my being.

Although my life with Patrick was characterised by traumatic emotional and psychic events, there were various aspects of ordinariness that brought the situation down to earth, and helped me to survive it. Many of his friends were very kind to me, and sometimes invited me to visit them in their homes, to give me a break from the pressure of my involvement with Patrick. Most of them were also involved with him to some degree or another, and understood how painful and stressful the relationship could become.

One woman owned a farm, and I particularly liked going there to relax in the countryside, and to relish the peaceful luxury of her home. Sometimes she would turn up unexpectedly, and offer me a visit just when I needed to get away, and take me back with me in her car.

Occasionally I returned to visit Father Edmund on my own. As he and Patrick were colleagues, mostly when I saw him I was with Patrick as well, and therefore could not share with him my bewilderment and distress. When I did see him alone, he listened in his characteristic way, waving his pipe and making a wise comment here and there. I remember him saying to me that the time would come when I would not need Patrick, and would leave him behind. I was aghast at this and simply could not envisage it at all, but how right he was. He could see through to the other side of the infatuation, and I am impressed now, as I recollect this, that he knew me well enough to foresee that I would eventually free myself from the intense involvement and the destructive hold that it had over me.

Another friend lived on a croft in Shetland, and I was invited to spend a week there with Janet, her husband Adam and her son Johnny. It was an exciting journey in the small plane that took off from Edinburgh Airport and landed at Sumburgh airport, near Lerwick. There was a gale force wind blowing across Shetland at the time of the flight, and it took the pilot three attempts to land safely. Many of the passengers, including me, were frightened by the bumpy ride and the two aborted landings. When we finally touched down and I entered the airport building, Adam was waiting for me. I burst into tears and fell into his arms with relief.

The visit was very interesting and enjoyable. Adam delivered meat at various locations in Shetland, and invited me to go with him on one of his trips. It was lovely to be able to see something of the natural beauty of the islands, and learn a little about the history and the people. I also loved staying at the croft, which was right on the coast, and was so peaceful and quiet. The peat fire in my bedroom gave a lovely comforting warmth, and the smoke rising from the chimney had a pleasant odour – completely different from the smoke of the Hapton chimneys. The wind was relentless, though, and being November, the evenings were long and dark. There was a quality of silence about this darkness that was deeply healing. For me it was like a receptive listener, absorbing all my distress and anguish into itself, giving my soul some moments of repose.

The family ate a simple diet, mostly of vegetables from their garden with a little fish, meat and cheese purchased in local shops. Janet was understanding about my problems with food, and somehow I managed to cope with the meals – with occasional lapses, such as pinching an extra lump of cheese, or slyly helping myself to a handful of biscuits. In spite of this, my eating pattern while staying there was much more balanced than when I was 'at home' with Patrick. When it came time to return, I was reluctant to leave this lifestyle and my friends, and re-enter the combat zone of life with him.

While I was living with Patrick, I had the opportunity to visit Ireland with him, also accompanied by Janet. Patrick had a large family, some of whom still lived in Ireland, and a family celebration was to take place. He invited Janet and me to go with him and share in the celebration, staying at a hotel run by one of his relatives. In many ways it was a special privilege. I would never have been able to afford to see Ireland if it had not been for Patrick, who paid my fare on the ferry to Larne, and for the free accommodation in the hotel.

There was much about the expedition that captivated my

imagination. The countryside was beautiful, true to the image of the 'Emerald Isle', with green fields and misty mountains, just like a picture postcard. People seemed very friendly, with rich Irish accents, and we were made very welcome at the hotel. I came across various quaint anomalies which one typically associates with Ireland – although I am sure that such things are not specific to that country. There was the signpost, which pointed to the same location in opposite directions, the toilet with the handle that flushed upwards, the pub sign hanging upside down... I really liked the feel of the place!

I also noticed a more obvious presence of religious belief than one generally finds in Britain. Shrines for devotions to the Virgin Mary were dotted along the roads, and the occasion of a funeral in a small town was honoured by virtually everyone. Shop owners, customers and passers-by paused in their tracks and lined up along the pavement to acknowledge the hearse as it went by, with a genuflection and a sign of the Cross. I thought that there was a marked difference between this refreshing reverence for the departed and funeral processions which in large towns go by almost unnoticed – except perhaps for a line of impatient drivers behind, eager to overtake. Whatever one's thoughts and feelings about religions and their effects upon that the societies that adhere to them, it cannot be denied that certain aspects of the moral codes involved appear to have a beneficial and positive socialising influence.

There were many gifts and enriching experiences that came my way during my time as Patrick's companion. I think that it is important for me to recognise and acknowledge this, as I could so easily write off the whole episode as a dreadful nightmare, and miss those aspects of it that were balancing factors. I feel that this is an essential lesson for facing up to those times in life when everything seems to close over us and there appears to be no light on the horizon. My salvation during that time with Patrick, and in other desperate times of my life, has come through being able to be open to the gift of the present moment, and thus somehow to retain the ability to tap into that great mystery of healing that exists within the universe.

During the time when I was living with Patrick, I came to know One Who Comes much more intimately. This being is neither male nor female, but can transmit energy of either gender or both at the same time, according to my need. Generally I relate to the being as 'him'. This is partly due to the lack of a pronoun that incorporates both masculine and feminine, and also because of the unfortunate misogynous habit of speech that gives precedence to the masculine identity. The character of One Who Comes is firm and penetrating, but his communications carry the utmost gentleness and precision, and he has a delightful sense of humour. His humour is always perfectly placed – never unkind or out of context – and always so refreshing and enlightening. Many, many times I have been aware of his interventions – saving me from disaster, and in many little intimate ways assisting my efforts at living my daily life. I leaned gratefully on One Who Comes, but I was aware that I was never allowed to lean too heavily, to be lazy or to offload my own responsibility.

I think that without One Who Comes and my training in community life I would not have survived the forces that assailed me while I was living with Patrick. The sexual dynamics between us were enacted in the context of a mythical construct of his own making, to which for that time I attempted to subscribe, although I think that I never believed in it wholeheartedly. This situation released tremendous forces of hatred and self-destructive violence in me, and I had no one to turn to for wisdom and help.

Patrick was a 'one man band', and he insisted that his methods of healing (so-called) and his person were above any correction and criticism, and that I needed no one else but him. At the time I did not realise that this position was bordering on being delusional and was the mark of extreme personal insecurity. I did, however, feel instinctively that something was wrong – just as I had done about certain aspects of community life. His approach manifested as a take-over bid, which I assume must have arisen from an unconscious aspect of his personality. Fortunately for me, he went too far when he tried to take control of my weight and eating, creating fantasies of a thin demon that possessed me, and that I had to let him decide what weight I should be. In some extraordinary adaptation of the doctrine of transubstantiation, he claimed that he would become the food that I ate, and that I would thus be 'eating Patrick'. This was like a red rag to a bull to the anorexic part of my nature. The taproot of my identity – my very survival – lay in the devotion to, and service of, thinness, and he was trying to uproot it! I felt that he was trying to destroy me, that he had deceived me and was yet another person who wanted me to be 'fat'. My fighting spirit was roused, and I put forth all my strength to do battle with him.

I had thought him to be my saviour and that I was utterly dependent on him for my health and sanity, but the extremity of his determination to control my food and my weight was a shocking revelation. I found a tremendous fire at the very core of my being that rose up to defend my integrity and my right to define my own identity, even if it was an anorexic one.

My daily life with Patrick was so different from my life in the community. It was a shock to my system on all levels, and left me floundering in a sea of unfamiliarity and unstructured time. I had no money of my own and had to rely on Patrick supporting me, which made me doubly dependent on him. He gave me a regular minimal 'wage' for being his housekeeper, which being well trained in all sorts of drudgery at the community, I did efficiently.

For a while it almost seemed as if I were his wife, and my life revolved round him totally. My thoughts and emotions fluttered around him constantly, like moths around a light. It felt strange that I was free to go out and initiate my own daily events, rather than having to adhere to the community's regular schedule, but I was not really free at all. I was bonded in a kind of slavery to this extraordinary relationship, and Patrick was my master. He envisaged the relationship that way, too, and made much of being the dominant partner in it. He was the Christ Man, and I was the Eve woman who needed his deliverance. I feel an enormous sense of gratitude and relief that I am no longer trapped by that particular interpretation of Christian doctrine! I can even laugh about it now. How I extricated myself from the whole mess I will never know fully, but I think, as I mentioned before, I have my anorexia to thank. My 'marriage' to this mysterious illness, which seems to have a life of its own, is very profound. This being the case, Patrick's charade never penetrated me completely, or convinced me, or took me over.

I soon discovered that there was a whole coterie of women, and one or two men as well, who were revolving round Patrick's powerful charisma and participating in his mental and emotional construct. We were like stars in a galaxy revolving round the centre, but at the centre was a black hole. For a time, Patrick was absorbed with me and I was the focus of his attention, but pretty soon the novelty wore off and he took up with other women. They disappeared into his bedroom, and I was left alone with my rage and jealousy. I became head cook and bottle washer, and felt like I was just part of the furniture. I was also expected to entertain, feed, comfort and pray for this flow of 'guests' – which proved to be a hefty challenge to my generosity of spirit and my integrity. I don't think I rose to it very well.

With no restriction on access to food, and in a situation where my real hunger was not being met, my eating became chaotic again, and once more my weight began to spiral out of control. Bingeing, dieting, more bingeing, more dieting, an encroaching layer of the dreaded flesh, sexual power-games, isolation, loneliness, financial dependency – this explosive mixture generated more and more powerful forces within my being until I felt, as I had done so many times before, that I could not hold myself together any longer.

Patrick's attention and affection for me waned progressively. He had wooed and courted me, drawing out my sexuality, and I had left everything that I had established in my life within the community in order to be with him. I had adored him and believed in him so much, but now I felt lost and abandoned – exposed to my own self-destructive violence that was bound up substantially with my sexuality. The fires of hatred and jealousy seared me to the place where soul and personality meet. I could not tell whom I most hated, myself or him, and torrents of murderous rage spewed out of me like flames from a dragon's mouth. It was a dangerous situation. I spent many hours planning how I would kill myself, and fantasising about what it would be like to be dead.

It seemed simpler to do away with myself than to struggle on. I had nothing to live for since my beloved had discarded me. Sometimes I wonder at the horrendous crimes that are committed as a result of 'love'. How could anyone do these atrocious things? I have felt such forces, though, surging fiercely at the walls of my integrity. It is perilous to deny our dark side and the energies of the shadow, for they are liable to rise up just when we are not expecting it, demanding to be let out.

It seemed as if psychic forces and entities were attracted to the energies generated by my conflict concerning Patrick, for psychic phenomena and unseen presences became frequent occurrences, and they filled my life with unimaginable terror. At that time I was so open to everything that was around, and unable to interpret it in any way other than demonic, that I had no means of dealing with my experiences. At least in the community there had been plenty of people around to talk to and to call on for help with this kind of thing. Patrick was almost invariably absent, and when he was around he responded in a typically religious authoritarian way, sometimes even shouting at me and shaking me to 'get rid of the demon'.

One of these dramatic incidents occurred on a day when I was on the verge of suicide. My survival energy was totally spent, and I had decided to take an overdose to end the nightmare that was my daily existence. Medicines and painkillers were kept in the kitchen and my room was at the other end of the hall. I had never really liked that hall. It had a strange feel about it, a bit like the long dark corridor in the North College of the Cathedral where I had first lived when I moved to Drumduish.

As I passed Patrick's room I noticed a strange, uncanny smell, and saw that it was billowing with smoke. I was paralysed with fear and astonishment. Then I saw that the bathroom was also full of smoke. Even though both doors were open, the smoke was not coming out of either room. It just hung there, like a malevolent fog. The smell was indescribable, something I had never come across before, but it maybe resembled that of burning flesh. As I stood there frozen with terror, I felt a very ominous presence drawing near to me. This galvanised me into action and I fled from the flat, ran down the stairs, and knocked frantically at my neighbour's door, trembling and white-faced. 'What's the matter?' she asked. 'Have you seen a ghost?'

She had lived with Patrick before me and was used to unusual occurrences. I told her of the smoke, and she came upstairs with me to the flat. I made her go in first, and followed timorously. The presence had gone, but the smoke was still there and we searched the flat for a possible source – clothes on a radiator, perhaps, or the gas fire, an electrical appliance maybe – but there was nothing at all in the whole place that we could find to be the cause. We looked outside to see if there was a bonfire lit or something else burning, but there was absolutely nothing that would explain the smoke.

We opened all the windows, and by the time that Patrick returned, the smoke had all disappeared and he did not believe my story. Typically he had left me alone to contend with the forces that he had been a party to stirring up. When my neighbour told him about the experience he accepted what she said, albeit reluctantly, but paid little attention to the trauma it had caused me. He dismissed it as some kind of 'little demon' that had visited me.

The smoke returned again on another occasion. That time I was out, and I came back to find it in the same places, although not so dense.

For a long while I was convinced that the forces which nearly propelled me to suicide had stirred up the smoke of hell – the traditional Christian concept hell which still held sway over my beliefs at the time. I still do not have an unequivocal explanation for the experience, but the likelihood of a blocked communal chimney belching smoke through an old fireplace that had been filled in has come to seem like a possible alternative interpretation. However there were no old fireplaces in the bathroom...

Whatever the actual source of the smoky drama, it did serve to distract me from the course of self-destruction upon which I had been set, and was therefore a life-saver. My guides and helpers on the other side would no doubt use anything at their disposal to keep my feet upon the earthly pathway of my destiny. If it was a handy demon, or a handy blocked chimney, what difference did it make? It worked, which was the main thing.

The stress generated by the life I was living with Patrick caused my physical symptoms to increase, and I became more unwell than ever. During my time on Drumduish, my physical illness had been largely dismissed as neurotic, since there was no obvious cause apart from a minor duodenal ulcer. The island doctors were of little help, telling me that once I sorted my problems out my physical malaise would settle down, and that there was nothing actually wrong with my body. How often have I heard this miserable diagnosis! Certainly I do believe that the mind has a profound effect on the body, and that essentially all illnesses begin on the subtle vibrational levels of anatomy before they manifest as symptoms in the physical body.

However, each level of our human manifestation affects the

others, and any change on one level can produce a ripple of changes throughout the other levels. In my view, the skill of healing, and of directing one's own healing, is the discernment of what changes can be made on what levels, and the precise order, timing and method of effecting them. The idea that 'it's all in the mind' is not a truly integrated understanding of what it means to be a human being.

It was so difficult for me to cling to my integrity, and continue to listen to the messages from my body which were telling me that there was definitely something very wrong. Therefore it was a great relief when I finally consulted an allergy specialist and found that I had severe allergies to many common foods and environmental pollutants. There is an essential distinction between taking oneself too seriously and respecting one's perceptions and judgements.

I do not really know what brought me through the unspeakably terrible experience of living with Patrick. My diary was my closest confidant, and my entries filled three large A4 files with my thoughts and experiences. I still have not been able to read through them all again. It was not that our everyday life was especially dreadful. Apart from the eruption of sporadic dramatic episodes, everything went on fairly normally. I did housework, shopping, cooking, cleaning and all the ordinary things of maintaining a home. We did apparently pleasant things together sometimes, like going for walks and occasional outings, or I would visit some of his friends.

I don't think that my family or anyone else, except a few very close friends, realised what was really going on. It was the underlying currents of passion, fear, rage, and jealousy, circling around that bottomless pit of despair that was nearly the end of me. Those unseen helpers were surely working hard to protect me and keep me treading the path of life! Friends and helpers seemed to turn up just when I most needed them, or sometimes the smallest chink of light would penetrate my darkened mind from an apparently insignificant event – a crow rolling a tin can along the path, cloud patterns in the sky, or a smile from a baby in the supermarket, for example.

Eventually I began to rise up and fight the emotional and psychic cruelty that was being meted out to me. I hardened myself within and toughened myself without until I walked out of Patrick's house and out of the relationship, shut the doors of my heart and never allowed him back in. I was totally disillusioned and completely bewildered as to how I could have convinced myself that I had been in a relationship of love. I was unable to explain to myself how my feelings of such overpowering adoration and deep devotion could have led me into such an appalling mess.

I have perhaps painted a picture of Patrick as a cruel and ruthless man, and in some respects he was, but in many other ways he was kind, generous and loving, and was highly regarded by many for his learning and wisdom. There are many archetypes that seek expression through us, and it must surely take many lifetimes to reflect the purified version of each one. I believe that it is a great mistake, in relationships or indeed in any encounter, not to be aware that all but the most exceptional human beings are capable of transmitting harmful and negative energies. I think that although Patrick may have sincerely believed that he had reached enlightenment, he was, like the majority of us, still on his evolutionary journey through earthly incarnations.

I continue to reflect, and to seek understanding on all levels, as to why I drew this experience to myself. What complex set of factors caused me to invite, accept and submit to the humiliation, fear and cruelty that was brought to me through Patrick, and how was it that the unconscious dynamics of two people could combine to produce such a nightmarish situation? I think that a substantial portion of the answer lies in the very fact that it was the *unconscious* thoughts, feelings, needs, attitudes, concepts and other such constructs of our personalities that were involved, together with their diverse origins. Social structures, religious doctrines and beliefs, parental upbringing and family life, karma and past lives are a few of the many possible sources of such origins. It was as if the nature of this combination drew in many other energies – archetypal, historical, ancestral, and forms from other planes – to participate in the meeting of two human beings.

Who knows what entities and consciousness were seeking evolution through these moments of earthly time played out between us? Whatever the configuration of forces operating during this portion of my life experience, Patrick provided me with a powerful impetus for change, and for that I am grateful. The great psychologist Carl Jung was of the opinion that to know oneself and to integrate one's shadow or unconscious dynamics was of the greatest importance in human development and evolution, and I agree with him.

As soon as I refused to engage in the particular dynamics that had been operating between Patrick and myself, neither he nor the situation had any more hold over me, and the form that the relationship had taken ended. My withdrawal had to be total. Merely ceasing to relate outwardly would have been insufficient to effect a change.

It would be too simplistic to say that I had chosen the situation of being with Patrick, together with its alarming interactive processes, or alternatively that I was the victim of circumstances. Had I been suffering from a different kind of illness, it is unlikely that I would have been drawn to Patrick, or he to me. In our relationship, as with certain chemical reactions in the body, it was as if one particular configuration of molecules fitted perfectly into another, setting a process in motion.

It is true that choices I have made in my life have led up to encountering a certain person in a certain situation. However, such decisions may well have been driven by subconscious material of my human make-up, or indeed my soul's choice – something of which I was unaware in my everyday personality. Further, no moment in life is disconnected from all the other moments, in this lifetime or in another. Neither is the individual disconnected from any part of the living universe, which is our matrix of existence. In the focus of my experience with Patrick all those other elements were gathered in. For this reason I do not pass any final judgement upon it. As I grow and develop in my humanity, my perspective of it changes over and over again, like patterns in a kaleidoscope.

I think that it is cruel and arrogant to assume that a suffering person has simply chosen their experience according to some kind of individual inner agenda. Did I choose to develop anorexia nervosa? Does a little child choose to be abducted and abused? Does a mother choose to see her children die of starvation? Does a young boy soldier choose to be mutilated in war? At the end of the day there is relief and humility in admitting that we do not have all the answers, and in maintaining a silent reverence and compassion for all that we do not understand.

Patterns

Nowhere to go and no place to call home,
Over the universe lonely I roam,
Seeking some planet or maybe a star,
Some nook or cranny, nearby or far,
Wherein I can rest and call myself me,
Where in my own eyes my self I shall see:
To escape the tormentor who clutches my reins
And tightens the bands to drive forth my pains,
Who laughs at my screams and jeers at my pleas,
Demanding submission as I on my knees
Cry out to a God who with promise of Light
Enticed me to follow, then vanished from sight.

Maimed and forsaken I wait for the kill,
Caring no longer if it bode good or ill
But only desiring the oblivion of death,
To breathe my last sigh and to sigh my last breath.
Memories jumble in kaleidoscope
And in the strange patterns I search for some hope,
But I find only puzzles and half finished designs,
Unanswered questions and nonsensical signs
Which led me, believing, across life's stormy way,
Seeking a mirage and an image of clay.

For the ardour that called me and kindled my fire
Was doused to indifference and made me a liar,
For I said that I loved but 'twas only a game
Which went out with a hiss like water quenched flame,
And billowing smoke arose like a cloud
Which draped like a pall and wrapped like a shroud,
Enclosing a body of death all around
As the dying embers of heart scorched the ground.

Jacqueline Kemp

Chapter Six

Concrete jungle

It had become imperative to find somewhere else to live other than with Patrick. He had set his sights on another woman and wanted me to go. When I first moved in he had said that I could stay with him as long as I liked – it could even be forever. Yet even while I was trying to find a way to store my meagre possessions in the flat, someone else was already hovering at the door.

At first I was deeply hurt when he had told me that I 'needed my own front door' – a euphemism for telling me that he didn't want me there any more – but I soon realised that I was desperate to get out of there and to find my own space. Where to go, though? Once again I had that awful panicky feeling that I had to move but had nowhere to go to. I started to search for alternatives, but every investigation drew a blank. I was cold towards Patrick, withdrawing emotionally, and disentangling the psychic cords that bound me to him. He did not like it and was often angry with me, but I told him he couldn't have it both ways.

Eventually the flat across the landing became vacant, and as I was considered to be part of this community stair, which had a special agreement with the council, I was allowed to move into it. I was very fortunate in this as it was a spacious three-bedroom flat, at the end of the block, and was the only one with a decent view of the sky. In retrospect I recognised how very lucky I was, and that this was another of those kindnesses from the universe that so often blessed my stumbling journey.

The flat had been the home of three men, and was not in the most attractive state, so I redecorated it and set about making it my home. These flats were old and in urgent need of repair, and

I had to cope with many eventualities for which I was not very well prepared. The heating system consisted only of an open fire with a back boiler, and did very little to heat even the living room. However, it boiled water vigorously at night – when I didn't need it – cheerfully rattling out a rhythm on the pipes and keeping me awake. It took a minimum of forty-five minutes to clean out the ash and build a new fire in the morning, a task I performed every day with a sense of gratitude to my community training in fire lighting! If the wind was in a certain direction it would blow the smoke back down the chimney and fill the sitting room, a little reminiscent of the smoky visitation in Patrick's flat. After a particularly windy spell, the chimney pot fell off, and since the flats were due for demolition, the council did not replace it. In spite of the misery of the cold and my battles with the heating system, having my own space opened up a whole new era of life and experiences for me.

In total, I lived in West Hapton for twenty-one years, the time I spent with Patrick being the beginning of it. It is such a large chunk of my life, and in spite of living a relatively mundane existence, there was so much that I learned and experienced that it is difficult to know how to represent it. In some ways it seemed like a life sentence, and I can view it very negatively, remembering the constant desperation of feeling that there was no escape from that restrictive situation in such hostile and depressing surroundings. On the other hand it gave me a view and an understanding of life that I will never forget, exposing my prejudice and preconceived ideas and forcing me to search for the very basics of integrity. Indeed I found a great many wonderful crumbs of beauty and drops of kindness, often in the most unexpected places and from the most unexpected sources.

The first thing I had to do was to find some sort of income, and thus began my practical lessons in negotiating the machinations of the Department of Health and Social Security – or Work and Pensions as it is known now. After 'signing on' for a couple of weeks, my doctor kindly suggested that I claim

Sickness Benefit, as it was called then, and this became my main income, and in some ways my identity, for the rest of my working life. I think that in many ways it was a mixed blessing. I was very fortunate – far more so than many folk, I imagine – and with various concessions and additions that came my way, my income, although low, was a lot better than 'the dole'. My family were generous and gave me gifts for all sorts of things, particularly for my cats, whom I shall introduce later on in this chapter.

I was grateful for the income. I am always grateful and appreciative of money, however little or however much comes my way, since I view it essentially as a gift from the universe, by whatever means that gift is delivered. However with it came the social stigma of being 'on Benefits'. Various assumptions are often made about people who do not have a Proper Job. Under this label I could now be viewed as being one of those 'spongers off the State' or 'using the taxpayer's hard-earned cash'. One person to whom I spoke, when looking for different accommodation, assumed that just because I was 'on Benefits', I would try to evade paying my rent! Generalisations can be very demoralising, and can also be the source of much strife and misunderstanding between people and groups. Also there was the constant dread of Brown Envelopes, containing perhaps a summons for an Assessment, or an enormous book-sized form with all sorts of questions to which one had to try to divine the right answer.

Later on, I was allowed minimal 'therapeutic earning' while still drawing benefit, and things became a little better. I enjoyed doing some occasional hairdressing for a while, and then I gave a few piano lessons. However, this by no means constituted the well-paid career job to which I had aspired. This aspect of my life was intimately related to my experience of anorexia nervosa, and is one about which I have the deepest and most painful regrets and a multitude of inner questions. My financial dependency on my family was an integral part of my anorexic experience. Somewhere deep within myself I believed that the only way I could 'earn' money was by being ill, that I had nothing to offer to society at large which was worth a decent income, and that in terms of marketable skills, I was worthless.

When I was a child, the unhealthy family dynamics had prevented me from developing a secure sense of myself as a person. All my immediate family seemed to need me in differing ways, and I was often ill, and often comforted or rewarded for compliance with gifts of money – a two shilling piece perhaps, for taking nasty medicine, or a half crown for my money box to cheer me up.

Events in my life often conspired to confirm and solidify my belief system about my lack of worth as a working member of society. That belief system caused such profound obliteration and anguish to my whole personality that it was not until recently that I could really face up to it, and acknowledge the devastation it has wrought in my life. I have wondered if had my family been less generous, would the resulting poverty have forced me into getting a job – any job – and holding it down, thus cleaving some sort of dignity for myself as being 'in work'. I will never know, but I doubt if I would have survived the challenge. The scourge of anorexia nervosa was so deep that I was always on the edge of losing touch with everything that held me together, and frequently broke down completely. The current social problems of drugs and alcohol misuse are no mystery to me, for there, but for an incomprehensible grace, go I.

Money has always been, and continues to provoke, a profound struggle in my soul. I imagine that a vast number of people worry about money or its equivalent. As a race, our beliefs tend to be about lack – about not having enough, or about hanging on to what we do have. In general, we do not believe in abundance, plenty, and sufficiency for everyone and every creature. For me this whole subject seems to go deeper, and the fear of not having enough money, fear of spending money and of not being able to have what I want – or what I think I want – is a major psychological and spiritual dilemma. The anguish and shame of never having been able to earn a decent living, and the guilty longing for wealth and riches, cuts through to the very heart of who I am in this lifetime. Barely a day goes by when I do not spend time worrying about it all and getting myself into a paralysing tangle, and even if I am not thinking about it, disturbing thoughts about it revolve round and round in the back of my mind. Nevertheless, from time to time through all of this, I find that a connection to the spirit world opens up. It can be anything – an unexpected gift, a cold weather payment, an act of generosity from someone, or maybe my own discipline of generosity – which tells me that the universe *is* a place of responsive abundance, kindness and plenty. I think it is my work in this lifetime to learn how to access this richness and to exchange fear for confidence, anxious hoarding for joyful flow and guilty longing for overflowing gratitude.

After I left Patrick, my religious beliefs began to change. It was not a deliberate attempt on my part to change them – on the contrary, I tried desperately to cling to my version of Christianity. This had developed from my early upbringing in a traditional Anglican church setting, going through the evangelical phase at university and then the charismatic phase in the community. The culmination of the process was my effort to appropriate Patrick's particular brand of Catholicism and mysticism – with a lot of his own ideas thrown in for good measure.

This accumulation of beliefs had acted as a kind of framework within which to conceptualise my experience of life, and was some sort of security for my fragile identity. Yet despite my best efforts, all that I had believed and followed devotedly all my life began to dissolve and crumble away. I began to read extensively, searching for understanding. I investigated as many different topics as I could find regarding the practice of religion throughout the human race. I delved into modern science, psychology, feminism, research into ancient scriptures, and various other religious traditions such as Hindu

Buddhism, and pagan beliefs.

It dawned on me that what had been presented to me, and what I had accepted as facts, were not necessarily facts at all, but were substantially only beliefs, concepts, opinions and constructs. This realisation was absolutely terrifying. There was nothing to cling on to any more, no one with whom I could speak the same language, no God to blame, hate and fear, and no recognisable Jesus with whom to have a relationship. Windows and doors in my mind began to fly open; questions and astonishment flooded in. While this was incredibly disconcerting, it was also a great relief. Extremes of guilt and resentment began to fall away, and I felt free to investigate and expand. Looking back I can see that this was a wonderful development in my spiritual journey. My attachment to the dogmas of religion began to change into the adventures of spirituality.

This process led me to question the validity of my religious experiences in the past – the voices, demons, angels, Jesus, God, the Holy Spirit – all of which had been the backbone of my religious life as a Christian. The concepts themselves, in which I believed, did not penetrate me in the same way as the Experiences. Yet, without doubt, the intellectual and the experiential aspects of my religious belief were linked. I find a great mystery in the way that our beliefs form and shape our reality.

There were the Experiences, as I would call them, which seemed to be at a level of reality that was different from the ordinary, and there was the experience – the daily living of life within the framework of my Christian beliefs. The Experiences were intense, vibrant and alive and had a lasting effect upon me, touching me at a far greater depth than was usual in my everyday life. An analogy would be the impact of meeting and interacting with a person, when compared with merely knowing about them. I sometimes wondered if, because my concepts had changed, this meant that I had simply imagined the Experiences, or indeed, that they had been generated by my concepts.

The human psyche is so complex, and perception can be an elusive and deceptive faculty. Our expectations, desires, attitudes, emotions and bodily state can influence profoundly what we perceive. Reality – that intangible, malleable stuff – is moulded and shaped by our beliefs and conditioning. One is left asking oneself, what *is* real? What does 'real' mean to us, anyway? I began to feel that the reality which I thought was solid, fixed and absolute is not so at all, and that somehow our *experience* of reality is woven from an apparent paradox of an ever-changing flow of events moving across an unchanging awareness.

I have wondered what was happening when I felt that I had perceived Jesus speaking to me, or felt the presence of angels and demons, or had visions and heard voices. Perhaps at least some of these experiences were projections of part of my own personality energy, or from parts of my being of which I am not normally conscious. However, in regard to the presences, both holy and unholy, I still feel that some of these were attributable to the manifestation of beings from other realms.

As I grappled with these questions, I moved further and further away from a traditional Christian outlook towards an inner pathway of seeking what it means for me to be incarnate in a human body. This seeking has not reached a final answer, and is a constant force which drives my passage of earthly moments.

I find it more rational to be open to the probability that there is more to life in the universe than in this very limited and short human existence, which we call 'being alive'. The awareness of some of the presences was unmistakable – as clear as when one is aware of another living person – whereas others seemed to be in a kind of twilight zone, and were not so easy to distinguish. My fears and concepts may have caused me to label some of them as 'demons' and class them as evil, when they may not necessarily have been so. I do believe that there are malevolent entities in other realms, but we are rather prone to calling things 'evil' when we cannot understand and control them. Some of the presences that I experienced were definitely hostile and were potentially devouring, but some humans are like that, too, and they are not necessarily evil people! Perhaps it is simpler to class things as 'evil' instead of developing the kind of personal and corporate awareness that would enable us to deal creatively with the forces involved.

Taking all this into consideration, I now feel that everything I experienced as a Christian was valid and real, but that I interpreted it according to my beliefs at the time. After this, I began to stumble my way to a greater sense of freedom, where all was not cut and dried, but where there is one intelligent universe of which we are all a part. All of us are moving towards truth and self-realisation and all of us have our own unique pathway.

As I continued my journey, experiences which I termed 'psychic' rather than religious still continued to happen, often with terrifying intensity. I would flee from my flat, shaking with fear, and dared not go back unless I had someone to accompany me. I lived in dread of these presences and experiences. I did not feel safe in my own home, and felt that I could be invaded at any time. I imagine that is how I had felt in my childhood home, too, and perhaps that had rendered me open to experiences of this kind. These psychic experiences were one of the greatest nightmares of my life, and even though I have learned how to control the manifestation of the presences, I still feel a shiver down my spine when I think about them.

I began to wonder if such experiences were connected to my anorexia, and that perhaps one of the deepest roots of my illness could be a kind of thin-skinned sensitivity, a lack of protection to the subtle layers of my being. I began to turn my attention towards seeking help, information and advice – whatever I could find to bring some light into the terror that haunted me.

The pathway was fraught with pitfalls in itself, and a couple of times I felt I got my fingers badly burned. The people who helped me most were those who did not try to deny, explain or exorcise what was happening to me, but who listened with interest and offered ways to try to cope, based on their own experiences and understanding. However, some of the so-called experts created further damage.

A certain doctor, who shall remain nameless, claimed to be able to dowse substances and spirits that were making me ill. He turned out to be quite incredible in his rudeness and egocentricity. He saw fit to accuse me of 'not trying' and then attempt to imprint me as his follower and subservient convert. He prescribed a strict diet consisting mostly of a few vegetables, pears and lamb, and to avoid any contact with water – even for washing – for a month. He did not seem to notice that I was a vegetarian. This abstemious process was supposedly designed to 'starve the spirits', after which time he would deliver me from them! When I returned home from this ill-fated visit, it was as if my flat was exploding with presences, and I could not stay in it until I had got someone to help me to calm the atmosphere. The denizens of the lower world had seen a golden opportunity! It was fortunate that I had seen through the doctor's pretence, and I wrote a rather direct letter telling him what he could do with his treatment. In retrospect, I felt that overall the whole thing had been an important learning experience, and had served to strengthen my self-respect and determination. I often find that what I intend to be one kind of experience turns out to be something quite different. Yet everything is of value, if I do not hold on to preconceived ideas and am willing to learn.

I was emerging from the effects of the relationship with Patrick with a growing realisation that the illusion we had set up together – of him as the Man Who Could Make Me Well and me as the Poor Sick Desperate Woman – was dying, and I began to seek help from other sources. I knew that complementary medicine offered a wide range of approaches. The National Health Service does offer certain types of complementary therapy, and some GP practices allow therapists to use rooms. However in the latter case it is usually a private therapist who rents the room and the treatment is not funded by the NHS. Therefore my choice of NHS complementary therapy was rather limited, and while I did benefit from homeopathy through the NHS for a time, it was not sufficient to provide me with a way forward with anorexia nervosa.

I tried many different forms of therapy – Postural integration, allergy desensitisation, homeopathy, acupuncture, polarity therapy, massage, art therapy, the Alexander Technique, psychotherapy, spiritual healing, radionics, dream work, herbal medicine, chiropractic, osteopathy, and past-life regression. There may have been others which I have forgotten! All the while I was still looking for the 'answer' – which I still saw as relief for my tormented mind and body. In my exploration of the therapeutic world I met some wonderful people who gave me a great deal of support, encouragement and help. I continue to discover such glowing gems of humanity, who while still being ordinary people, have a way of giving of themselves and their skill that reaches through to the core of me, helping me continue my work of reconstruction and repair. On the other hand, some experiences of therapy could be extremely negative, in that I fell for an attractive 'product' and did not see through to the person behind until it was too late. Such a person may have been well-meaning, but not sufficiently integrated to avoid relating to their client in ways which were unsuitable, and not conducive to healing. With each encounter I learned something new, and my vista broadened – even if an experience was not what I had been hoping for.

One particular example stands out in my memory. A certain healer was recommended to me by another professional. He was reputed to be very powerful and able to achieve amazing results. I was captured by this report, and hoped that he could help me. I made an appointment. The healer offered home visits, and came to see me in my flat. From the very first time we met he took a fancy to me, and led me to believe that he wanted to develop a relationship with me – a sexual one, of course! I was somewhat flattered, and my tremendous need to be loved and wanted, coupled with the naiveté of my childlike self, disposed me to make myself vulnerable to this man. I later realised that although I had been paying him for help, in truth he had been abusing me – both sexually and emotionally. Once again I am so grateful to the fighting spirit that arose from my anorexic persona, which eventually enabled me to rise up angrily against this abuse and confront the 'healer'. Needless to say he disappeared, post haste, followed by a volley of scathing letters from me, which I expect he threw away without reading them.

It took me at least a year to recover from this foray into the tangled world of self-styled 'healers', who have no recourse or aspiration to self-knowledge and thus no means of self-control when dealing with vulnerable people. Even if they do not realise what they are doing, such 'healers' are at risk of exploiting the behaviour patterns of people who are desperate for help. There are of course many wonderful and entirely responsible healers who offer dedicated service to those who come to them. For many years I tried to work out why it was that I had somehow attracted one of the other kind.

I began to see that my inner concepts and attitudes – often those which were largely unconscious – were a contributing factor to such experiences. I noticed that as soon as I said 'no', from a position of integrity, both the man and the abuse vanished. However, it was essential that the thrust of the word 'no' came from my whole being. At one point when the 'healer' was carried away by his desires, he had pushed me on to my bed and was lying on top of me. He was a big heavy man and I could not throw him off. In a split second I was conscious of a dithering inside myself. Should I be letting this happen? Isn't this what is supposed to happen to women – to be carried away by a man's desire? Isn't this a neat way in which I can evade responsibility for my own choice in sexual matters – by being forced into a sexual enactment? Is it more exciting this way, than with a true partner – with a shared desire and a joint decision? Am I more desirable because he is forcing me? Have I the right to resist? Do I want to resist? All these and many other questions flashed through my mind. Then a great surge of self-definition rose up in me, and I freed myself.

I am not offering here any simplistic answer to the tremendously complex issue of rape and sexual abuse, nor implying that the incident forever released me from making unwise judgements of sexual situations. Nor am I implying that the man was not entirely responsible for his own decisions and actions. I just knew, in that moment, that I had a choice about my intentions and my identity. The outcome was not a foregone conclusion, of course, but in this case it was one with which I am now well pleased.

Many of the therapeutic encounters were deeply meaningful to me, and involved so much more than the treatment itself. The practitioners who gave of themselves within the context of their skill became special people for me. These were people whom I loved, and still love, and for whom I made a lasting place in my heart. When I say 'loved' I don't necessarily mean 'in love', although that did happen sometimes – but those relationships did not usually lead to anything creative. The love which I felt for most of these special people was born of gratitude and of recognition. It was so important to me that there was a real person reaching out to me from behind any therapeutic function.

One such person was an acupuncturist with whom I had treatment on and off for many years. I was very fond of him, and often felt a great deal of pain and frustration because of the limits of the therapeutic situation. Periodically there would be an eruption, and I would stop going to him for several months or so, but I was continually drawn back to him, and I was touched by his willingness to continue the relationship and to reflect to me his own feelings about it. I felt that he saw me as an equal human being, and this in itself was a healing experience. At times I felt wounded by the exchanges between us, and finally I stopped going to him for treatment when I felt that there was no further possible development of our relationship. As I look back on this particular therapeutic relationship, I would still say that it was a rich experience in my life, from which I had learned a great deal. The boundaries which chafed me at the time no longer seem important and did not devalue the experience in the long term. I was sad when I learned that he had died. I had not seen him for a long time, and wished that I could have said goodbye. Yet I know that whatever was true and wholesome about the love we exchanged as therapist and patient will persist into the life or lives beyond.

I have often wondered why this deeper connection could take place, whereas in other relationships, therapeutic or otherwise, things have gone very wrong and left a great deal of wounding. I think that it may have something to do with the way in which all relationships have their time, their place, their boundaries, and their ebb and flow. If one is attuned to these dimensions and flows with them, rather than trying to hold on to a particular form of the relationship, it is possible for that relationship to occupy its appropriate place in one's life. It is then a creative experience, in spite of all the hurts, frictions and mistakes that can arise when two people seek to be real and to grow with each other. But if the relationship is pushed beyond its appointed dimensions at a particular time, it can become destructive and stultifying, and can hold one back in one's spiritual evolution.

It is amazing to find how, at times, difficult situations can lead on to something which turns out to be creative and life enhancing. In the midst of one of my periods of strife and tension with this particular acupuncturist, he told me rather forcefully that I needed to learn to swim. I was furious and walked out on him and did not go back for some time – until I had learned to swim! I had always been terrified of the water, and various compulsory classes at school had left me more frightened than ever, and still unable to swim. I used to feel weak at the knees with terror when I approached the swimming pool. Yet I loved the element of water, the sound and intoxicating smell of the sea, the rolling waves lapping the shore, bubbling streams, great flowing rivers, even the splashing of rain, as long as there was not too much of it! After the confrontation I decided to have another try at learning to swim, and something inside me told me that this time I would succeed.

I enrolled for lessons at the local baths, but found them a terrible ordeal as the teacher was not very sympathetic to cowardly mature learners like myself. She stood on the side of the pool and poked a pole in for the struggling swimmer to grab if she or he went under. I did not find this to be very reassuring! Inflatable armbands were not allowed, and there was much splashing up and down the shallow end, clutching a tiny float that did not seem large enough to support one's flailing body. However, I was determined to overcome my terror of the water, and I persevered.

Disregarding the teacher's disapproval, I bought some armbands and went twice a week to practise in the children's pool, pretending that I was someone's mum. Each time I went I prayed to the Angel of Water to help me in my attempts to master some little step, to disperse my fear and to learn to swim. Thoughts came very clearly to me as to what to try, and each time I had a measure of success. I didn't feel so embarrassed when I was splashing around in the company of children, who seemed to accept my clumsy wallowing in a friendly and uncritical way. How lovely children can be, in the simple enjoyment of whatever they are doing, rather than trying to achieve something. I think this sense of relaxation enabled me to trust myself to the water, and with the Angel's encouragement I paddled myself a short distance to the side. I'm swimming! I thought, with a sense of exultant joy. Little by little I desensitised myself to my terror of water, with the Angel's untiring patience and help, and after six months or so I could splash and splutter my way from one side of the pool to the other without the help of armbands. I went on to improve my strokes, taking lessons on and off for a few years, from more flexible and friendly teachers, until I grew to love swimming. I will never have the confidence of the children who jump in and dive to the bottom without a trace of fear, but I feel that in this work of learning to swim, I also learned one of life's lessons.

The transforming power of creativity can flow through anything that presents as negative or destructive, whether a trifling irritation or a major catastrophe, to reinvent it in a wonderful way.

Many of my therapists have become friends, some just for the time that I was in therapy, and some continuing long after I ceased to be a patient. I could never see the situation of being with a therapist as purely functional. Each therapist is a human being, an individual with a unique soul, with a personal history and purpose. That person and I were brought into contact and happened to be walking this Earth's pathways alongside each other for a while. My teacher of the Alexander Technique was one of these special people – a dear lady, who went out of her way to offer me kindness and friendship. Her firm but gentle touch was so reassuring and non-invasive and became a profound source of healing. Her loving touch helped not only my posture, but also allowed me to exist in the body I had presented to her, without demand that I conform to her own needs. I found that this reached me at the level of my desperate craving for the kind of accepting, formative touch that would give me a sense of my own shape and the wholesomeness of my body – the kind of touch that had been missing in my childhood.

I have had extensive experience of the National Health Service, from the age of four, when I began to be ill with bronchitis, through all the various ramifications of anorexia nervosa, until the present day. While certain interactions have been dismissive and humiliating, I believe that we are fortunate to have such a service, and through it I have received the healing ministry many a time, in many forms. For around fifteen years, I benefitted from regular monthly consultations with a senior NHS psychiatrist. The interaction between us always remained very formal, but I was grateful to him for giving me his time so consistently over such a long period. During that time, I managed to withdraw certain emotional needs that I had hoped would be met, and appreciate the kind of support that he was able to offer me. This in itself was a form of healing. I have learned that healing can come in limitless ways and forms, through any kind of source. The healing force is eternally creative, rising fresh and new in every situation where people are open to it. The NHS is no exception to this.

Each one of us will attract healing in different ways and through different channels, according to our individuality. For that reason it is as well to be open-minded as to all possibilities of healing, while retaining discernment at the intuitive and rational levels. When one is sick and desperate, one can be very vulnerable and perhaps clutch at straws, or sometimes be taken in by presumptuous claims, so it is important to be aware that counterfeit offers exist. Even authentic forms of healing may not always be helpful for the current stage of one's journey to wholeness. In my view one of the key factors in recovery is to be able to discern the inner timing of one's own healing process.

In the Secret Places

The dying embers of my heart
Glow for you.
If you could tiptoe near to me,
Blow on them,
They might flicker into life,
So once more
The fire blazes high.

Cat's eyes watching
From inscrutable feline faces
See the anguish flowing forth
From my secret places.
Without judgement they respond
To my raw depravity
Accepting the tormenting pain
That makes my life a travesty,
Fleeing from the violence
Of my inhumanity,
Comforting the dark despair
Of terrified insanity,
Pardoning the arrogance
Of my blind stupidity,
Compelling me to see myself
In frightening lucidity,
By honesty and humbleness
Teaching me humility,
Hiding nothing of their needs
Return me to gentility.

Cat's bodies softly
Brush against my skin,
Purring their contentment
From music deep within.
Neither they nor I know
When our end will be,
But now I know that cat souls
Will always wait for me.
I tread my lonely pathway
With the creatures of the Earth,
Together as companions
Seeking our new birth.

Coming close to touch you,
Hold my breath,
Poised upon this brief encounter,
Life or death.
Dare I ask you for a kiss?
Yes and no.
Question and answer come to rest.

Jacqueline Kemp

Chapter Seven

Cats and kids

Some of the greatest healers in my life have been the creatures of the Earth, and indeed the living entity of Earth herself. Soon after I left Patrick and established myself in my own flat, I met up with a stray cat. Some of the local children brought her to me, knowing me to be an animal lover. She was a poor little thing, only about six months old, starving hungry and dreadfully thin. I was not sure what to do. I felt that I could not cope with the responsibility and expense of owning a pet, but I could not turn her away and refuse to help her. I decided to feed her and let her stay the night, and this was the beginning of our long relationship. For a month she came and went, roaming about on the rough ground behind the flats and coming to me for her food. I dithered, unable to make up my mind as to whether or not to take her on as my cat, but finally she won me over. It was not that I didn't want her, but more the fact that I love animals so much that to give my heart to one is a lifetime commitment, one which always involves me at a very deep level.

I called my little new friend Tinkerbelle. At first she was not easy to live with. Her constant demands for attention, and tremendous neediness, seemed to drill a hole in me and made me feel unreasonably angry, which upset me greatly and made me feel really guilty. A great deal of soul searching finally revealed to me that she was reflecting the enormous neediness which lay denied, buried and rejected beneath the surface of my consciousness. This was a difficult realisation, and I was not sure how to deal with it in relation to Tinkerbelle.

I made a contract with her in my thoughts that I would willingly give her attention and comfort each day whenever I could manage it, but that would have to be enough. I could not go overboard to try to meet her overwhelming desire for love. I found that this decision relieved my sense of guilt and therefore my anger, and we began to settle down together. I fed her well, and she filled out to become a beautiful sleek dainty little cat with a loving and gentle nature. In learning to care for her I was somehow learning to care for myself, and she was my teacher. She had come to show me, at great risk to herself – for I could have refused her, or harmed her – a part of myself that I hated and could not bear to see.

Although we had always had cats when I was growing up, I did not know much about how to look after them properly, so I did not get Tinkerbelle neutered until three litters later. The first time she went on heat, I wondered what was wrong with her and was terribly worried. I had been keeping her in, and she had been quite content with that, but now she was desperate to get out. I could not bear the piteous yowls, so I went down the stairs with her, and who should be waiting outside but a large tom cat. After a few introductory spits and sniffs they were off, and I did not see Tinkerbelle again for two weeks. I was convinced that she had been harmed or killed, and I mourned for her every day, looking out of the window and calling, feeling so guilty and anxious.

Some time after I had given up all hope of every seeing her again, I got a phone call from my neighbour. Tinkerbelle was on her window ledge, looking very thin and dirty. I was overjoyed. I collected her and brought her upstairs to my flat and gave her food, which she devoured eagerly. She then settled down and set about cleaning herself in front of the fire. We were together again. Not surprisingly, she was pregnant, and her appetite grew enormously as she prepared herself for motherhood. I was overawed by her acceptance of her state, her humility, and her dependence on me to feed her. It touched a chord of anguish in my heart. How could this lovely little creature allow herself to be dependent on me, a human being, for the essentials of her life, and thus open herself to whatever I might be? The trust she had in me gave me great pain. I fell over myself to provide for her, and as I did so I became more and more inwardly aware of the plight of animals. What an enormous and horrifying potential there is for their abuse by humans, and what a wonderful and glorious opportunity there is for us to serve them and do a tiny bit to redress the incomparable debt that we owe them.

I had come face to face with my own arrogance towards animals, and now a profound recognition of the shattering truth that divinity manifests in all life forms was dawning upon me. I felt disgusted with myself for my ignorance and lack of recognition of the dignity and magnificence of the animal realm. How could I ever have thought that Tinkerbelle was 'just a cat', or a pig 'just a pig', or a tree 'just a tree'? This was a major turning point in my life, as if a veil was peeled away from my eyes. In some ways it would have been more comfortable to remain blind, for the seeing was more than I could bear. My mind and heart floundered under the strain, and I feared the thoughts that flowed into the caverns of my awareness, but I could not turn back without denying my essential self. I think I was so blessed in that somehow I managed to reach forward into this awareness, as it became the source of much healing in my life.

As Tinkerbelle's kittens grew inside her, she became increasingly contented, spending most of her days eating, sleeping and grooming herself. I watched her belly getting larger and larger, her acceptance and peacefulness contrasting starkly with my own horror of pregnancy. With her, though, it seemed to me to be a beautiful and wonderful process, the age-old mystery of spirit becoming embodied in form. Tinkerbelle began to look for a suitable place to have her family and I made her a cosy box, which I tucked away inside a cupboard. I kept peeping in, anxiously, not wanting to disturb her but wondering when the kittens would be born.

One night I heard a loud MIAOW, and jumping out of bed I hastened to the cupboard to find the first kitten climbing on to Tinkerbelle's belly in search of milk, and the little feline mother looking up at me with huge unfathomable eyes. Soon she was in her element with three lovely kittens, washing them, suckling them, and purring her happiness to me. I was in awe of her – this wonderful teacher and loving mother. I quickly noticed that right from the start, each kitten was a different personality, a distinct individual. Thinking of the millions of kittens that come into this world, this was nothing short of mind-boggling. And that is only one species! I began to think more carefully about my own individuality and uniqueness. Who am I, amongst the myriad of human beings that have come and will come to this earth? I had no difficulty in loving each kitten simply because it was itself; why then could I not love myself simply because I am myself?

Tinkerbelle had three litters before I had her spayed, and each birth was a special and wonderful sharing between us. She was the only one of my cats that had kittens, and in that she gave me something deeply healing for my soul. I am not in favour of allowing cats to reproduce *ad lib*, as finding loving homes for the kittens is a difficult business, and so many end up unwanted or in a situation where they are not well cared for. However, with Tinkerbelle my procrastination with neutering turned out to be one of the ways in which she served and healed me so profoundly. I was lucky with homes for her offspring – for each one the right person seemed to appear. There was only one kitten for whom I made a mistake, and I regret that to this day. The owner did not behave in a responsible way, and the young cat wandered off, never to be seen again. I can only hope and pray that some kind person took him in. Two of the kittens made it plain that they did not want to leave, so I kept them, and I found that each one had something special to teach me. The profound depths to which an animal can take us are amazing. By and by I acquired another cat – a stray young male – so we were quite a houseful. Tinkerbelle, and her two daughters Tiger and Lizzie, plus the new boy, Corky, were my closest companions for many years, and we went through so much together.

I wondered how I could cope with four cats, food, veterinary care, litter, their clawing my meagre furnishings to pieces, and lots of worry! Yet they filled my home with love and comfort – their playful antics lifting my heart, and their unquestioning companionship filling my anguished mind with their affectionate presence. Later on I came across the Cat's Protection League, which was an invaluable source of help and friendship to me as I struggled to care for my feline companions.

Corky was so lovable that he quickly found his way into my heart and made himself part of the household. The girls grudgingly accepted him, except for Tiger, who always had to be in charge and put him in his place with a swipe of her paw. Corky had an incurable passion for food and ate at every possible opportunity, going round the others' plates to hoover up any leftovers. I wondered sometimes if he had come to me especially for this, to share my obsession with food. Every time I went to the kitchen, he appeared and sat on the stool with his paw hanging over the side, ready to hook me as I went by. Sometimes he sat on the counter, purring expectantly. At first I was exasperated with his apparent greed – or what I labelled judgementally as greed – but gradually I began to find comfort in his very solid presence, and I suspect that he was making a great sacrifice for my sake, by being somewhat on the heavy side and a food junkie.

I had always found the kitchen to be a place of lonely torment – the compulsion to eat tearing at my terror of fat flesh. Mealtimes were a nightmare of isolation and fear, more so if I were with people, so I preferred to eat alone. Perhaps only an animal or an angel could have drawn close to me and penetrated the shameful and secret despair that disguised the core of my anorexia. I always fed the cats before I ate my own meals, and somehow their satisfied smacking of lips and contented washing after they had eaten brought a little light into the darkness of my experience of food.

The cats with whom I shared my living space are the only beings on this side of life who have seen me at my worst –

violent, raging, shrieking with grief, agony and fear, cursing and foul-tempered, on the point of suicide and lying for hours utterly exhausted with the struggle to stay alive. Their eyes were great pools of universal acceptance, and the love they returned to me is something that I will never comprehend. Living with them has been one of the most humbling experiences of my life, and still is, with my current companions.

In the early days I easily became angry with Corky. He seemed to be born clumsy (like me!) and had a way of choosing the most inopportune time to knock something over, trip me up, scratch up the carpet, or appear covered in coal dust. At times I felt so frayed at the seams of my sanity that this would trigger an explosion from my desperate self. I am not trying to make excuses for myself, and to this day I am ashamed of my outbursts. Seconds after an eruption I would be in tears of remorse and shame, rushing to comfort him and begging his forgiveness. Always that wonderful purr would soothe my heart and pacify my mind. I wondered how I could possibly deserve this kind of love and forgiveness, which far surpasses anything that I could achieve myself. Can an animal be a spiritual master? I think so. At night Corky took to landing on my bed with a great thump, and sitting on my chest to gaze into my face with eyes like windows into the universe. I have never liked any human being looking at me, never mind gazing into my face, yet Corky's gaze was like a shaft of pure love. He often wedged himself under my chin and purred me to sleep, and sometimes in my desperate hours I have woken in the night to find him still there, still purring. When I think of my suspicious nature, which never forgets a slight or an insult, and certainly not an outburst of temper, I feel that there is something in the souls of animals that we humans have never grasped. Corky's humility and forgiveness, receiving me back time and time again, and continuing to love and trust me is an example before which I stand speechless. Some would say that it was purely survival instinct on his part, that he had no other option, or that it was just a learned stimulus and response, and so on. Well, let them say it. The way we treat our fellow creatures on this planet must be a source of great sorrow in the universe.

The other cats, and those I have had since, served me uniquely in their own ways. My Lizzie taught me patience and understanding with her nervousness. I had tried to find a loving home for her, but was unsuccessful, and I worried about keeping her because of the extra expense. The uncertainty must have unsettled her, as she used to urinate frequently on the carpet, causing even more stress and tension between us. Finally, I saw the fear and unhappiness in her eyes, and I felt mortified. I said to her 'Right Lizzie, you are going to be my cat, no matter what happens.' From that moment she never urinated on the carpets again. She must have had a frightening experience when she was neutered, as she was never the same afterwards. It grieved me to see her so fearful when she came back, and it took years of work with her before she became confident again. It was such a wonderful reward when she let me hold her in my arms again and started purring.

Tiger was the most spirited and intelligent cat I have ever known, and this made her a difficult girl to handle. She related to me on her own terms, and only gave me her affection when she felt like it. She loved to play, and we would think up all sorts of crazy things to do together. One of her favourites was a large cardboard box, in which she could hide and then rush out and catch the other cats off guard. She suffered all sorts of unusual feline illnesses all of her life, but she never lost her spirit. I admired her tremendously, and she was an example to me in many ways. She did not have a large appetite, and was very selective in what she would eat, being something of a connoisseur. When my father came to visit, she used to hang around him at mealtimes, looking at his plate meaningfully, until he gave her some of his fish or meat. She was even known to hop up on to the table, while we were not looking, and start licking the butter! I worried about her constantly, and we made frequent trips to the veterinary surgery together, but she taught me that we had to take one day at a time, and for her, my love and care in that day were sufficient.

As a group, these wonderful creatures protected me in yet another way. As I became closer to them and their presences became part of my life, the psychic disturbance that took place around me began to diminish. The discipline of caring for the cats helped to regulate me and bring a sense of balance to my personality. I also knew that the cats could see and sense beyond my range of perception, and thus I knew that if the atmosphere was okay with them, it must be safe enough for me, too. The gentle sound of them going about their daily lives was a tremendous comfort to me, in contrast to the threatening and intrusive noises of human activity that pervaded my space. When the times came, saying goodbye to each one in their own special way was an opportunity to acknowledge the unique relationship we had shared, and to experience and accept each grief and loss in the form that it came to me. However Tinkerbelle gave me a very special gift when she died. Up until then, when looking in a mirror – which I did frequently – I had always seen the grotesque and distorted image of a face superimposed upon my reflection. It did not appear to be a human face and I could not discern its origin. When Tinkerbelle died, she took the face with her and I never saw it again. It was her last service to me and I am forever in her debt.

Many cats have passed though my life as well as these four friends who kept me company in my flat. Various hungry strays often turned up for meals, and my neighbour and I fed some of them for years, or managed to find them new homes or a place in a cat shelter. It was a privilege to serve them, to be face to face with hunger and be able to do something to help. I have empathy with hunger in all its forms – hunger in all creatures and vegetation that is hungry for light and nourishment. The archetype of hunger lives deeply in my soul, and I often feel that my particular experience of anorexia nervosa is in some way an intercession for the immeasurable extent of hunger in our sorrowful world. What a joy to be able to help even in tiny ways.

One day a friend arrived at my door holding a box containing four tiny orphaned kittens, which he had found after he had noticed a cat killed on the road and had so kindly stopped to bury it. As he looked around for a suitable place, he spotted the mother cat's offspring, which she had no doubt been on her way to feed. How such things pull my heartstrings. There is sometimes so much pathos in life that it overwhelms me. Seeing the little mewing kittens in that box, I could not turn them away. I am sure my friend would have somehow looked after them if I had not, but he already had a houseful of cats, rescued in one way or another. Thus I took on the role of mother and nursed my little charges until they grew up into lovely healthy cats. It was a task full of joy and of challenges.

One of the poor little creatures was like limp rag, seeming to have given up on life now that her mother was no longer there. I had to coax her to take the baby milk and vitamins that our vet had prescribed, feeding her from a dropper. The others soon realised when food was on offer and swarmed over me as soon as I sat down, mewing and scrabbling until they were full. Titch, as we called her, took longer to accept the dropper, but as soon as she decided that life was going to be worth living after all, she fought for her place amongst the others and didn't hesitate to swipe with a tiny paw if she thought she wasn't going to get her turn. I admired her determination to live and get her fair share. I often laughed at the kittens' antics. When they were weaned, Titch became quite aggressive at food time and would rush to the plate of food, defending her portion with growls and claws. Everyone got plenty, of course, and then they would retire with round tummies and fall contentedly asleep. Why was this so beautiful and acceptable in my eyes, when I condemned myself so fiercely for the desire to eat and for the slightest bulge in my stomach?

When my little 'children' started to grow up, I realised that I could not keep them all, along with my own cats. It was a real houseful of hungry, lively felines, and I could not cope with them all long term. I worried about them like an anxious parent, wondering how I could get a loving and responsible owner for each of them.

Our Titch got a home quite quickly with a minister friend of my neighbour, and it was lovely to be able to get news of her. She lived happily with the minister and his dog, ruling the roost, I believe, until she was a ripe old age. The one fluffy kitten also got a fine place to live, but no one suitable came for the two dark tabbies. I began to feel desperate about it, as by now I loved them so much that I could not bear to give them away to just anyone. Many prayers and heartfelt pleas went up for these two pussies.

Later, while I was dozing, I had a dream that someone phoned and asked if I had two kittens looking for homes. I woke with a start and felt with certainty that the kittens would get homes. True to my dream, a few days later the phone rang and a man asked about the kittens. I asked him how he had heard about them and he said someone from the church had told him. I wondered who that was... Maybe it was an angel. The man came round with his wife and I knew that the kittens would be happy with them, because they were so warm and gentle with them. So that was all of them settled with new owners and the flat seemed empty without them, but I have to admit that it was a relief! They had been such a blessing to me, giving me an intense experience of motherhood that I could never otherwise have had.

Though I have not kept dogs or other animals, many different creatures have come to me throughout my life to give me gifts of comfort, love, recognition, friendship, or to touch my heart, bringing me healing and helping me on my way. A passing dog with wagging tail perhaps, thrusting its nose into my shopping bag and making me laugh, penetrating the gloom of toiling through another day of life beset with the symptoms of anorexia nervosa. Horses have connected with me many times, sometimes coming over to me unbidden and gazing at me through their enormous pool-deep eyes, or blowing down their noses into my face. I remember one time when I was in a particularly bad mood, walking with a friend and feeling out of sorts and estranged. We came upon a horse looking over a fence and I began petting him, chatting and feeding him handfuls of grass. Suddenly he gave me a playful shove with his great head and sent me sprawling backwards into the undergrowth. I could almost see him laughing. I wasn't hurt, just discomfited by an undignified landing, and anyway it jolted me out my grumpy mood of self-pity!

Birds too can be messengers of joy. When I lived on the Isle of Drumduish, the call of the curlews soothed me to sleep and the squealing gulls filled the air with the music of the sea. In the city, I grew to love the harsh calls of the crows – jesters and clowns of the town, without whom my life would be that much sadder. I loved the armada of swans, which gathered at the mouth of the Almond River as it flows into the estuary – those lovely huge white birds waving their graceful necks as they waddled up out of the river to snatch morsels of bread from my hands. The flight of the wild geese, heralding the changing seasons, is beautiful beyond words and never fails to lift my heart. Now that I have a home with a garden, I delight in feeding all my feathered visitors, from lumbering pigeons to tiny finches, and of course the ever-present crows that wait on my garage roof for left-over cat food. The humility of hunger goes to the core of my being.

Various people have suggested to me – sometimes in the name of therapy – that my love of animals is a substitute for satisfying relationships with humans. It is true that I find that my relationships with animals touch my heart in a way that my human relationships do not, but I would not agree that there is a substitution going on. I do have many people in my life that I love deeply, but it is a different aspect of love. The nature of every relationship, be it with human or animal, is unique, and I do not think that generalisations and comparisons can be made between a relationship with one being and another. We humans are animals, after all, and there is a continuum, not a separation, between species. One person can never be a substitute for another; neither can one cat be a substitute for another. Were I to have a houseful of animal friends, I would still want relationships with people, and were my life to be crowded with human relationships, I would still need close relationships with animals.

I think that the view of humanity has become too narrow in the concept of relationship. The illogical conclusion of this often seems to be that there is only one Relationship in one's life which is central, and one can spend one's life looking for that person or trying to hold on to them. We are in danger of forgetting the richness and diversity of relationship, not only with each other but also with the many other life forms on this earth, and with beings in the spirit world, too. The expansiveness of heart that comes from such a wide ranging love and variety of relationship is lost when we focus exclusively on one Other as the main source of meaning in life.

I believe that an inability to connect with each other and with the earth and her creatures lies at the heart of so much of the cruelty, greed and violence that is a major issue in our world. A terrifying, numbing encasement of the individual, especially if not consciously recognised, triggers a desperate effort to escape from this confinement and make contact. Violent energies can build up, which may also attract energies of the same vibration from other levels of reality, and burst out to manifest in a variety of destructive ways. There is such a great urgency for us to return to our earthly and spiritual origins and to remember in essence who we are. This is especially so in these times of climate change and environmental destruction which threaten our very existence on this planet.

In my relationship with my cats and to the many animals that cross my path, I am seeking to do my own small part to redress the wrongs perpetrated by humanity upon the creatures of this earth. Although I find some animals easier to love than others, I

218

regard all animals as creatures with dignity, individuality and worth equal to my own, with as much right to lead their lives on this planet as I have. I aspire to do things that promote the harmonious evolution of human animals, where respect, understanding and compassion are the groundwork of human and animal relationship. To live with the awareness and complexity of such wide issues of abuse as animal testing, the inhumane use of animals for food, animal products used in cosmetics and so on, is a tremendous weight of grief for me.

I think that so long as humanity gives itself permission to abuse the animal realm, for whatever justifications, there can never be a peaceful and creative harmony of all life on earth. Abuse is abuse – wherever and however it happens. One cannot say that it is acceptable to abuse one category of manifest life, and not another, for the categories that are created by human beings can easily be changed or adjusted, to justify any actions deemed to be necessary or desirable. I need to remember this central fact in relation to myself, too. Abusing myself in any way cannot help anyone or anything. Further, permission to abuse stunts the impetus to discover other, non-abusive, methods of research, development and production. Necessity is one of the drivers of invention, and the human race is immensely inventive. If necessity points to a more respectful, compassionate awareness of our fellow creatures as our only way of survival, humanity will have to respond, or will lose its privilege of living upon this planet.

It is not that I am devoid of similar feelings of compassion for issues of human suffering. I do feel the greatest sorrow for all forms of suffering, but my mission is to help animals, and I think that while human suffering is largely acknowledged as something which needs to be eliminated or at least alleviated, that of animals receives less attention and is often dismissed as irrelevant. Exploiting animals, or people, or any of the earth's resources for that matter, to try to solve human dilemmas can never be viable in the long run. The end does not justify the means, and as we are seeing today, the means that we have been using are leading to economic and ecological crisis, and a great deal of suffering.

I am often greatly challenged by the awareness that my own thoughts, attitudes and actions contribute directly to world issues. What is the use, I ask myself, of condemning the injustice of governments or lamenting the plight of the underprivileged if I close my eyes to the needs around me and do not face up to my own fears of not having enough, or to my own greed and materialism? It is no use bemoaning the state of the environment if I do not treat my own surroundings, however humble, with respect. In the face of the immensity of our world's problems, it is so hard to feel that one really can have an effect, but I believe that one's daily life is where the effect is greatest. It is where values of compassion, respect and kindness for all living beings could change the world – for the better.

Some people think that it is a cop-out to work primarily on oneself, when it seems that so much action is needed. Is it so easy, I wonder, to confront oneself systematically with relentless honesty – to allow life to touch one's deepest fears and impulses of self-rejection, to seek to heal, and to change oneself by working things through in everyday life and relationships? It is the most profoundly challenging and exhausting work that I know. I agree that action is necessary, but from a standpoint of self-knowledge and acceptance, not as a means of denial and projection of those buried parts of ourselves. To bring peace we must *become* peace.

* * * * *

Very early in life – somewhere around the age of ten years – I decided that I would never bear children. I am not sure what caused me to make this major decision at so tender an age, but I think that I may have known instinctively that I would not be able to tolerate the presence of another being growing inside my body, taking up my space and altering my shape in a way that I could not control. I did not like children – more so when I was a child myself than I do now – and felt that I could never give a child a good start in life, maybe because I had had such a distressing one myself.

As a child I was afraid of other children, both younger and older than me, and felt that I must be of a different species. They seemed to live life on a different plane from the regions that I inhabited, and though I tried to keep up and join in, I was so often mocked, left out and left behind.

As I grew older and the knowledge of pregnancy and motherhood impinged upon my understanding, I began to develop a horror of it – the whole ghastly business, as I saw it then. I found babies especially repulsive, and as I became more aware and honest with myself, I had to acknowledge a strong hatred and violence within me towards them. However alongside this was a strange sort of compassion and understanding of children, not so much within my personality, but from a part of myself that I did not recognise. I felt sorry for them, having to come into this world that I hated and feared, and having to struggle with the sorrows and complexities of life. I always felt like a child inside, and in some ways I still do.

Children seemed to me to be not a different stratum of humanity but were just like the rest of the people in my life that I had to try to get on with, only smaller. Age and size did not seem to make any difference to the troubled and difficult exercise of relating, and most of the children I met seemed a lot more confident and self-assured than I have ever been, even in my adult life. Of course I have only met a minute proportion of the world's children, and no doubt there are many who are just as confused and terrified as I was, if not more so.

Along with animals, children have been some of my greatest teachers in life. I was often puzzled and somewhat infuriated, for although I professed not to like children and tried to avoid the necessity of relating to them, for a large part of my life I have been obliged to interact in a variety of ways with them. In many cases this has been a bumpy ride, and has caused me a great deal of anxiety and heart searching, but in many cases there have been profound and delightful interactions and relationships with life's little ones.

My healing in relation to children began when I was with the Community of Transformation. At the time there were a fair number of families, from different walks of life and with varying numbers of children. According to the community rules of fellowship I was obliged to relate to them in an appropriate manner, and I found this surprisingly rewarding. I had contact with almost all of them I think, through my role as the community hairdresser, but in addition, many of them went out of their way to be friendly to me. I became interested in their lives as individuals, and was deeply touched by their confidences. They accepted me as one of them, perhaps seeing more perceptively than the adults into the frightened child concealed within me. The community life had a very beneficial socialising effect on the children of its members. I was struck by how expansive and accepting they were in their relationships to all the adults. There was far less segregation than in the kind of society to which most of us are accustomed, and this was one of the aspects that I missed most when I left.

Moving to West Hapton was a different story all together. The area was part of a large council housing estate, which at the beginning of my residence there was very run down. Row upon row of grim flats – many of which were boarded up – unkempt gardens, a few uninspiring shops and the awful flat-roofed school was the sight that greeted me when I first went there. Each time I went back down the road that led to my part of the estate, I always used to feel that I was going back into prison and the gate was clanging behind me. Yet even here there was beauty and kindness, often hidden in the most unexpected places and people.

On the whole, the local children seemed to me to belong to a different race from the ones I had known back on Drumduish. What a culture shock it was. Many of them came across as tough, wild, aggressive, foul-mouthed, and apparently without any kind of conscience or sense of responsibility. This was no doubt due in some measure to my perception of them. I was fearful, prejudiced and unable to relate to them, and I could not see beneath the surface to the real people underneath.

Whenever the weather was decent, or school holidays were on, hoards of them emerged like ants from an anthill and swarmed over the estate. I dreaded the summer holidays – six weeks of screaming, swearing, shouting kids at the back and front of the flats, often until very late at night in the long evenings. Probably having little constructive direction and no creative environment to channel their youthful flow of life energy, they were disaffected, and had little alternative other than to let off steam in whatever ways they could find.

It was likely that there was very little money around in their families to pay for interesting hobbies and instruction, or to send them off on activity courses and the like. However there *were* some resources provided by organisations or the council, and I observed that it was not just a material poverty that affected these young people, but a kind of poverty of soul that made a significant proportion of them uninterested in making use of what was available – instead preferring to spend time in gangs, or in destructive or antisocial activities. I can't pretend to understand all of what underlies the development of this kind of subculture. It was hard not to judge, and very hard to live with, and to maintain some sense of recognition for the real human beings that perpetrated the chaotic and anarchic elements of the social environment.

The unruliness and destructiveness of the Hapton kids angered and frightened me. They were largely out of control, and threats and violence seemed to be the only means that those who sought to rein them in knew how to use. I quickly learned to speak their language. In most situations there was no point in being polite, as they simply did not listen. A healthy peppering of four-letter words, when addressing them, was the very minimum that would command their attention. One time I noticed two young lads cycling round our garden at the back of the flats, churning up the grass, flattening plants and knocking washing off the lines. I leaned out of the window and called:

'Hey lads, this isn't a cycle track. Off you go and cycle somewhere else!' All they did was to mimic me. Furious at their insolence, I marched out of the back door, gesturing angrily and bellowed, 'Fuck off you bloody little bastards! Go and cycle your fucking bikes elsewhere or I'll get a couple of the men to come and knock your heads together!' They cycled off unperturbed and did not return.

I was surprised at myself, and felt a bit guilty. I could guess that they would be well used to such verbal abuse. It would be like a second language to them – or even their main one. Many such children would be those that just 'came along', without being planned for or really wanted. Single teenage mothers were the order of the day. Perhaps these girls had no other prospects, no interesting future to work towards, and no position in society. Pregnancy was, and still is, a way of getting money and a place to live, and who can blame them for using this as a means to an end. However, it did not make for a constructive situation for the raising of children, and from the cradle, the child might experience shouting, foul language and violence, with parents who may well be dependent on drugs or alcohol. I could see this early habituation of children to such behaviour happening in the streets all the time.

When deemed to be old enough, the children would be turned out into the streets to amuse themselves, with no supervision or creative involvement from the parents. Thus abandoned to their own devices, what amused them most was to cause havoc and distress to others.

An underlying sense of powerlessness, non-recognition and the degradation to self – caused by the habitual perpetuation of abusive behaviour from one generation to another – is a breeding ground for social decay. This way of life seemed horrific to me, but with some reluctance, I found myself admiring the resilience and raw energy of those kids that shouted, cursed and punched their way to some sort of maturity.

The neglect of children was of course not true across the board. Many parents tried their very best to give their children a decent upbringing within the limitations of a very challenging environment, and some youngsters I knew went on to achieve great things. Despite the fact that I had been brought up in the cotton-wool protection of a middle-class suburban background with the benefit of top quality education, these particular children achieved far more than I have. To these parents and kids I give my utmost respect.

In spite of the chasm that apparently separated me from the Hapton kids, I did manage to form some kind of relationship with some of them. Nationality and language was a major barrier. It never occurred to me that my English accent would be seen as something which identified me as an object of suspicion and even ridicule. Although I learned a useful selection of swear words and idioms, I could not use them with a Scottish accent, nor could I understand the street lingo which was common parlance. If a word began with 'f', I knew what was intended, but other than that it was often an inspired guess as to what was being conveyed.

I found that before I had lived in the area very long, I had been labelled as a 'witch'. If this had not carried concomitant victimisation, actually I would have been quite flattered. I had made one or two contacts with members of the Wiccan organisation, and found their beliefs and practices both interesting and enlightening. I was impressed with their reverence for the Earth and all creatures, and fascinated by the apparent ability to mobilise universal energy for various purposes, none of which seemed to me to be in any way negative or harmful. Once, I was even invited to a Shabbat, and found it to be a beautiful and respectful celebration of the times and seasons of the Earth. This was a far cry from the group imagination of the local children, whose idea of a witch was an old woman with a big nose, riding a broomstick, stirring a cauldron and chanting evil spells. The origins of this image are deeply imprinted, stemming in part from a fear of feminine power, and political and religious persecution. This matter is worth another book in itself, so I will not explore it any further here, but simply mention that, as I experienced it, the caricature of the witch was a convenient way for children to label and persecute someone who was different from their concept of an ordinary woman.

I dreaded Halloween and Bonfire Night. As soon as darkness fell on Halloween, the procession of kids, most often dressed in black plastic bin bags, would begin. Somehow they managed to get into the stair, probably pressing the service button, and banged relentlessly on every door, requiring a suitable reward for a generally very uninspiring performance. A few visitors were a bit more imaginative, having managed to get hold of an ugly mask, or a devilish pair of horns, or some other piece of ritualistic equipment. Even though I shut the curtains, turned off the lights and pretended to be out, they would not give up, and if the door was not answered there might well be retaliation in the form of a kick on it, or rubbish pushed through the letter box, or some other vengeance. I wondered if other people experienced this kind of thing, or if it were just me who attracted it. Even though I hated and resented this apparent persecution, I still felt sorry for the perpetrators. They had so little to excite and stimulate them that Halloween must have seemed like a golden opportunity to them. The younger ones had a look of eager expectation in their eyes, and I didn't feel that I could disappoint them.

After several years of avoidance tactics, I decided to try to outwit them at their own game. I went shopping and prepared a large 'cauldron' of treats – mostly sweets and cakes unfortunately, but I didn't think that they would be very pleased with healthy snack items. Then I turned off the lights and lit candles in hollowed-out pumpkins with sinister leering grins. I had bought a cheap witch's hat, which I balanced precariously on my hair, and donned a long black wrap over my black jeans and sweater. Then I waited for the visitors to arrive...

My little dramatic production was amazingly well received,

and I was touched by the thrill on the young faces, and their gratitude. The word soon went round, and there were seemingly endless knocks on the door from local children coming to see the 'witch'. I was relieved when the visits subsided and there was peace at last, but reflected that joining in was certainly a more positive experience that avoidance and resentment.

Bonfire night was a more dangerous event, an opportunity for wild and irresponsible behaviour with fireworks, and setting fire to whatever was available. The young arsonists were amazingly creative with their 'bonfires', which could sometimes turn out to be a major disaster. Sirens or fire engines and police cars seemed to be sounding late into the night, and from time to time the newspapers would report a tragic event the following day. I feared as much for the animals as myself, and for other people who found it an endurance test. Before regulations on fireworks were passed, the season might begin at least six weeks beforehand, and go on for several weeks afterwards. Enormous bangs would rock the neighbourhood, amplified by fireworks being let off in the rubbish bins. The remains of many a charred bin could be found the next day. Whining fireworks would shoot through the air and explode terrifyingly close, if one was unfortunate enough to be out walking. Some of my acquaintances seemed fairly impervious to all this fiery chaos, or at least took it in their stride, but I could not help thinking that it held reminiscence of a war zone, and how much worse it must be to live in a real one. Fire is a fierce and beautiful element – it can serve us and greatly assist us in our human development, and can create stunning displays of its glory and wonder. Yet used wrongly or without respect for its power, it can turn on us and wreak horrific damage and cause terrible suffering.

It is interesting to consider how much language shapes and defines us, and creates what we experience as reality. Words which enfold the energy of thoughts and emotions have great power. It was always a very precious moment – a kind of miracle I would say – when I made real contact, person to

227

person, with these children. It is the kind of moment that evades description and eludes the passage of time, and stays there as an eternal recognition.

There was one boy in particular who triggered off a great deal of violent emotion in me. I first encountered him and his pal when they were about four years old. Our rubbish bins, in two rows of bin nests at the back of the flats, were constantly in a filthy mess. I often had to wade through rotting rubbish, ankle deep, to get to my bin, and no matter how many times I cleared up the mess, it appeared again two or three days later. Complaints to the Council and Environmental Health Board were largely ineffective, as they said they had no power to prevent the problem. I did not really believe this, for had it occurred in one of the more well-to-do districts of Edinburgh, no doubt a way would have been found.

One day I found the four-year-old vandals doing their dirty work. 'We've turned out the bags,' they said, 'and we're not fucking clearing up.' What could I possibly do? I felt frustrated and furious, as I knew very well what I would like to do. But if I laid a finger on them I would be accused of child abuse, or there would be serious repercussions from their numerous relatives. Complaints to the parents would most likely be ineffective, as they had little control over their children, and at worst would cause hostility or be met with further abusive language. These children were abusing me, and the environment in which I lived, and I wanted to teach them a lesson.

The problem of the bins bedevilled me for years, and I could not understand why few others seemed to get as upset about it as I did. Aside from the health hazard, I could not see how it was helping these children to let them continually get away with something that was so destructive and insulting to the environment and the occupants of the flats. I felt that they were actually looking for limits to be laid down, and that being free to run wild and destroy everything in their path made them somehow feel formless and insecure. They did not stop at the bins, either.

For several years – until they grew up and turned probably to more exciting forms of antisocial behaviour – they conducted a vendetta against our stair. Broken glass was thrown on the paths, filth put through the letter box, windows broken, plants stolen and destroyed, window boxes turned over and smashed, drains blocked up, locks glued, ash bins overturned, coal stolen and scattered around, and so on. How utterly desecrated must have been the sense of self of each of these little people. I felt totally besieged and invaded by the destructive attack, and helpless to prevent it. I could see no reason for the stair in which I lived being singled out in this manner. Everyone in the stair was kind to the two boys and very likely treated them with much more tolerance and respect than they received in their own homes. Maybe this was the reason.

I did everything I could to form a relationship with them and to understand why they were behaving in this way – talking to them, playing games with them, buying little odds and ends for them to play with, giving them money for helping me wash the stair, and more. My efforts must have seemed paltry in the face of the enormous deprivation that characterised their lives, and in fact, only seemed to make matters worse, attracting more abuse and victimisation. I felt both compassion and rage. The red-headed boy personified a desperate, wild, deprived and uncontrollable part of myself, and I struggled daily in prayer and meditation with my hatred for him. There was no point in trying to suppress this hatred, for it was too overwhelming.

I felt that if I could somehow experience these powerful emotions fully, while at the same time releasing them to the angels, then perhaps I would not damage myself, or the child, and maybe eventually some light would come through to the situation. I began to see certain things that I admired in him. He was very inventive, and so eager even for the basic materials with which to construct props for his play, or, unfortunately, to use to annoy people. He had a kind of defiance and courage, which while it was probably born out of a complete lack of relatedness, was also a remarkable defence against the crushing of his person.

A crisis came one day when the two boys overturned my ash bin, spreading heaps of dust and ashes all down the stair from top to bottom. It is providential that I did not catch them doing it, for I doubt if I could have controlled my extremely violent reaction. Shaking with fury, I went round to see their parents, and required them to come and see what their sons had done. To my surprise they came, and were apologetic and helped me to clear up the mess, though the stair needed to be hosed down a couple of times afterwards before it had all gone.

I am not sure what repercussions fell upon the boys, but after that things took a turn for the better. I did not see them for a while, and their friends said that they were afraid to come up. I was rather relieved! Some time later they appeared cautiously, one of them holding an ancient piece of broccoli, which he offered me as a gift of recompense, saying that they were sorry. He thought that the yellowing vegetable was a flower, and so it was, for in my heart I was more touched by this than if they had given me an expensive bouquet. I cannot see into the fabric of this meeting of persons – the whys and the wherefores of it – but there was a profound lesson in it for me. I hope that somewhere in the memories of these children, who will now be adults, some little gleam of light may remain.

There have been many such trouble-makers in my life, both children and adults, and I wonder about this. Is it because I am so unable to ride the punches of life – so thin-skinned, that I crumple in the face of any form of aggression – or do I need an enemy to fear and hate, and therefore attract such people? I do not have the answer, but it does not seem to get any easier to deal with this kind of thing.

The influence of the macho culture was so prevalent in Hapton, and there was little place for gentleness and sensitivity, especially amongst boys. In the light of this, the gesture of the broccoli was all the more precious. At a very early age the boys learn that they must be a 'hard man' or a 'head case' or suchlike to survive, and to join in with a gang to avoid being ostracised or bullied. It must be a very wise and mature mother who can give her children the confidence and resources to negotiate such an environment and still be true to themselves. A primitive fear would rise up in me when I saw – all too frequently – gangs of boys, often many of them quite young and small, running down the street brandishing sticks, bits of metal, golf clubs or whatever they could find to use as weapons, shouting, chanting, swearing and hitting at everything in their path.

We do not seem very far from the earliest stages of evolution, and we all have this kind of primitive aspect to our nature, even if it is buried deep beneath the layers of 'civilisation'. It was, and still is, very difficult to see the outward events of my life as a kind of 'mirror' that reflects something of my inner self back to me. Accepting this is a fundamental key to growth and maturity, and as far as I am concerned, one of the hardest tasks I shall ever undertake.

I am not very surprised at the aggressive behaviour of children in this kind of environment. With what floods their young minds – both in terms of role models and entertainment, now so readily available and vigorously promoted – what else can we expect? Maybe in this context there is an element of a kind of natural selection – survival of the fittest. After all, in the natural world, differing species are substantially formed by this dynamic. Can we hope for anything else, I wonder? These profound conundrums occupied much of my thinking when I lived amongst them, and I am glad of that, as it has broadened my mind and I believe it has made me less judgemental. As human evolution progresses, it may well turn out that spiritual and emotional development are as much elements of survival as competition and aggression.

*　*　*　*　*

I find myself wondering about the failures in general social understanding of the whole subject of abuse – in its widest form. Abuse begins long before it shows itself in the form of sexual misconduct or physical or verbal violence. It finds its way into all areas of life, and the full impact of abuse upon the young human being is unfathomable.

There is nothing in life which does not have its shadow side or its counterfeit double. For instance, that which is deemed to be a virtue may cross an invisible boundary and become a vice, if it is applied unthinkingly in every situation. Suppose, for example, that someone considers humility to be a desirable and virtuous quality that they aim to manifest. While a true understanding of oneself and one's place in the created order leads to the development of wholesome relationship with all life forms, excessive self abasement misinterpreted as 'humility' may lead to subtle or overt forms of self abuse – which could be liable to engender abuse of other life in its wake. Thus the shadow side of humility is inverted pride – pride in one's humility.

Love is another aspect of life in which many counterfeits can be hidden. I have already discussed one manifestation of this, in the tendency in my early years to mistake sexual desire for love itself. Since love is a limitless quality, the possibility for counterfeits is also limitless. This is because the application of love can never have an absolute definition. To take a simple example, one may think that it is an act of love to listen sympathetically to a friend in distress. However it may be that this friend has become so preoccupied with their personal agony of mind that they are repeating the same issues over and over again, like a broken record, and cannot break out of the cycle. It could be that in such a circumstance, sympathetic listening would perpetuate the cycle and drive the friend further into the trap of their own mind, such that they become unable to see any way forward, and thus evolve through their problem. In this case the application of love may call for a more incisive and confrontational approach to direct the friend's mind toward creative possibilities.

These illustrations are of relatively simple situations. The wider picture is of course much more complex, and the difficulties of finding one's way along the pathway of Light are immense. At the end of the day, one can only have the intent to do so, and the confidence that all mistakes will eventually transform into one's higher and greater good.

Whenever a child, adult, animal, plant or any living thing is treated merely as a commodity, this constitutes a kind of abuse. Without recognition and respect of the uniqueness every living thing – children, adults, animals, vegetation, and the earth itself – there is potential to possess our 'commodity' as an extension of ourselves, and to use it only for our own conscious or subconscious purposes.

Unless parents are very aware of the origin and constituents of food, and sound principles of nutrition, and also have adequate financial resources, young bodies are assaulted with the damaging effects of distorted food right from the start. This constitutes an abuse in its own right. Foods designed to attract children often contain many undesirable ingredients such as artificial flavourings, colourings and preservatives, high levels of sugars or salt, refined carbohydrates, and trans fats. The effect of this on the body, mind and even personality has recently been coming to light. It is a promising sign that attempts are being made to encourage people to limit their intake of such substances, and that more attention is being paid to the kind of food that children eat.

The ice cream van that came around the council estate was one of my greatest trials, arriving many times a day and until late at night, with bells at full blast right under my window. I called it 'The Poison Wagon' – a purveyor of sickly-coloured soft drinks, sweets of all kinds, crisps and snacks, as well as the swirls of white stuff that masqueraded as ice cream. The children ran eagerly out into the road to buy from the poor overweight lady who was selling it. I could not help feeling sorry for her. Probably she was trying to scrape together a meagre living to feed her family.

There seems to be a trend in our society to applaud and advocate lack of self-restraint – 'Just do it', 'Buy now and pay later', 'Shop till you drop', and so on. As I see it, to let children run wild, with no limits, no consequences, no discipline, no consideration for the environment in which they live, and giving them everything that they ask for, is as much a form of abuse as is controlling them with violence and threats. Both of these extremes reflect the loss of a sense of recognition and respect between persons in all strata of society, and consequently the loss of a sense of community and responsibility. This extends from the microcosm of family life to full planetary awareness, and the results are far-reaching.

Children of our perniciously abusing society can themselves become abusers at a very early age. Some cases hit the headlines and cause a national furore, whereas much abusive behaviour goes on without repercussion. Playground bullying, ostracism and mockery, cruelty to animals, endangering lives by hurling missiles at passing vehicles… All of this behaviour may be frowned upon, but perhaps is not recognised as seeds of that which touches us all at some time or another – the struggle for power, the strong and the weak, the victim and the oppressor.

I don't think that it is helpful to pretend that all children are little innocents, and to draw an artificial line between the age of innocence and the age of responsibility. To excuse abusive behaviour of any kind with 'but he/she is only a child' does nothing to recognise the opportunity to teach a child from the earliest age to choose creative and resourceful ways of relating to the world in which they are destined to live. Unless we face up to the wars in our own hearts, and attempt to resolve them, our ability to give children the opportunity to bring peace to the world is limited. I suffered so much from the war between my mother and father that these issues are very close to my heart. In the years I spent in West Hapton I experienced both abused children and abuse from children, giving rise to a great deal of strong emotions and questioning in my mind.

And out of the Ashes

My prayers echoed emptily round heaven's vault,
Bouncing off the planets
And fleeing from the stars,
They returned to me unanswered.
God is dead, I thought.

Now driven by relentless force,
Confusing compulsion runs its course,
And in its vice-like grip of pain
The shriek of agony will rise again,
Echoing down ancient halls,
Thrown back and forth between blank walls,
Returning to its tormentor.

O flesh upon this tortured frame,
That writhes in solitary shame,
And screams its protest silently
In depths of bitter agony,
Taking on itself disgrace
Until it loses any trace
Of goodness once intended.

Mind and body lying in stuporous submission,
Blanketed in apathy and protective inhibition,
A limbo place of semi-life,
Where death draws sweet and near,
Yet dark unknown looms threateningly
With paralysing fear.

And out of the ashes of ruined life
In the face of triumphant death,
A new and beautiful form arose
To which the Spirit gave breath.
A treasure of eternity, from suffering is won,
A mystery begun.

Jacqueline Kemp

Chapter Eight

Out of the ashes

She was on holiday with her partner, in the beautiful Emerald Isle, staying at a Rudolph Steiner village. It was so lovely there, with its harmonious buildings, creatively decorated rooms and productive gardens. It seemed like a haven of peace and tranquillity. She had been worried about food, though, even before the trip. How would she cope with unfamiliar food while in unfamiliar places? It was a potentially dangerous situation. She did not say much to her partner about her fears; she wanted so much for this to be a wonderful trip for both of them, and she didn't want to be a nuisance. After all he had paid for most of the trip, and it was a marvellous opportunity.

She was shown to her bedroom in the guest accommodation. It was delightful, with an open view of the countryside from the window. She started unpacking a few clothes to put into the wardrobe next to the bed. Opening the doors she noticed two large plastic drums lurking at the back of it – what on earth could be in them? Curiously she opened one, just a little bit, and peered inside. Oh no! Horror of horrors! It was full of the most delicious muesli she had ever seen – bursting with all kinds of nuts, seeds, grains and dried fruit! The other was just the same. She backed out of the wardrobe and shut the door, her heart pounding. She started to panic. What was she going to do? At the end of their stay the drums were half empty, and she did not dare tell anyone. Shame, guilt and remorse silenced her.

Having my own flat, albeit in a very challenging and uncongenial environment, gave me a personal space in which to begin to try to pull together the ragged threads of my life. I was still battling with anorexia nervosa, often severely depressed and extremely anxious. Yet in spite of this, creativity began to emerge from within me.

I lived in Hapton for twenty-one years, which while I was enduring it seemed like a life sentence. Looking back, I can see that while outwardly I did not accomplish what I would have liked – further academic qualifications, finding a good job and developing a secure intimate relationship – it was a very formative time in my inner life and in my journey with anorexia. This is a long period of time to review, and it did not have many high points. I will therefore focus on experiences which seem particularly significant to me.

Desperately driven by the spectre of the symptoms of anorexia nervosa at my heels, I continued to search for a 'cure'. I undertook treatments of many different kinds, until treatment was 'coming out of my ears'. I will not dwell on that here, as I have already mentioned some of the more important experiences. As I have said, it was always the input of the practitioner as a *real person*, rather than the treatment itself, that made a difference, if any difference was to be made. I am not trying to diminish the importance of knowledge, skill and expertise in the arena of therapy, and I am certainly not of the opinion that 'all you need is love'. It was just that for me, knowledge, skill and expertise administered without love had no effect. I don't mean love necessarily in the form of feelings. Love is such an all-encompassing word, with so many shades of meaning, that using it here is perhaps misleading. I think what I mean to convey is that the intent of the heart is central to the effectiveness of the therapy, rather than merely employing the intellectual application of a therapeutic technique.

It felt wonderful to have my own flat, and even though I did not own it, I invested a great deal of energy, love and thought into making it a nurturing, beautiful place for me and my cats to live in. The continual battering from the external environment made my endeavours hard going, but to some extent I think I succeeded. Quite a few people who came to visit for short or longer times, or even dropping in, commented on the sense of Presence that they felt there. This was an affirmation for me of my efforts, and I felt rewarded for my work. For a short while I continued to receive unwelcome visits from the apparently malevolent presences that I had encountered in previous dwelling places, but gradually this subsided, and the atmosphere of my home became strong and light. This must surely have been due to a major contribution from the angels, together with the long-suffering tolerance of my beloved cats, as my mood and temper were often far from peaceful.

About a year or so after I had taken up tenancy of this flat – which was opposite Patrick's – the council made a compulsory purchase of the block for renovation, which was urgently needed. We were moved to a freshly renovated block of flats just around the corner. This was a big bonus for me, as we received a substantial compensation payment for the compulsory move, and the flats were so much better. At last, I had a proper central heating system, windows that closed firmly and a decent bathroom.

I was so lucky to have this large flat, which being at the end of the road and on the second floor had a fairly open aspect and I could see the sky from both sides. Often there were glorious sunsets, or sometimes a rainbow set against the dark sky, arching over the gloom and disarray beneath.

The communal garden was quite nice, too, with a large patch of grass, some bushes and a few trees, although it was constantly beset by invaders from the neighbouring stairs. Some of us cared about the garden, and tried to make it as lovely as we could. However, any kind of beauty seemed to attract those who felt compelled to attack and destroy. Perhaps they could not bear its exposure of their ugliness, blotting out the ability to recognise and affirm their own beauty. Plants were constantly being uprooted or knocked over, window boxes stolen or overturned, items thrown into the trees and bushes, and even large branches being sawn off the trees by boys building tree houses. These tree houses were the bane of my life, being right opposite my window, and a source of constant disturbance and invasion of privacy. I managed just a little sympathy for the poor kids, starved of green spaces and a natural environment in which to explore and adventure. Even so, the garden was a green patch and a source of consolation for me in our concrete encasement.

Ordinarily, as a single person I would have been offered only a flat with one bedroom, but because I was part of the original Star Community, I had a flat with three bedrooms – the same size as those tenants who had a family. Looking back I can see that this was a gift, a grace that had come to me in the midst of my struggles to repair my life.

The Star Community started its life as a group of people with high ideals of living a Christian life-style in an area of social deprivation. There were six flats in the stair, inhabited by families, married couples and single people. Although I was not around at its inception, I gathered that there was some kind of organisational structure and constitution. I think that this had worked well for a time, but the inevitable stresses of living together as a community began to take a toll, and various members left for one reason or another. At the time, the Star Community had a 'special let' from the council, and under this dispensation, was able to influence who came in to take up residence in the flats. Usually someone of religious orientation was chosen, and I was lucky to be one of them, when the flat opposite Patrick became vacant. For a time, communal prayers were held in one of the flats, and this was a stabilising factor in the life of the Community. This kind of community lifestyle was very much more flexible than the one I had lived before, and I appreciated having some measure of contact with my neighbours, while being free to live my own life.

As time went on, the nature of the Community became more dispersed, as people became increasingly involved in the direction of their own lives. Various tensions arose between neighbours, and I found it challenging to relate to some of the occupants of the flats. The woman who came to live with Patrick after I had left appeared to be hostile towards me. This situation went on for several years and caused me a certain amount of anxiety and distress. Since I was living in the flat opposite to Patrick's, I found this very challenging to deal with. However, it did help to reinforce the complete separation that I had made from Patrick. Towards the end of my time in my flat, I was glad to find that communication improved, but I never really understood the reasons for the earlier difficulties.

Some members of the Star Community became close friends, and it was good to be able to visit from time to time, for a chat and for mutual support. When I left the community to live in my own house, I really missed this. Having such people close by, to whom I could turn for help or to whom I could offer help, was a great source of comfort and stability for me.

There were five children in the Star Community during the time I was living there. Two families each had two young boys, and one family had a little girl. Unlike my general stressful and unhappy experience with the children who lived in the area, I found that my relationships with the community children were positive on the whole. There could be conflict over such things as noise, bicycles left around, mess in the stair and so on, and the needs of the families with children could be at variance with the needs of the single people. However, the children were nice to me, often chatting and telling me about themselves, which I considered to be a compliment. Sometimes I went down to the shore with one or two of them, and some of them came to me for piano lessons. I lived in the Star Community for so long that I could observe the youngsters growing up into young adults and starting to form their own lives. This is always a privilege for me, as not having my own children, I feel that this aspect of life would be empty, were it not for relationships with other people's children.

All in all, although my time in Hapton was difficult, being part of the Star Community was instrumental in helping me to survive this very challenging time of my life.

I undertook various courses of study to try to widen my horizons and enhance my chances of returning to employment. Although I never did return to full-time employment, the desire to learn, to pass exams and get qualifications was definitely a positive force towards healing in my life, not least in relation to the people with whom it brought me into contact. I also tried to develop various artistic pursuits in which I was interested, such as shell craft, sand painting, marquetry and candle making. I found that I enjoyed this kind of creative work, even if the results were not especially brilliant. I felt that I had externalised part of myself and made it visible, with form and shape, as a creative offering to the rest of the world.

Whilst living on the Isle of Drumduish, there had been little opportunity for me to exercise my driving skills. I rarely drove further than to the town, sometimes in an old taxi, to pick up members of the congregation for a church service, or occasionally on an errand to collect someone from the ferry slip. Consequently, when I came to live in Edinburgh, I found that driving in and around the city was by contrast a hazardous nightmare, and longer drives taxed my concentration considerably.

After some years of living in Edinburgh, I acquired a small car, and I decided to take the Advanced Driving Test with the Institute of Advanced Motorists, both to improve the safety of my driving and with the hope of reducing my insurance premium. I started by taking regular lessons with an instructor from the British School of Motoring. He was a pleasant man, and after the lesson was over, used to invite me for a cup of tea at a convenient roadside café. I began to look forward to this, as I found that I enjoyed chatting to him. I sent him a couple of letters, written in a friendly and conversational way, but subsequently his behaviour at my lessons became noticeably cooler. He started making excuses not to stop for tea, such as having another pupil straight after my lesson. I suppose that I should have been able to predict this, but it took me a while to get the message. When I did, I stopped going for lessons.

At this point, I had to search myself to discern my true intentions. Had I been looking for a relationship, or did I want to pass the Advanced Driving Test? I am glad to say that I decided on the latter. I researched other possibilities of instruction, and signed up for lessons with a retired Class 1 Police Driver. This man was a really superb instructor, and I learned a great deal about driving skill from him, as well as enjoying the lessons on a more professional basis. When teaching, he used his own car – a modern, fast, comfortable vehicle. I can still hear him saying 'No rush, kid' when I was anxiously trying to get his car into fifth gear – a refinement which my little old car did not possess. Whenever he drove, with me as a passenger, I observed that he displayed an impressive combination of skill, confidence and knowledge. I felt that even if I absorbed only a small quantity of this from him, I would become a much better driver.

In order to discover more about the requirements of the Advanced Test, I joined the local group of the IAM (Institute of Advanced Motorists) and went on regular drives with their Observers, who were trained members of the IAM. Unfortunately, when I took the test, I was so nervous that I made many foolish mistakes that I never usually made when driving, and I failed. I was devastated. However, my struggle with myself concerning the first instructor stood me in good stead, and I returned resolutely to my intention to pass the Advanced Driving Test. I continued with the IAM, this time with another Observer, who was a very kind and reassuring man. He took me out driving over and over again, until I had enough confidence to retake the test. This time, I passed! I was overjoyed, and so was my Observer. He sent me a congratulations card. I am grateful to him to this day, for the empathy he showed in sharing my distress over my initial failure, and helping me not only to pass the test, but unbeknown to him, to help me to move beyond an emotional *faux pas* and achieve my goal.

One of my major endeavours, which was to have far reaching effects in my life, was to take up my studies in music again. I had loved playing the organ while I was on Drumduish. With a church organ close to hand and the motivation of services for which to prepare, I had a ready context for my practice. However, studying the organ while living in Hapton proved to be much more difficult. I did play for a while at a nearby church, to which, coincidentally, a priest and his wife from the Community of Transformation had moved. Practice times were much more difficult to organise. I did not have a car at the time, so I had to get a bus to the church, fetch the key from the vicar and go back to the church. Then I might find that it was an inconvenient time to play the organ, for example if someone was cleaning and hoovering the church. A practice session could easily take a whole morning, with only a small proportion of the time being spent actually playing the organ. However I was able to help out with playing for the occasional service, wedding or funeral, and I was glad to be able to make a small contribution in that way.

I took lessons for a time. These were funded by the church and were excellent, being provided by the organist and choirmaster of St Mary's Cathedral in Edinburgh. I remember feeling rather intimidated by this illustrious musician, and I suspect that he was accustomed to far more adept and high flying students than I. Although I was toiling under the weight of depression and anorexia, I appreciated his instruction and did my best to win his approval. I am not sure if I ever did, but there were occasional comments of 'that wasn't too bad' or 'you have improved with that one'. Such comments were rather like finding gold dust along the road of my musical endeavours! He even once allowed me to play on the organ of St. Mary's Cathedral, when I had learned a piece of music to his satisfaction. This was a great privilege. It was a wonderful experience to hear that great instrument come to life at the touch of my fingers. I have returned to the Cathedral from time to time, and heard it being played expertly, and every time I find the sound truly thrilling. The great thundering bass pipes vibrate the structure of the building, the magnificent chorus of diapasons peel out though the stillness, and a multitude of tones from the ranks of pipes colour the music with every conceivable hue. The sound of an organ such as this one touches the depths of my soul.

The difficulties with practice, and my changing concept of spirituality, made it impractical to continue as an organist, so I turned my attention to the piano. I have never really felt that I was well suited to the piano as an instrument, as so much of the music written for it is expressive in quality, and my body is not given to fine expressions of feeling. Somehow I could never feel involved with the music, as I could with, for example, playing Bach on the organ, and there seemed to be some kind of abyss between how I understood the music should sound, and what was produced by my fingers. Throughout my life I have felt intensely the pain and frustration of this abyss, which affects all areas of my life and not just music. It was as if I just could not connect up with my body, and could not dwell in it, but rather felt it to be a clumsy 'thing' which I had to try to make work in the correct and acceptable ways. However, I persevered, often feeling totally discouraged and descending into fits of violent fury when this 'thing' would not do what it was supposed to do – that is, produce the glorious music that I could hear in my head.

I took lessons from several piano teachers, eventually ending up with Dr Gardener, who was an eminent musician and performer in Edinburgh. I am certainly enormously grateful to him for the meticulous quality of his teaching and his patience in getting me through professional diploma exams, and helping me to qualify with a Diploma in Music at the Open University. With the benefit of his tuition I gained the Associate of Trinity College London (ATCL) and the Licentiate of the London College of Music (LLCM), both exams being in piano performance. The experience of taking these exams was extremely nerve wracking, and I do not know how I ever managed to force myself to go through with it, twice over. However the reward of obtaining the diplomas outweighed the temporary stress and terror of the examination procedure. Unfortunately, I never found anything in Dr. Garderner's lessons which could give me confidence in myself as a musician – with a contribution of my own to make to the world of music. It was quite the opposite. I would frequently leave the lessons feeling depressed and unrecognised, my fragile dance with the spirit of music undermined and overpowered. I began to see that this relationship was a mirror of how I felt in relation to my father in general. This insight helped me to deal more constructively with the situation and stay with it so that I could continue to benefit from the knowledge and skill that was being offered to me.

However, teaching is more than just putting across knowledge and skill, and when I started to take pupils of my own, I found that I had to be willing to learn from them and to enter into a two-way relationship with them, where their input was of as much value and significance as mine. I had to learn to make a listening space for each one in my heart, where I could allow my pupil to explore and develop their own unique relationship to music, affirming and guiding that wherever I could. With some pupils, their approach to the learning of music was not at all what I thought it should be, and I learned some hard lessons myself through recognising and accepting that there is no 'right' way which suits everyone.

I encountered numerous problems with pupils, who were mostly children, and also their parents. These often involved painful inner confrontation with myself, and much anxiety. Thoughts of what I had or had not said or done went round and round in obsessive spirals in my head, and sometimes I would dread the next lesson. The relationship with each pupil was always a gift to me, though, and I grew very fond of some of them, finding it a wrench when they stopped lessons for one reason or another. I taught one family of Chinese girls for thirteen years, and had the privilege of being involved in a small way in the process of their growing up from little girls into teenagers and then young women. It was almost like having my own daughters, and I am really grateful to them and their family for this experience.

It was always difficult to know how to blend discipline and sensitivity – to be a teacher of music on one hand, and a fellow human being sharing music on the other. Sometimes I did not get the balance right, and either there would be complaints that the pupil was not making enough progress and I should be more strict, or else that I was too strict and the pupil did not like it. With each one the delicate balance would vary from lesson to lesson, and had to change as the child matured.

One boy in particular constantly put me the test with his rudeness and uncooperative behaviour, and I often found myself feeling angry with him. He was the middle son of a fairly well-to-do family, a bright and intelligent boy, and his mum kept her boys on a tight rein. On one occasion I was feeling weary and unwell, and the rebellious lad tipped the balance of my temper. I gave him a sharp dressing down and marched him off to his mother for retribution. After the lesson, I felt depressed and somewhat guilty, feeling that I should have had more patience, but to my amazement this tense encounter proved to be a breakthrough, not only in our relationship but also in his progress. I wondered if he had wanted to find out if I cared enough to get angry with him and define realistically the boundaries of our relationship. The vagaries of human interaction never cease to amaze and trouble me.

One of the other studies I undertook while living in Hapton was Remedial or Swedish Massage. My attunement to the sense of touch as a medium for healing had developed during my years with the Community of Transformation, with my natural abilities in hairdressing and back-rubbing being popular with a good selection of the members and visitors. Formal training in massage presented itself as a possibility for income, and I signed up with a college course that led to a recognised qualification. This proved to be a lengthy undertaking, as one studied at home and then took weekend practical courses at the delightful resort of Blackpool. I have to admit that I found the sea shore more attractive than the lecture room and practical work, where one nervously avoided the scathing tongue of the instructor, and wielded towels with varying levels of dexterity to protect the practice client's modesty.

I finally got the certificate, and was rather proud of it, but sadly never managed to use it to earn any money. Hapton just wasn't the place to establish a massage clinic! Any mention of massage conjured up a seedy image of back-street parlours where clients – mostly men – went for a different kind of massage! After a few uncomfortable misunderstandings in my makeshift massage clinic in my flat, I gave up trying to make a living from it. I was so insecure and so easily discouraged that I failed to establish myself as a massage professional. Perhaps someone else might have forged ahead and attained a prestigious position in an up-market sports centre, or something similar. I have many regrets and self-condemnations.

I think that the sense of being imprisoned in my own body, combined with an anguished longing for the kind of touch which would communicate peace and healing, made me particularly sensitive to the qualities of touch that I experienced. Occasionally someone's touch seemed to reach right through to my soul, thus bringing a sense of integration and wholeness – a feeling of being alive. I both craved and feared this kind of touch, for as soon as I received it, I could not stop myself from falling in love with the one who gave it, and wanting to possess that person. More often than not, though, a touch would only reach the superficial layers of my perception, and at worst was an unwelcome intrusion and demand. I began to realise that when people touched me, they were not necessarily touching *me*. It could often be that they were merely touching my body. Of course, this was appropriate in many situations, such as visiting the doctor or dentist. However, even such health professionals have very different styles of touch, and I have encountered respect and gentleness in this arena which in itself has been a source of healing.

In my experience, physical proximity does not necessarily give rise to a feeling of being close to someone. In fact, it often made me feel more isolated and empty than ever. When I accepted proximity because I thought I ought to, I could even pretend to myself that I wanted it. Such pretence was so cleverly devised that I did not recognise how I really felt until years later. Actually, I found certain kinds of touch, usually that which was sexual in need or intent, to be draining, as such touching could be more for the gratification of the other's need than anything that truly reached out to me. In this case I am not trying lay blame at the other's door. In some ways, I am probably a very difficult person to connect with, and there is nothing wrong with a need, sexual or otherwise. The meeting of each other's needs can be deeply fulfilling and a means of giving and receiving love. I think the problem was that my needs were never really met, and that I was unable to identify them sufficiently at the time to ask or insist that they be recognised.

For a long time, the lack of the kind of penetrating touch which I craved was like a physical pain. I felt myself to be a huge, formless, bloated thing, floating miserably above the earth, caught between spirit and matter, and unable to feel at home in either. I am so grateful to my cats and to many other animals during those dreadful times. My own cats so willingly offered their furry bodies to be stroked, brushed and caressed, and generally returned my proffered affection with purring, head rubbing, winding round my legs or landing with an unexpected thump on my lap while I was dozing or reading. No matter how many times I frightened them with my descent into hellish and violent distress, they always came back, forgiving me and generously offering their love. I am deeply humbled by this memory. For me, physical contact with an animal is something very special, yet I do not have an explanation for why this should be so. It is like an instant soul meeting, person to animal.

Another very creative and beneficial opportunity came my way while I was living in Hapton. During my search for an answer to the problem of the mysterious visitations that bedevilled me, I had taken a short course in London with Ruth White, a spiritual teacher and healer. I had read some of her books, and had been very impressed with them, and I wanted to meet her. At some point in the course I asked Ruth for a personal conversation, during which I poured out my troubles to her. I was deeply comforted and reassured by her wisdom and understanding, and decided that I must see her for a longer appointment. This I did, and after a few meetings I began to feel a wonderful sense of relief, so deep and compassionate was her understanding and that of her spirit guide, Gildas. It stirred a longing in my heart to become a healer myself, and when I was offered a bursary to study on her course in spiritual healing, based in France, I accepted eagerly.

I went four times to the beautiful healing centre in the south of France, each time for a fortnight, and I can truthfully say that each visit was one of the most wonderful adventures that I have ever had. Not only did I have the opportunity to visit a different country but also I participated in the rich, diverse and deeply nourishing environment of learning and healing. Though group participation was quite an intimidating venture for me, I was surprised and gratified by how readily I felt accepted, and how my efforts to become part of the group process were affirmed. What a difference from group therapy at the mental hospital!

In addition to our instruction on the spiritual healing course, we were treated to some lovely outings to the French countryside, towns, and places of interest, and I even found the courage to make hesitant conversation with French-speaking people, using my rusty A-level French.

There were problems for me with food – wrestling again with a deserted kitchen and with fabulous French cheeses – and I experienced various health problems, but somehow I managed to surmount these setbacks and the whole course was a very positive experience. It was during one of these visits that my interest in nutritional science was kindled. Later on, this lead to personal research, from which I gained much useful knowledge that helped me in my struggle to change my attitude to food and eating. The overall effect of the course in spiritual healing was an affirmation that I had something of value to give in the field of healing. Although it took a long time to develop, it was a seed that bore fruit, and which I sincerely hope will continue to grow throughout the rest of my life.

The Trust that funded the course in spiritual healing for me also generously offered finance for three sessions of psychoanalysis from a well-known Jungian practitioner. My first session with Mrs. Potter was very engaging and I looked forward with anticipation to my next appointment. I felt that I got on well with her, and a rapport was quickly established. After the three sessions were completed, I was delighted when the Trust offered further funding for a whole year of psychoanalysis. Letters were exchanged between the Trust and Mrs. Potter, and she agreed to undertake my treatment, which was to begin when she could make a regular space in her schedule to see me. I waited to hear from her. As the waiting extended into weeks, I began to feel anxious, and plucked up courage to phone her to enquire about appointments. To my horror, Mrs. Potter responded that she could not find a regular space, and in any case, had decided that one year of psychoanalysis would not be beneficial to me. She had not consulted *me,* as to whether *I* thought it would be beneficial. I was devastated, and it took me a long time to get over this crushing disappointment. I could never fathom the reason for her sudden reversal of attitude towards me, and inevitably, I assumed that it was something about me that she did not like, or something about me that was 'wrong'. I have had this kind of situation occur more than once, when I have been eagerly anticipating the attention of someone whom I thought would be able to help or teach me. I am always left with the question in my mind: 'What if …?'. I think that it goes to show that one must not rely too much upon the outward form or channel for that which one seeks to draw to oneself, but to look for the essence of it, and to be open to whatever means by which that may be transmitted.

Gradually, as I became more centred in myself and more aware of the balance of my own masculine and feminine energies, my need for touch changed. I was no longer a beggar for affection, selling myself for a drop of the perceived touching nourishment which I had thought would give me identity. It became more of a need to be in touch with my true self, and to be touched by life itself. However that longing for the true touch, the meeting place, has never left me, although now it is not limited to physical touching. I think that we all long deeply to be in touch, and that that longing finds so many conversions and perversions within our social conventions.

If we were all willing to be truly touched by the processes of life, how different our world would be. The numbing, the isolation, the noise and multitudinous diversions of our modern world have lured us away from our deepest needs, and have enchanted us into a fairytale of materialistic pursuits. The reverence and awe of truly meeting another being, be it human, animal or vegetable, is all but buried under a maelstrom of clamouring voices telling us who we ought to be, what we ought to have, and what we ought to do. As I began to penetrate this veil of the outer structure of life, a deep sorrow invaded the core of my being. Yet at the same time I felt that I was being shot through with shafts of incredible joy and wonder. I still wait for that same kind of seeing to penetrate fully the outer mantle of my being, so that I can finally accept myself as one of those glorious thoughts of the infinite mind.

In many ways, living in Hapton was a tremendously gruelling experience – like being in exile – and looking over those many years that went by, I wonder why I was unable to change things more. The sense of alienation from anything which felt compatible with my needs and longings was a constant source of striving within myself, but I feel that it is significant that in an area of poverty, which was rife with social problems, so much inner richness came my way.

Although I berate myself for not doing anything much during my stay there, perhaps I was doing a great deal on the inner levels of being. The lessons that I learned there are invaluable, although I must confess to a great deal of complaining and resentment in the learning of them!

Soon after I began my life on State Benefits, I realised that I had become one of the invisible members of society. I was stuck in the sickness and poverty trap, and unable to find a way of becoming better off financially. Even if I could have found a part-time job I would probably have received only a low wage, for work that could have crucified me. My psychological and physical health problems, coupled with a high level of environmental sensitivity made the more readily available part-time jobs, such as supermarket cashier or shop assistant, an unrealistic proposition. The complexities of such a mode of survival wrapped themselves round me and dragged me down in a vicious spiral. They were not just practicalities, but were thought forms with a life of their own – which seemed to take root even in the cells of my body.

I became disgusted with admonitions of 'Why don't you just …' and found that I was reluctantly forced to have an increasing respect and compassion for those people at whom I had often looked askance. 'If only they would do such and such, they could get out of their predicament' was the kind of judgemental attitude to which I was prone. The alcoholics, the junkies, the street beggars, the vandals and other of society's catastrophes – I shared an inner secret with them. Although on the surface I might appear respectable and polite, I was just as much of a drop-out. I am not trying to absolve anyone of responsibility, least of all myself, as we all have a choice as to how we deal with what life brings to us. It is just not as easy as it might look to the outside observer.

Places like Hapton with many people on a low income or State Benefit did not seem to exist in the mainstream concepts of society, except as Problems that need help or tighter control. So much of the concept of what is seen as desirable and right is aimed at middle class, substantial wage earners, and so is a large proportion of the complementary medicine and New Age movement. What person on a minimal income, which does not even cover the weekly bills for basic necessities, could pay the fees charged by private therapists, even if the therapist is kind enough to offer a reduction? What such person can afford to buy healthy organic food, or non-toxic eco-friendly products? But a therapist needs to earn a living and must therefore charge a reasonable fee, organic food and eco-friendly products are more expensive to produce, so there is no easy answer to this conundrum.

To my way of thinking this no-win situation can only be solved by a complete reorganisation of social values and what we hold to be important for the quality of life of everyone, every creature and the survival of life upon our planet. Where is the healing for a place like Hapton, one of so many, where people are piled on top of each other in concrete blocks, where children run wild in the streets causing havoc and destruction, where noise and litter are the order of the day, stray dogs and cats search for subsistence, and shouting, swearing, violence and poverty are a way of life? This chaotic subculture of human existence will insist on making itself heard one way or another, and will disrupt any attempts by our society to paint a veneer of niceness and success over itself.

Whenever I went away from Hapton for more than a day, I would begin to relax, and my hyper-alert, on-guard watchfulness would begin to subside. It would feel as if my whole being began to soften at the edges. Yet as soon as I returned, I felt my inner hackles rise again as the hostile and depressing atmosphere of the place enveloped me, and I would have to harden myself all over again. The very first time I that went to France for the spiritual healing course, I wept long and copiously because it was so beautiful, so peaceful and so open, and all my sorrow flooded out into the quiet and receptive space.

Other sorties in search of a gentler environment to soothe my soul were not always successful. I could never escape from the anxious, desperate and craving self which followed me, like a pack of hounds. It caught up with me wherever I went. One time I had decided to take a short retreat at Holy Cross Abbey, a monastery set in the beautiful East Lothian countryside. I had often visited the Abbey for an afternoon trip with Dad when he was staying with me. He loved the sung Vespers and the devotional chants. Afterwards he liked to visit one of his favourite pubs, where he often reminisced and told me his stories.

I was hoping to find a similar feeling of a haven of rest and quiet on my retreat, but sadly it did not turn out that way. Although I was received pleasantly, there was no effort on the part of the monks to make me feel at home, and I was shown to a rather cold, uncomfortable little room and left to my own devices. Probably they would think that someone taking a retreat would want to be left alone, but the complete absence of any warm human contact, and the austerity of the unfamiliar surroundings, left me an easy prey to the dragon lurking in the subterranean caverns of my mind…

The communal meals were simple but generous, especially in the provision of bread, which was not just your ordinary, everyday bread that was available in the supermarket, but an amazing, fragrant, home-baked creation, cut into doorstep-sized slices that had a delectable, chewy consistency. What is more, there were ample supplies of homemade butter, jam and honey to spread on it. Oh what a recipe for disaster that proved to be!

My aspirations of quiet prayer and contemplation evaporated rapidly as my retreat disintegrated into an orgy of bread and butter, bread and butter and honey, with more bread, more butter and jam to follow. This combination was served at every meal, and after the first couple of days I was in complete panic and despair. There was no one I could turn to. I could hardly go to the Guest Master, or even the Abbot, and say, 'Please help me, I can't stop eating your bread and butter.'

I tried going to Mass – perhaps the Holy Food and Drink would calm me and help me to get myself under control. As I approached the altar and was about to kneel down, a monk drew close and informed me, in a discreetly subdued tone, that as I was not a confirmed Catholic I could not receive Mass. I retired ignominiously to my pew, embarrassed and humiliated. What price the love of God? I thought. I had been accustomed to the inclusive and ecumenical attitude to the celebration of the Eucharist in the Community of Transformation. I cut short my retreat, and returned home the next day, sneaking away without saying goodbye or giving my reason for leaving.

This, and many other instances of seeking to escape from Hapton, from anorexia nervosa and from myself, only brought home to me more forcefully that there was no escape, and never would be. The only way forward was inner transformation.

These days, whenever I go away from my current home and stay in another place where I have to eat food, I am overcome with wonder that I can now do so without the slightest desire for the fleeting pleasure of bingeing on excess food. For me, that pleasure always immediately converted to an experience of torture, when I lost control of my relationship with food. Yet I can never be complacent, for sometimes that torture seems only a breath away, and my balance is maintained only by the very strictest and intensive attention to the needs of my body, my personal integrity and my spiritual journey.

The longer I lived in Hapton, the more I felt the trap closing over me. The ugliness and destructiveness of the environment so infused my existence that I began to fear that I would not be able to see beyond it. I felt with painful empathy the panic and desperation of the caged or trapped animal. The constraints and the nature of my illness made it very difficult to rise above the situation, and I felt that life had given me too much to bear. The longing for the healing vibrations of the countryside and the sea, and the steadying embrace of Mother Nature, became like a physical pain.

Yet Hapton, in all its degradation, is part of nature. Mother Nature embraces all life on earth and we are all part of her body, and however much we would like to think ourselves in control of the systems which govern out lives, we are dependent on her life-giving rhythms. Thus, in Hapton, there is the deepest of lessons to be learned. Beauty, kindness and grace are everywhere, even in the most unlikely places.

Having experienced the paralysis and hopelessness of extreme despair, I would now never make a superficial assumption that change was purely a matter of choice, and that someone, if they *really* wanted to, could get themselves out of their distress – whatever its origin. There seems to be a certain kind of simplistic assumption – particularly amongst New Age thinkers and personal growth experts – that each person is the sole creator of their reality, and can therefore change it at will, in any way that they please. While I do believe that we have much more control over our experience of what we consider to be reality than we generally think we do – although I can't say that I am very good at it myself – I don't see how we can be in total control of everything that happens in our lives. There are a whole lot of people involved in creating a corporate reality experience, thus involving a complex interweaving of co-creators.

There is a kind of polarity between the view that deems everything in a person's life to be something that they have ultimately, by some diverse means or other, brought upon themselves, and the view that holds Fate or God as the supreme master of destiny – with a person as a mere pawn on the universal chess board.

Training the mind to create thought patterns and beliefs that manifest and generate abundance might be possible, and if so, this would certainly be desirable as a means towards eradicating poverty and lack. However, it is somewhat arrogant to assume that those people whose only experience is poverty, and whose lives are steeped in the struggle for sheer survival, would have the time, energy and determination to practise this very difficult discipline. I know this from my own personal experience, because I have been trying it for a long time!

Until we have a greater understanding of life and its hidden mechanisms, it is perhaps more prudent and more humble to admit that we do not have all the answers, and cannot find solutions to every problem. We can only choose how we will respond to each and every moment in our lives. We can look for the point of transformation in each situation where new energy can flow in, and where the flow of kindness, compassion and creativity is opened up.

Every one of us needs to look deeply into our own heart and recognise how we ourselves are contributing to world deprivation and suffering. We have our fear of not having enough, our need to have more and more in order to stave off the inner emptiness, our estrangement from confidence in connectedness with the universal source, and our sense of unworthiness that makes us deeply fear that our needs are not valid. All these subterranean beliefs and many more, contribute to the manifestation of inequality, exploitation and impoverishment.

Among the many lessons that I have learned through living in Hapton, one of the greatest is that which demonstrates to me that living on the edge, for all its apparent limitation, privation and threat to life, can itself become a creative thrust to the broadening and deepening of the experience of life. Poverty, illness, humiliation, despair and suffering of all kinds can become transformed into riches. Such riches are not simply of the material world, but are of an eternal and enduring nature.

It is not that I think that suffering is the *only* way to promote spiritual growth, or that it needs to be courted as some kind of initiation rite into the higher dimensions. Whatever life presents, whether it be of joy or of sorrow, can be the route to a different way of being alive in the world – one with a wider perspective and a greater soul quality. I still complain vigorously about these broadening and deepening experiences which life brings me, and the 'ordinary me' would much prefer a comfortable life! But looking back on the lessons I have learned, I count them as priceless, and am deeply grateful for them.

The great variety of challenging experiences that I have had through living in Hapton testify to a commitment of pursuing the pathway of incarnation, with the intent of living it as well as possible. In my experiences, I have been rewarded. I do not regret the time spent there, and I am grateful to so many people and creatures that helped me through it.

Many Waters Cannot Quench Love

O Love! You found me once again –
Beneath the hatred layered in years,
Taught in suspicion and fears,
Love came as pain.

Many waters cannot quench love,
Neither can the floods drown it.

I thought love's pain
Was more than I could bear.
Lodged in my soul
The seed of love caught fire
And burned with searing flame,
Searching out my shame.

In panic from love I fled,
Tried all I knew to hate instead,
Doused the flame with indifferent pride,
Ran to my secret places to hide,
Covered myself with an angry façade,
Made the outer shell ugly and hard,
Did violence to self till my features were marred.
To my prayers for love to cease – no reply,
The Author of Love would not hear my cry,
But the flame of love burned more fiercely still,
No power could quench it, nor could the flames
kill.

Many waters cannot quench love,
Neither can the floods drown it.

I turned towards love, the fire to placate,
To co-exist peaceably, each in its own state,
But the flame of love could not be satisfied,
It spread and grew and consumed me inside,
It ate up my fear and my hate and my sin,
Refined and purified me within,
Enticed me and melted me, till I became
Love myself, one living flame.
Captured, defeated, glad prisoner I
Of the Author of Love, who had heard my cry.

Many waters cannot quench love,
Neither can the floods drown it.

Jacqueline Kemp

'Many waters cannot quench love, neither can the floods drown
it'. Quotation from Song of Solomon, Chapter 8, verse 7
The Holy Bible (King James version)

Chapter Nine

Love and loss

As I continue to pursue the transformation of anorexia nervosa as it manifests in my life, I contemplate that love and loss, in all their differing forms, are some of the greatest catalysts to that transformation. For many years, the two went hand in hand. I could not experience love without the concomitant devastating anguish of loss. Having experienced the painful and bewildering loss of my brother at an age when I was too young to understand, all subsequent losses resonated with that, until I was able to bring the buried feelings into consciousness and internalise them. It was only as time went on that I began to understand the kind of love that loss cannot destroy, and be able to love without seeking to possess the object of my love. This was, and continues to be, extremely difficult for me, and I regret that I have not yet perfected the art of being able to offer and receive unconditional love. However, elements of it have begun to form in my nature – to set me free from the consuming fire of need that was a driving force of my anorexic experience.

Throughout my teenage years and adult life, a series of different men, and one woman, have been the focus of my longing and anguish. These relationships have manifested through diverse roles and forms – dentists, doctors, psychologists, therapists, priests, healers, pastoral leaders, lovers – all with a similar ingredient of unrequited longing for recognition, affirmation of uniqueness, and being wanted. The emotional absence of my father in my formative years, and his inability to affirm and nurture my personhood, underpinned all such relationships. Each one has been permeated with a whole gamut of powerful emotions such as grief, rage, fear, rejection and despair which brought me face to face with aspects of myself that I could hardly bear to admit. Illusions were ripped away, challenging me more and more deeply as to the understanding of love, and leaving me naked to the fierce blasts of self-hatred emanating from the hidden depths of my nature.

I have spent many years pondering this violent war waged within myself, for each belovèd was also a projection of the enemy within. The inner saboteur sought constantly for her victim, finding that projection in a succession of amazingly inventive and ingenious dramas. Not that the relationships were all entirely destructive by any means. Love was there, in the background, guiding, purifying and teaching me, as I battled my way through what seemed to me to be a baffling and dangerous maze of interactions. All of these relationships gave me back something of myself, and contributed significantly to the growth and strength of my own masculine energies, my inner animus. Many of the relationships led to a profound sharing of hearts and minds, and occasionally bodies, the recollection of which remains with me as an enduring gift of love. I would not have believed it at the time, but it is this gift that remains with me in my heart, while the dross of all the struggling slowly burns away to nothing. I think that from my perspective now, I am grateful to be free of this kind of emotional involvement and very wary indeed of resurrecting it in any shape or form. I know my limits, and realise that with my obsessive and addictive tendencies, I have to be very careful of the kind of interactions in which I involve myself. I am still learning of course, and still healing, so it could be that such changes will bring about different kinds of closeness in my life. I hope so, for the tearing feeling of longing for warmth and intimacy conflicting with the terror of my boundaries being invaded and losing control is very hard to live with.

Learning to hate was a big part of my journey in the world of relating. As a Christian, I had thought that it was very sinful to hate and to be angry, and that there would certainly be a terrible punishment in the offing if I allowed these feelings to surface. My upbringing did not help, where hate and anger were unwelcome emotions in the extreme, upsetting my mother and making her unhappy, and far too dangerous to express to my father, whose suppressed hate and anger could so easily be triggered and deposited on the unresisting persona of my mother. I did not learn to deal with the so-called negative emotions in a capable way, and so grew to fear them.

As time went on I explored the more mystical dimensions of Christianity. Gradually growing into a broader understanding of spirituality, I ceased to worry so much about hating. Long years of therapy of so many kinds compelled me to begin to address the enormous volcano of rage and hatred buried deep inside me, and once it started to pour forth its fire and brimstone, there was no stopping it. It has never been an experience that I enjoyed, and indeed continues to cause me a lot of anxiety when it recurs in the present day, but I realised that for the sake of my sanity I had to find a way to deal creatively with this enormously powerful energy within me. I began to see that hate and anger could be a transformative energy, if I chose to handle it in that way.

It is not easy, far from it, and I am not sure of the energetic and spiritual mechanism involved, but I found, and continue to find, that there is a way to hate without directing the hate at the recipient with intent to harm, and of somehow routing it towards the transformative angelic powers, so that it may transmute into creative and healing energies. This is not necessarily a simple or instantaneous event. It can take years of hard work on the psychological and practical levels as well as the mystical and spiritual. I am not a person who can forgive easily. Sometimes the force of hate that I had to allow to surge through me was so great that I feared it would take me over, and I would become the embodiment of hate. The pain of such force to my body, mind and spirit was unspeakable.

After years of a great many repetitions of what was essentially the same drama, with variations of plot, characters and costume, I began to wonder exactly who or what it was I was adoring or hating – these being basically two sides of the same coin. I began to make myself take a seat with the audience and observe the unfolding of dynamics as the action took place. I noticed that the heroine (me) had an extraordinary knack of attracting heroes (them) who offered her a combination of abuse consisting of some kind of humiliation and rejection, together with some kind of seduction and demand. What is more, the heroine actually solicited this kind of behaviour in the most nauseating and calculating way, and unquestioningly accepted it, imagining herself to be in love with a kind of god-like human being (well for a time, anyway, until the unwelcome realisation dawned that she had got it wrong again). She was pathetically willing to sell off her dignity and autonomy for a few crumbs of dubious affirmation, and would readily perjure her identity for a fleeting experience of being wanted. So, who was it that I really hated? After lengthy consideration of various possibilities, I came to the very painful conclusion that it was this snivelling wretch of a heroine that I really hated. The agony of self-hatred is so difficult to face, in whatever guise it presents itself. For me at least, it has never been a one-off realisation, but a life-long wrestling with self, the little self or the concept of self.

I will reiterate that I do not have any intention of defaming any of those persons with whom I formed relationships of emotional and physical love, in which I felt myself to be 'in love'. In each one, from the briefest encounter to the more enduring involvement, there were those higher values and aspirations of caring and understanding, and a desire for reciprocal support in life's journey. My struggle with hate was like a poison, which infiltrated them all to one degree or another, eventually bringing the involvement to a close. With one person, the initial friendship that had drawn us together reformed over a period of years, and that which was born of caring and mutual respect reawakened, making us better friends than before. I am very grateful for that restoration, but I continue to regret the times when I betrayed my own nature and chose compliance over self-definition, in whatever relationship or circumstance the choice arose.

Reflecting upon the years of my road of relationship, I can see that boundaries were a major problem. My upbringing and anorexic manifestation made it very difficult for me to have any awareness of my physical, psychic or emotional boundaries, and I felt like a formless thing, ready to be moulded into any shape which the other intended. Living in the experience of separateness, which is a part of the human condition and learning experience, I believe that it is crucial to understand the nature of boundaries.

Philosophical and scientific explorations of the nature of matter and its ephemeral state are interesting and necessary, and do give a different perspective on what we normally understand as reality, but we still have to live day by day in the current experiential dimensions of the average human being. Today we understand more and more about how the created order is one gigantic organism, and that everything is energetically connected to everything else. This is exciting, and expands the horizons of how we relate to everything that enters our perceptive experience, but at the same time, in everyday life and everyday relating, boundaries are still a functional concept that have to be observed if one is to make one's way though life with some degree of what is normally considered to be sanity.

Perhaps in different cultures or different eras, those labelled as insane today would have been regarded as possessing divine inspiration, or would be trained as shamans, or some other kind of revered spiritual role. For me, to examine my understanding and attitude to boundaries was a mandate of health, and to leave this great question unanswered would have meant a life of deterioration into irreparable mental disarray. I cannot say that I have answered the question once and for all. Does one ever answer a question once and for all? No sooner than one thinks it is answered, or humanity thinks that it has got it all solved, something arises to challenge the answer! I think that questions must be lived, and answers must remain flexible.

As I approached this arena of boundaries, I realised that I

was afraid of saying 'no'. I can hardly ever remember my mother saying 'no' to me, and somehow it felt that any 'no' was a rejection of the worst kind. It still doesn't feel that great, but why should it be any worse than 'yes'? I felt that I had no right to say 'no', and that my life and identity were of no account. I was simply there to please others and to do their bidding. Who did this amorphous blob think she was? How dare she say no to what was being required of her? She had nothing better to do in the universe, so she ought to make herself useful by saying yes to every wish and command. I was afraid that if I said no, I would arouse anger – a terrifying barrage of words that would sweep over me and obliterate my little bubble of self. I was afraid that if I said no, I would not be wanted. I was afraid that if I did not meet all the other person's needs, I would be made to feel guilty and feel a failure. Unfortunately, in many instances my fears were justified and my suppositions correct. Yet, learning the hard way, I somehow managed to clumsily 'no' my way to some sort of self-respect. This was not just on the level of personal interaction but very much in the mind and spirit as well.

Most of my involvements with males, not solely in terms of intense emotional relationships but on other levels such as professionals, acquaintances, local boys, piano students and so on, have taught me something more about myself as a person. Often, such encounters have challenged me to the roots of my identity and caused me to seek through a furore of emotions and attitudes. Yet at other times there has been pleasantness, an easiness and almost camaraderie, offering me a sense of balance in my perception and understanding of the whole spectrum of gender identity and relationship. It has been hard to come to an appreciation of myself as a woman in her own right, not dependent upon a male for description, fulfilment or individuation. I resented bitterly the commonly interpreted function of woman as the helper of man, devoted to serving his needs. What a cheek, I thought. If that's what the Bible says, then I'm not going to take any notice of it! I have since explored that interpretation of scripture, and have generally come to the conclusion that it is really more of what *man* thinks than any ultimate spiritual injunction.

Inhabiting a woman's body, I am largely subject to the formative influence of current and historical female gender roles, and the consequent effects this has on personality and self-expression, and perhaps even on biological determinism to some extent. Conditioning from an early age will affect thought patterns, and consequently the way the brain works, possibly leading to some of the observed differences in the way that male and female brains operate. Genetics has a part to play, but the outcome is not as fixed as maybe was once thought in the worlds of science. The nature/nurture debate continues.

All these explorations, and my continuing interest in such matters, had a certain freeing effect on me. At times, a sense of relief would flood through me, even amusement, as if I had discovered some wonderful secret. I became increasingly aware of being both male and female inside myself. I have to behave and generally act as a woman to conform to social expectations – although an increasing number of women do not – but inwardly I cannot really identify myself as one or the other. Such realisations have led me into an ongoing exploration of the curious value judgements made about 'masculine' and 'feminine'.

I found myself puzzled as to why certain qualities should be attributed to males and others to females, and why these qualities should be considered desirable in some instances, and deplorable in others. The more I thought about it, the more ridiculous it seemed, yet the inbuilt social conditioning is so strong that I can't help continuing to judge myself for qualities that are not part of the acceptable parameters. Take 'soft' and 'hard', for example.

Living as I did in a strong macho culture for many years, I was always struck by the social pressure on boys and young men to be 'hard', as if that were the epitome of maleness.

They are supposed to be aggressive, show no gentle or affectionate feelings, never cry, defy the law, be insolent, throw rubbish around and never put it in bins, and generally behave in an antisocial way. 'Street cred' is the order of the day, and the very thought of being 'soft' is a terrifying anathema for these poor lads. Yet the soft parts of women's bodies are glorified to obscene and ludicrous extremes, on sale and advertising everything from fast cars to ice cream. How daft can we humans get? Yet this is a deadly serious matter. Fear and oppression of the feminine have led to some of the most gruesome episodes of human history, and continues to permeate language, attitudes, self-images, social structures, and even our eco-system.

I realised that I had grown up with the unspoken expectation that to be a good woman, according to the Christian doctrine – which was the pervasive definition of life and its meaning in which I had been raised – I had to be meek, self-sacrificing, never show any anger or aggression, never insist on what I wanted, never have the hubris to define myself or look for self-determination in my life, and instead look to a man to authenticate and give meaning to my existence. What a desperately narrow, restricting outlook for a woman. No wonder I did not want to be one, and did everything in my power to remove my soft bits! It was only as I began to throw off this pseudo-spiritual straightjacket that I could begin to breathe in the life of self-knowledge, and with it, the experience of real love.

I have always loved, but that love is necessarily a maturing aspect of the human character if it is to progress from the simple need of love in the very young, or the obligation of an imposed self-sacrificial love, or the focused projection of the in-love experience, into a broader, all encompassing embodiment of love. The very word 'love' carries with it such a wide range of meanings, implications and understandings that it is difficult to use it at all to convey what one really means. There must surely be some sort of qualitative difference between loving chocolate, for example, or 'making love', or loving those people who come into our lives bringing with them challenges and problems. Maybe these multiple meanings of love within the English language are an unintentional linguistic representation of the infinite manifestations of love in our human experience. In some other languages, there are several different words that convey different aspects and qualities of love.

As I pursue my pathway through life, I become more and more amazed, awed and humbled by the way that love manifests to me, in an infinite variety of forms, through an infinite variety of agencies, and in an infinite variety of ways. There really is no limit to love. But what *is* love? I keep asking myself that question. It certainly isn't always that nice, pleasurable stuff that we are habitually persuaded to believe in. I think that because it is limitless, it cannot be defined, and it cannot be tied down by the formulations of the human mind and the encapsulation of language. It can only be recognised. To me, it is that which forms us more truly into the likeness of our original divine spark, but of course, that can be anything if we choose to allow it to work in this way. So love can be anything and can reach anything, an all-pervasive creative energy that we can appropriate to ourselves, but it also has its counterfeit, as I found out to my cost.

Perhaps for me the deepest area of confusion as to the nature of love was the common misconception that feelings of love are love itself, and that the ultimate expression of love is sex. Of course both the feelings and sex can be an expression of, and the conveyance of, the love energy, and I am glad to have had the opportunity to experience something of that, but they are by no means necessarily so. In some of my experiences of relationship, I was astonished to discover that the powerful feelings of adoration – apparently love – could so easily turn about and become a violent storm of hatred. I wondered if I had really loved the person in the first place. Certain sexual encounters, which at the time had occupied my thoughts with feelings of longing and what I took to be love, turned out to be a kind of symbiotic exploitation, empty of any real lasting depth of understanding or commitment. Yet they were sincere at the time, at least for me, although I can't speak for the other persons concerned. I gradually came to the conclusion, which may not be entirely correct, that these others were persons upon whom I could conveniently hook my projected fantasies and needs, and the strength of the emotion or passion was fuelled by a need to find myself. I was continually trying to reclaim lost parts of myself by loving (or hating) the reflection of those parts in the other person. I think that this does not deny the authenticity of the encounter, provided one aims to act with integrity, nor the service rendered by the recipient of the projection. However, unless one realises what is going on, it can all go horribly wrong, and lead to complicated entanglements, a long-lasting wounding, and in the worst cases, a gross and uncontrolled outpouring of untransformed archetypal energies. One only has to look at the TV soaps for five minutes to see it all in full swing.

The love in friendship has always sat more naturally with me than the love of sexuality. My limited experience of sexual partnership has always triggered a kind of primitive possessiveness and need, as if somehow the partner assumed a guise, and became to me someone other than who they really were. I did not seem able to internalise the person with whom I was in love, and every parting was like a loss. Since I did not know myself, I never really felt known. There was an internal guard defending my space, and at every meeting the guard would have to be overcome. I needed constant reassurance that I was wanted, and that the other person would be there for me, which I am sure made me clingy and demanding – even if I strove not to show it. I remember one of my belovèds calling me a psychic vampire! Maybe he had some justification for this, and I can laugh at it now, but it certainly hurt a lot at the time. However, I understand now that this experience was an indication that the relationship had neither sufficient emotional and spiritual foundation nor staying power for *my* needs, for it to be able to sustain the sexual aspect.

The people I chose for sexual partners were those with whom I could not enter into the relationship on the levels which I desired and needed, and perhaps they themselves were unable to, or did not desire it. Thus, sadly, at the deepest levels of my being, I experienced sexual relations in some respects as invasion and loss, even though on other levels there was love and caring, and I could convince myself that it was what I wanted. This confusion had a very damaging effect, such that all my sexual relationships caused me intense anxiety and emotional agony. The upsurge of such strong feelings would inevitably result in my bingeing on food, in a useless attempt to push them down, with the resultant upsurge of disgust and self-loathing.

Trying to share my body with all this going on needed a momentous effort of denial on my part. It was many years before I was able to bring the conflict and confusion into my conscious awareness, and make more creative decisions in the way I chose to relate. The times of happiness were always underpinned by this component, and though I do not regret in any way the real sharing and love that was woven through these difficult relationships, I would not like to repeat this kind of experience.

Friendships have been of great significance throughout my life, playing an invaluable part in the formation of my personality and the growth of self-knowledge, and also keeping my wandering spirit anchored to the earthly life. I would venture to say that friendships are the 'bread and butter' of my relationships, the everyday sustenance by which I survive. I have and have had friendships with children, animals, plants, my therapists, doctors, dentists, and other professional helpers, with hairdressing clients, piano students, and my own teachers, and with people of all ages in a variety of walks of life. This is indeed a privilege, and I count myself very lucky to participate in such a wide range of friendship. By 'friendship', I mean that real meeting of persons by which one knows in one's heart that one has encountered another being. This kind of meeting is one which, even if it sinks to the forgotten levels of the mind, lasts forever, and can be reawakened in an instant. These friendships of mine would not all be intimate or long term, but nevertheless each is a recognition of a fellow traveller with whom I tread the pathway of life, for anything from a moment of time to years, or even a whole lifetime. In this recognition, time disappears and the eternal enfolds the meeting. These fellow travellers are a light on my pathway, helping to lift the burden of my incarnation.

While my friends become part of my inner existence, there is always the need to understand and respect the dimensions of a friendship. There is a right time for everything, a time to be close and a time to move apart, a time to hold and a time to let go. The other being is always a sacred mystery who cannot be described, analysed or controlled, but whose individuality must be revered and respected. Even with the understanding of this, I have not been very good at letting go. Something in me wants to hold on to that precious friend, and feels a terrible sense of loss and grief when the outward nature of the friendship has to change, or even cease. However as the years have gone by, I have become gradually aware of a more stable part of myself that remains relatively undisturbed by such traumas and more able to allow for the inevitable ebb and flow of life and death. This underpins the difficult emotional response, and while it does not exactly make it any easier, it is a steadying aspect of my awareness that eventually balances the roller-coaster of my feelings.

Recently I have become more experientially aware of the cellular capacity to store long-buried memories and feelings. A couple of years of doing Dr Frank Lake's Clinical Theology, or primal work, gave me an introduction to this. During this time I was able to access pervasive feelings associated with my childhood, even including a certain amount of prenatal and perinatal recall. This consisted more of impressions rather than actual memories, and as such, were not easily verifiable, except by information that I had later accumulated. Maybe the information coloured what I had experienced in the therapy. I cannot really be sure about that. However, my experience felt authentic, and I imagine that that was what was important, in addition to the verifying aspect of someone taking my distress seriously.

Later on, other body therapies, such as cranio-sacral therapy, began to show me how the form and structure of my body had taken on, and in a sense manifested, what I had experienced. I have yet to explore in more detail the nature of the human aura and chakras, in terms of how this part of the human being acts as a memory bank and stores energetically memories and experiences of the past. This can also be true of past lives, so I understand. This is a field of enquiry which holds great potential – another adventure, of which I am on the threshold. Reawakening distress is never easy or pleasant, and indeed, in my opinion, should be undertaken with caution. In my case, I drew near to the edge of self-destruction many times, when the pain of it all became more than I thought I could bear.

It is amazing and awe-inspiring to contemplate how wonderfully we are made, and how complex and intricate our whole being is, in all its layers and its journeying.

* * * * *

Some of the most painful losses of my life have been the passing away of my dearly loved cats. These beautiful creatures, who shared my life so intimately, became as close to me as any human friend, if not closer. When I was growing up, we always had cats, and I remember that their death brought such sadness for us all, especially Dad, who I think had similar feelings for them as I do, although he never spoke about that.

It was not quite the same when I had my own cats, and was responsible for them, and shared every detail of their lives. That was when I became so deeply aware of the divine presence manifest in them, and was so moved and humbled by their love, and their dependence on my care for them. Each parting was a terrible grief, yet also a profound honour – to escort that creature to the doorway of death and see him or her through. It was always at the veterinary surgery, or with a visiting vet, when I had to make that heart-wrenching decision to end the suffering of my dearest friend, and hold the furry body in my arms as the final injection was given. In an instant, that presence whom I had loved so much had gone, and I was left holding a lifeless body, in floods of tears for that darling cat that would never purr for me again. After a burial, and a little dedication and thanksgiving for the gift of that life so generously given for my comfort and companionship, the sharp pain fades, but the questioning and the longing always remain. I have heard that some animals return to their owners, when they have been much loved, either in spirit form or by taking on another body. This is something that I have not experienced as yet, although I still hope to. However, I have occasionally met my furry friends again in dreams.

The death of my father was a profound event, and proved to be a major turning point in my life. Dad was a strong and healthy man right into his old age, and only in the last couple of years of his life did he seem to experience some of the weakness and fragility which was my lifelong inheritance. We grew much closer in his later years, and this was a precious time that did much to ameliorate the damage of the past. His visits to me in Scotland became a time of anticipation for us both, when we would share all sorts of mini-adventures, and the daily chores of life became a joint endeavour. I have so many happy memories of these times – the things that gave him joy and pleasure, the recollections he shared, and the intimate glimpses into who he really was. I still wrestled with the anorexic force, though, and could never really share that devastation with him. I could not confront him with the anger and anguish that his conduct and attitudes had caused me, how they had shattered my sense of self and crippled my personality. Those matters are still being worked upon, and in the reaches of time I feel confident that there will be complete harmony between me and my dearest Dad.

He would come in May and October. Latterly, he came with Mum in May, and on his own in October. I suspect that he liked coming by himself, as then he could escape the tensions and difficulties of the family home, where he lived with my mother and sister. His last visit to me was in 1984, when I was forty-five years old, and it was one of the best times that we had together.

Dad and I had a similar kind of nature in some ways – the way we liked to do things, a similar sense of humour, almost a camaraderie – and I think that he felt at home in my home, the little haven I had created for myself. We worked well together, and he enjoyed doing DIY jobs for me while he still could, and advising me about finances and other practical matters of life of which I had little skill or experience.

We had such a special time during his last October visit. The weather was kind to us, and we had many pleasant trips into the countryside, going to his favourite places and sharing the joys of nature. He was ninety years old then, and though quite frail, was alert and interested in life, and still able to enjoy a short walk holding my arm. The feel of the grip of his old hand, strong and vibrant to the last, will remain with me forever. Dad loved life and did not like being old. He hated having to ask for help, and felt very uncertain, I believe, of what death and dying might hold. He often said that he could not imagine anything better than some of the beautiful places that we visited together, and that heaven could not surpass them.

He remained true to his Christian beliefs, but had begun to question them more and more, as the reality of mortality pressed closer in upon him. We had long discussions as to the nature of the spirit world, but I was never able to reassure him concerning life after death. Our relationship changed greatly towards the end of his life, rebalancing itself into more of a friendship, although he was always, and still is, Dad. I was always sad to say goodbye to him when he returned home.

Not long after his last visit, only about a month in fact, I learned that he had fallen in church and had not been able to rise. Someone had taken him home, and thereafter he began to deteriorate rapidly. My mother and sister looked after him for as long as they could, but it became necessary for him to go into hospital, as by this time he had lost all use of his legs. At that time there was no certain diagnosis, and this made the situation worse for everyone. I felt so desperately anxious about him, and often felt him in my spirit, calling me to help him. My mother, sister and brother helped him on the practical side far more than I was able to, but I think that perhaps because of my own suffering I was able to draw near to his soul in a different sort of way. I felt the weight of his dying process very heavily as he leaned on me in spirit, and I feel that this was a great privilege and a great source of healing in our relationship, and also in my own anorexic journey.

On one of my visits from Scotland down to the hospital, my brother's wife (now also passed over) suggested that I ask for a private word with one of the doctors, and this I duly did. The doctor told me that the prostate cancer for which Dad had been previously treated had spread, and had invaded the rest of his body, causing the base of his spine to collapse. There was no hope, nothing that could be done, and it was just a matter of time until the cancer took him away.

I think that they had already told Dad, as one day when we went in, his mood had changed. He had seemed unhappy, and had amazed us all by making my sister and me trustees of his accounts. Having been an accountant all his life, conducting his financial affairs was something that he still enjoyed doing. Money, and its usage, was important to him. Now he was relinquishing control, and at that point, although I did not then know the verdict, I knew that something was up.

When the doctor told me that nothing could be done for Dad, I was in floods of tears. I went straight home and told Mum, my sister and brother.

It still is a source of incredulity to me that they had not been told first. Why did the medical profession think that we had to be protected from the truth? Poor Mum was devastated. All her life she had depended on Dad, her Jack, to look after her and things pertaining to home life, and this he did very well, although he could never bring himself to give her again the love and affection she longed for as his wife. Like the courageous trooper that she was, she rallied her strength, and she and my sister supported Dad faithfully until the time of his death in hospital.

The day before I learned the diagnosis, a rather astonishing and somewhat alarming thing had happened to me. I had gone to the toilet for a bowel movement, and since the lavatory in my parents' house had a kind of flat pan, I was in the habit of inspecting its contents after using it. Not a very savoury practice you may think, but I have always been anxious about my bodily functions, and this was just another manifestation of that anxiety. To my amazement and horror, entwined in the sections of faeces was an enormous roundworm, at least ten inches long! I could hardly believe my eyes, and poked at it to see if it was still alive. It was not, and I imagine that the nutritional treatment that I had been having for digestive disorders had killed it, and it had come away. How long it had been there, and how it had got there, I have no idea. I reflected on the revelation of the existence of this large parasite and its death. I wondered if there was any significance in it.

I think that my love for Dad, and our special relationship, had allowed him in some way, unintentionally of course, to be an unseen drain on my life energy. He fed from me emotionally, as he was so unable to form close emotional relationships with others in his personal network. I understood him, without knowing quite how, even as a child, and could draw near to him when he kept everyone else at bay. I am not claiming any credit for this – it was simply the way it was. Who knows why? Maybe there was some kind of karmic link, and I think that there probably is, but in some ways unless one is really sure about this and its nature, I am not certain that it is very helpful to dwell on it. As I grew up, I just had to get on with the business of trying to dredge up from the bowels of my personality all those things that had complicated my relationship with Dad. I had to examine, understand, accept and forgive, both him, and myself, and this process is still ongoing. It is no mean task, as those who have made similar journeys will well comprehend.

Sometimes when I went down to visit Dad, I would stay overnight in the hospital so that I could be with him if he needed me. On my last visit, I had stayed in one of the guest rooms, and the staff called me to go to him as he was asking for me. He was upset. 'Why can't I die?' he asked. 'Please God, let me die.' I was so vexed for him. I held his hand and sung his favourite hymns for him, and prayed. At the time, my beliefs in spiritual matters were changing, and I did not know quite where to direct my prayers for help, but I had recently been reading about angels, and had a solid foundation of experience with these wonderful helpers from a different dimension, so I prayed to the Archangel Michael to cut the cord that bound Dad to life. It was not that I knew this being or had any special relationship with it. It was just that I felt that the name represented a kind of ray of energy that would come to our aid.

As Dad and I were praying together, I heard a sharp crack, somewhere that I could not locate. My tears flowed copiously, and Dad rested back on his pillow. 'You'd better go dear,' he said, two or three times. I didn't want to go, and asked him if he wanted his hospital buzzer in his hand so that he could call me, but he said he wouldn't need it now. I though that this was strange, as before he had been so attached to it, and had wanted to have it in his hand all the time. I left him, and went straight to the chapel, where I howled my heart out.

I had to return to Scotland the next day, and a few days later, Dad died. My mother and sister had just visited him – my poor dear mother longing for a word of love from him, but he gave her none. He died alone, and I think that he had wanted it that way. I went to pay my last respects to him at the funeral parlour. It was a strange experience – his body lying cold and still, in a coffin. This is one of the most evidential experiences for life after death, I feel, in that the person you knew and loved, whose presence was so palpable and whose soul you had met, has gone from their physical house and is no longer at home. You wait there for a little while, as if hoping that they will come back and open their eyes and say hello. Although the intellectual knowledge of death is present, the emotions take a while to catch up. On the day of the funeral, when the hearse arrived with his body, and the cremation service eventually drew to a close, the final goodbye dawned upon me, and I wept unrestrainedly.

For some while after his death, I had an agonising pain somewhere in the region of my solar plexus – not in my physical body, but a little distance from it, in my aura. I felt as a bee must feel when it stings and its intestine is ripped out, and I went around my flat screaming in pain, off and on for a few weeks. Not long afterwards, I began to feel Dad around my flat, in the room where he had stayed, and which he liked so much. When he was dying, and feeling fearful of what lay ahead, I had told him to come to this room if he needed to, and we would talk just as we used to. So I talked away to him, even though I could not see him, and I often felt a tickling in my hair, as if his presence were ruffling it. I wished so much that I could see him, yet in truth I was a bit afraid, still carrying the memories of those dark presences that had invaded my space so often before. This is a curious thing: the person I most longed to see and touch again was my Dad, and yet I was afraid.

The event of his death started me on a road that was to have far reaching influence in my life, and opened up to me many new levels of perception concerning our relationship and its continuity. It was also a turning point in my anorexic experience, from which I gradually and very slowly began to get control over my eating behaviour and recreate my attitude to food. I will write more about Dad later, as my search for him and our meetings beyond the grave were to develop into an exciting and mystifying journey.

In the penumbral years of my Dad's death, related events and my thoughts and feelings concerning them were like a shadow in my life, surrounding the time when he made the transition from one form of existence to another. During this time I had begun to go through the menopause, and this was a time of profound emotional and physical change in my life. On one hand, the physical changes in my body were uncomfortable and disturbing. My menstruation became very irregular, occurring anything from between two to six weeks apart, and the flow varied from a veritable flood with blood clots, to a minimal spotting of blood. My breasts were constantly painful, and though I was fortunate not to suffer from hot flushes, I felt bloated almost all of the time. This was not helpful to my anorexic horror of my stomach swelling up with food, and once again my body felt out of control. At the time I had not done much research into nutritional supplements and I now know of certain supplements which may have alleviated some of the symptoms. However, my doctor did prescribe Evening Primrose oil, and unusually for a GP, also prescribed a homeopathic remedy, which helped to take the edge off my discomfort. The doctor I had at the time was a warm and pleasant man, who was easy to talk to. I felt that he cared about me, and this in itself was a comforting and stabilising factor in this difficult time of life.

In contrast to all the physical upheaval, I began to experience a sense of relief at the emotional level. The 'danger' of pregnancy was passing, and I no longer felt that I had to present myself as a sexual object, available for assessment by the opposite sex. This was not entirely a conscious realisation at the time, and took several years to settle down into a different perception of myself as a woman. Sadness also accompanied the realisation. At a very early age, I had made the decision not to have any children, and I still believe that it was the right one for me. However, at the menopause I became aware that I could *never* have children, even if I had changed my mind and wanted to conceive, as my body had now also made its decision, which could not be revoked. There was a sense of loss, and a sense of loneliness in the subliminal parts of my awareness. In contrast, I felt freer in my relationships with men, more able to see them as individuals, rather than as persons who might be attracted to me sexually. This helped greatly in my efforts to disentangle myself from relationships which were unsuitable and therefore potentially damaging. It was also instrumental in gradually helping me to develop a more balanced and respectful attitude to food, and to my body.

My mother lived on seven years or so after Dad had gone. My sister remained with her to look after her. This was perhaps inevitable, as they had become inseparably entwined in reciprocal feelings of responsibility towards each other. On the one hand, it was a good thing that Mum had someone to look after her and could remain in her own home, but on the other, the *status quo* was preserved, and neither one could develop their own life in any different kind of way. The space created by the loss of Dad could have been an opportunity, but it seemed to be more of a trap for them. However, one cannot make any judgements about this, and I cannot know the inner workings of their relationship and choices.

My loss of Mum was more of a long drawn out process, not like the sharp agony that I went through with Dad. It was not that I loved her any less, or that the parting was any easier, but to do with the different kind of bond that I had with her. I was very close to her as a child – too close, such that I absorbed her thoughts and feelings too easily, and became both overly dependent upon her and responsible for her in a subconscious way that I did not recognise at the time.

My illness, and my efforts to survive it, continually required me to examine and face up to this internal and spiritual entanglement, and as the years passed I became gradually freer, and therefore closer to her in a more mature way. It was not without great pain, though, and I know and regret that it caused her great pain, too. When I first left home, it was perhaps one of the greatest losses for both of us, and when I joined the Community of Transformation, there was a further level of separation, insisted upon by the community. At the times of its greatest intensity, this process caused me a great deal of guilt and agony, but when I look back upon it now, and realise how much I have reclaimed who I really am, I am deeply grateful. I know that she is, too, from where she is now, in the next life.

Once Dad had passed away, all of us in the immediate family began to lose our Mum in a different sort of way. Whereas she had always been the loving, sweet half of the partnership, always wanting to help people and thinking well of them, she gradually became bitter and negative, and she allowed long buried resentments and pains to surface. Grief was a long march for her, and the loss of Dad had not just been at his death, but had taken place a long time ago, when he took his German lover. Although, in practice, he returned to Mum, he never returned to her as her loving husband. All this resurfaced to trouble Mum as she struggled on alone, and her once strong faith in God crumpled underneath her. I found it so desperately awful, seeing her go through this process, and perhaps understanding it from a different perspective from the rest of my family, as I had been required to delve so deeply in order to save myself. It was difficult to get time alone with her, as my sister had really become her guardian, and was understandably protective towards her, often censoring her conversations with others and controlling her in other ways.

Yet in spite of everything, Mum's spirit remained a bright flame in her suffering body and personality, and although she was not in one sense the Mum we used to know, she was still

Mum, and remained so until her dying day. In contrast to the loss of Dad, her death was a relief to me, and to all of us, I suspect, for although there was the inevitable grief of her departure from our lives, she had been so unhappy and so unwell, and every time I saw her she would ask me to pray that she would die. Those last visits and meetings with her were precious ones, even though the circumstances were so difficult. Always there was a little special moment, given by the angels, I am sure, when she was just Mum and I was just her daughter, and we loved each other.

I feel that it is a great honour to escort a person, or any creature for that matter, to the doorway of death and to stand by respectfully while they pass through it. A dear friend of mine, whom I met through classes at the Centre for Continuing Education in Edinburgh, asked me very early on in our friendship if I would be there for him when he died. He suffered from heart disease and did not have a good prognosis of years left to live. I assured him that I would certainly do so, if at all possible, knowing that death has its own timing and cannot be organised to fit into a convenient time slot when the loved ones can be present.

From the outset it was not an easy friendship. Watson fell deeply in love with me, almost to the point of obsession, and I found this very difficult to handle in a way which was respectful of his feelings but true to my own as well. I have to confess that at times I wrestled with a desire to hurt, exploit and humiliate, as had been done to me when I had found myself overtaken by similar feelings in other circumstances. I think, and I hope with all my heart, that I managed to avoid this, simply by being conscious of it, and setting my intent towards love and kindness. I know I did not achieve perfection in this, and there were times when our friendship was very troubled and stressful, but somehow we came through it each time, to a deeper and more mature way of loving each other.

Watson was not used to my direct style of communication,

and the sword-like nature of the self-awareness that perforce I had been obliged to develop, and I became aware that I had to work very hard, in a very short time, for us to develop that heart to heart love that characterised our friendship towards its earthly close. He wanted the traditional kind of man and woman relationship of physical intimacy and being 'in love', but having had many experiences in my life where this just had not worked, and had ended in misery and despair, I refused this kind of relationship, and instead tried to steer it into a closeness of heart and mind. While Watson would have probably still preferred the former, I think that what we eventually shared was a new experience for him, and I hope it was a good one. As for me, he gave me something that I had never had before, a complete devotion and respect, with recognition and admiration of my personality and gifts. Dear Watson! What a great gift he gave me – something I shall probably never have again, but which I shall remember for the rest of my life. I called him my 'heart husband', and he truly was that.

When he developed cancer, and it became evident that the end of the road was not far away, we drew even closer. It was only then that I began to realise how much he meant to me, as while I knew that I loved him, I had been unable to feel anything of love. With the agony of previous encounters, it was as if my feelings had been scoured away, and there was nothing left.

The night that I went to his flat and found him dying is forever etched in my mind. There were two other friends with me, as we had been going to meet together to talk. The wait for the ambulance seemed endless, and the wait in the hospital while they made him comfortable, even longer. I was named as his next of kin, as he had no living relatives with whom he wanted to be in touch, so I stayed on until I was allowed to go in to see him. I am not sure whether he knew I was there or not, as by that time he was unconscious. I waited into the late evening until I was exhausted, and then the hospital staff said that he was stable, and that I should go home and rest. They promised to call me if there was any change, but said that he could remain in this moribund state for a long time. I thought differently, but I was too weary to stay, and had had nothing to eat since midday, being unwilling to avail myself of the usual hospital snacks and drinks. I went home, had a little food and went to bed, and I prayed for Watson with deepest intensity. At 4 a.m. the phone rang to say that his condition had changed, and that they thought I should come.

I raced to the hospital in my car, and found Watson labouring for breath. I knew that the end was near. I stood by him, telling him all sorts of things. What does one say at times like this? I thanked him so much for being my friend, telling him to let go, as previously he had told me that his greatest fear in dying was leaving me. I felt a presence, then Watson raised his hand to me and I took it, and he breathed his last breath. For a while I stayed holding his hand, feeling his spirit leave his body, and when I felt this to be complete and that he was stable outside his body, I called the doctor. She came and confirmed the diagnosis of death, and kindly let me stay a bit longer with him. When I left, a long, subtle process of grieving began for me. It was not sharp, but an intense, heavy missing of him. I felt as if the ground had disappeared from under my feet. It was only then that I realised how much he loved me. All our differences had been 'ripples on the surface of love' as he had always said.

Following this, there was the funeral to organise, the executor business to be done, his flat to be cleared and cleaned, his friends to be notified, and many other duties, which kept me very busy, and for a while filled the emptiness left by his absence. It was not that I did not have other close friends, but more that he had come into my life with a priceless gift. I was left holding it, but he had gone. To add to the sorrowful matters of my life at that time, my belovèd cat, Corky, also developed cancer, and died soon after Watson. The two male presences in my life, who had always been there for me and had always wanted my company, no matter what sort of mood I was in, had left for another dimension.

About six months later, I became very ill with glandular fever, and have still not completely recovered. I do not resent this physical manifestation of grief, although naturally I desire to be well. It just shows me how very profound is the nature of love, how it cannot be defined or fitted into descriptions of what relationships ought to be, and how it is woven through the very fibres of our whole being.

I think that in relationships the nature of love can reveal itself in so many ways. While those 'in love' episodes of my life have been the most powerful in terms of the emotions that were stirred up in me, those loves that have grown quietly, sometimes in the most unexpected of circumstances, have found a deeper place in my heart, and have had a more lasting influence on me. At times I have not liked the person who appeared on the scene of love, and found little of compatibility that would draw us together. Nevertheless, that great essence and enigma that we call Love cheerfully ignores such trivial human preferences, and establishes itself in the work of loving. We may ponder at the why and wherefore of such a work, but such a Love does not permit itself to be defined and analysed, and merely gets down to business.

Perry is my long term friend and companion whom I met quite by accident, if there is such a thing as an accident in these matters. Many years ago I was feeling lonely after the breakup with the partner I had at that time, and I had put an advertisement in a local paper for walking companions. Perry responded, and we met.

On our first meeting I was perhaps more than put off by his manner, and while remaining polite and friendly, mentally decided that this person was not for me. We said goodbye, and I thought little more of it until I received a huge bunch of beautiful flowers with a note saying that he had enjoyed the meeting and would like to meet again. I did not know what to do, as I did not want to pursue the connection, and yet I felt sorry for him and did not want to hurt him. So we met again, and to cut a very long story short, we are still friends, having gone through hell and high water together in respect of the relationship and events in our own lives.

I think that what drew me to him was his love of nature and his devotion to animals, his deep understanding of them and the lengths he would go to in order to help and to serve them. In those respects we are perfectly matched; in all other respects we are polar opposites. He is the sort of man who would stop his car abruptly in the road having seen a dead cat lying on it, and take the poor creature away to give it a decent burial. He would go out of his way to rescue pigeons whose legs had been tied together by cruel and ignorant fools looking for a cheap laugh. He would get himself wet and dirty going after a dying rabbit, and hold it gently until the little creature passed away. These and countless other acts of compassion and kindness are commonplace for Perry.

The steadfastness of our relationship led us to an unusual kind of partnership. Outside observers may consider our style self-defeating or perhaps frustrating. Yet within the loyalty of this relationship, I have been able to experience being myself in many ways which would have not gone down well in other liaisons that I have made. Although I feel that I have to be on my best behaviour, or at least my better behaviour, in order to be accepted and loved, I have let Perry see the less attractive sides of my personality – getting angry, agitated and depressed, moaning and complaining, and various other unwelcome states! I have been able to say no, and refuse to be compliant. I have been bad tempered, and have even made an occasional verbal attack. Yet every time I find that he is still there, most often without condemnation or reproach. This kind of self-sacrifice for my sake seems inexplicable. To me, it is yet another priceless gift. In my turn I have made many sacrifices for him, more in the inner world of the heart and spirit, where such gifts are not always recognised. This person that I had considered to be a very rough diamond turned out to have a heart of gold, and while looking upon that heart, year after year, love grew like a carefully tended seedling, found springing up against all odds in a neglected garden.

* * * * *

There are many forms of love and loss other than personal relationship, but all involve a relationship or relatedness of some kind. One can experience this in any aspect of life, as life is about relating to each other and to the world in which we live. All forms of loss, even the smallest, carry with them a degree of sorrow and fear for me. It can be a life passage such as the menopause, or something like the loss of money, the loss of a place which I have grown to love, the loss of teeth, or the loss of a way of doing something. Even the loss of a favourite pen draws my attention to my fundamental sense of loss – the loss of that sense of oneness with everything and the loss of the sense of self. My experience of anorexia nervosa is itself based on loss – the loss of that recognition, respect and loving acceptance of my individuality, which led to a loss of self, and the concomitant narcissistic loss of flesh in a vain effort to recreate and love the self that had vanished from sight.

In my view, learning to love is very hard work, but the most rewarding and the most mystifying. It never ends, and the more one loves, the more love there is to be discovered. The form in which the love manifests may change, and indeed must change, I believe, as change is a fact of our human existence and a fundamental movement of the universe. Yet, paradoxically, alongside the change is something that does not change, and that is Love. For this reason love will always involve loss, and if we resist the experience of loss, the loss will seem a finality, but in truth the two are dynamically interwoven. Love and loss are partners in the eternal dance of life and relationship.

Valentine

Love you always in my heart,
Two souls life's journey cannot part,
Though changing fortunes, scenes and places
Come and go with many faces,
Still remain the hidden graces,
With us from the start.

Love evades the bald description
Of society's prescription,
Transcending all the well known rules,
In human eyes we are but fools.
Yet we have shared those precious jewels
Forged in deep affliction.

When I leave my house of flesh
The memory will rise afresh
Of gardens, fairies, frogs and you,
Spring buds and flowers bursting new
From Mother Earth in which they grew,
And love will reinvent itself.

Jacqueline Kemp

293

The Shore

I stand alone upon the shore
Gazing out to sea,
The vast expanse of ocean calls
A question from the depths of me.
How shall I frame this question
In the language of humankind?
A wordless query of the spirit
Flutters the edges of my mind.

The waves roll in to play with my feet,
Splashing fractals, exquisite,
Dynamic patterns, infinite,
I lose myself in endless light
Where questions end and joy begins,
Washing me free from close held sins.
Love's sword which pierced me to the core
Gave me to myself once more.

I wander through the interface
To a different realm,
And fascination draws me
From my earthly helm,
Loosening the tightness
Of my thought horizons,
So I may sail onwards
To a new sun rising.

The gentle wind lifts my hair,
Inviting my soul to fly
With the birds that wheel and squeal overhead
In the wondrous clouded sky.
Unveilèd their divinity,
At last I recognise
The answer to my question
In my own disguise.

Jacqueline Kemp

Chapter Ten

Beyond the veil

For as long as I can remember, I have always lived with thoughts of death and dying. Even as a child, my mind would play around the edges of the life/death doorway, wondering what was beyond it, but not daring to allow my thoughts to go too far. The world of the child seemed so much more circumscribed in those days, or perhaps it was just the type of fearful family environment in which I was raised that prevented the exploration of conversation and thought that seems available to children and young people today. The traditional Christian explanation of going to heaven or hell when you die, depending on whether or not you believed in Jesus, did not really satisfy me. For years I struggled with the concept, trying to penetrate the logic – which did not seem at all logical to me.

Yet the experience of death was something quite different from the thoughts about it. It became a sacred mystery – the presentation of an event for which there was no adequate description, and no answer to the question that filled my mind. However sorrowful and desperate the occasion, a kind of beauty hovered over it. People who have lost loved ones in harrowing circumstances, or have seen the results of violence or tragedy, will perhaps disagree with me, and I can certainly understand that. I think that it is only if one is able to go beyond the outer circumstances, and this may not be for a long time, can one see that death is something other than the ogre it has been characterised to be by our society.

The first inkling I had of death being a rite of passage was when my paternal grandfather died. Grandad had stayed alternately with us and with my aunt over the road for the last years of his life. This was difficult for us all, and especially so for him. I regret that I was not fond of him. I resented his presence, as Mum's attention was diverted to looking after him, and so I could not have her all to myself whenever I wanted.

Grandad was not easy to get on with. His presence increased the tension in our home, as Dad did not like him either. Yet I was sorry for him, and when he fell ill I used to go into his room to take him a cup of tea and talk to him. Maybe it was because I was so troubled myself that he felt he could talk to me and ask me what happened when one died. I had very little with which to reassure him at that time, but I tried. I think he must have been grateful, as I believe he connected with me when he knew he was about to die. At that time, I was living in a small flat not far from the family home. I had not been told that Grandad was close to death, but suddenly I knew he was dying, and fell down upon my knees to pray for him. Not long afterwards I heard that he had passed away, and I was glad that I had been able to offer that final little service to him.

While I was in the worst throes of anorexia nervosa, in my late teens and early twenties, I diced with death many a time with repeated overdoses of prescription drugs. I think that at that time I did not have much idea of what that great unknown could hold, although I was passionately interested in all things metaphysical, and read everything I could find about life after death, ghosts, witchcraft, shamanism and many related topics. This numinous world of the unseen mesmerised me, yet terrified me. When in an agony of tortured mind I craved oblivion, although I did not really know what would happen after the event of my death, except that I was sure I would be punished, and maybe suffer more than ever. Well, I am still alive in this world, and although the inevitable process of ageing brings the reality of mortality ever closer, death remains a mystery, and I wonder with a certain amount of trepidation what it will be like when it actually happens to *me*. It is not so much what happens after death that I fear, but the process of dying itself, which so often seems to fall within a mantle of incapacity and suffering.

* * * * *

It was really the death of my father that prompted me to search more actively for contact beyond the veil. After he had died, I felt his presence very strongly in my flat, where he had stayed with me, but it was not really the kind of awareness that gave me any sense of being able to communicate more tangibly with him. My friend Watson, who was still alive at the time, had several very striking experiences of Dad after his death. Although I did not have the experiences myself, I had no reason to doubt Watson's word, as he was not only a devoted friend but also a highly qualified and experienced psychologist with a precise and rational mind. He wrote out each experience for me in detail and gave me a signed copy, and I have kept these to this day. The first one was about three months after Dad had passed over, and I will quote it in Watson's words as he wrote it out for me.

"I arrived at Old St. Paul's yesterday morning, perhaps a bit overwrought: the bus had been late and I was in a lot of pain. Being Mothering Sunday, there were a lot of children there, several in front of me and behind, naturally restless and a little noisy. Usually that wouldn't have bothered me, but when it came time for Holy Communion, I felt that I did not want to go to the altar rail. So I was left alone at one point at the back of the church. The thurifer must have been very active for there was quite a veil of incense. I sat with my eyes closed for a few minutes. When I opened them, I saw, in front of the altar and behind the three priests moving along the line, your Dad, exactly as I recall him from that evening in October. He seemed to be looking directly at me, and he had one hand outstretched. I stood up and walked towards the altar. I cannot describe how I felt, but as I walked up the aisle, I said 'Are you all right, Jack?' – mundane I suppose, but spontaneous. I must have said it aloud (though I don't really remember), because in the hall afterwards I saw a few people looking curiously at me. I got to

299

the altar rail and was alone for a minute, with the priests at the other end of the line. Your Dad <u>smiled</u> (I will never forget that smile). He said 'I kept my cap on so that you would know me!' I said again, 'Are you all right, Jack?' He said 'Yes, Watson, we never did have that talk did we? I know a lot of things now I never have before... I am sorry about many things... Here is your Communion coming.'

"At that point the Rector popped the wafer on my tongue and moved on. There was a gap for a moment but the image of your Dad was fading. I called out (but silently I think) 'Pray for us both, Jack.' He smiled again, and although he was going the smile was so overwhelming in its warmth and reality. Then the African priest put the chalice to my lips and when he went, your Dad had gone also. I knelt on, trembling quite violently, so that Fr. Jonathan came back and touched me on the shoulder, and then it was all over.

"On soul and conscience, this is what happened at about 11.30am on Sunday March 26th."

This stunning report was like a light flooding into the heavy darkness of my grief. The bond between Dad and me was very strong, and when the components of that bond broke, it caused me intense pain on all levels of my being.

Watson was also stunned by his experience, and we mulled it over together, wondering and puzzling. I felt that Dad would come again to Watson, and he did, five times over a period of several weeks. The second appearance was as powerful as the first, and poor Watson was almost floored by it. He was unwell himself, and though we did not know at the time, did not have long to live. The subsequent appearances were less strong, and Dad was not so clearly materialised. I imagine that it became more difficult for him as his spirit body changed form and vibration. Through these wonderful communications he conveyed his love and continuing concern for me, and reassured me that he was well and safe. What a gift this was to me! My only sorrow was that for some reason he did not seem able to appear to me in person. However, as time went on, he found other ways of getting through to me.

I went to various spiritualist meetings, mediums and séances, all the time looking for Dad, but there was nothing really satisfying, just the occasional unconvincing message, and sometimes messages from other spirit people. I accepted these with an open mind, prepared to believe that they may be authentic, but I was not particularly convinced. One séance with a well-known medium was dramatic and evidential for certain of the participants, and although I received a message from the medium's sister to convey to their mother (with whom I was staying overnight) for which I felt quite honoured, there was still no contact with Dad. In a personal trance session with the medium the following day I asked if I could contact him, but was told that it would only happen when I was ready. I was disappointed, somewhat frustrated, and wondered what this meant. I felt that surely I was ready; I had been searching for Dad since he died.

A breakthrough came for me when I obtained an invitation to the home circle of another medium living in the Midlands. I was really hopeful and excited by the prospect of going there, but my journey to the house where the circle was held turned out to be one of those nightmares that one hopes will never happen. It was during a time of heavy flooding, which was especially bad around York, the principal station to which I had to go. Chaos abounded, trains were cancelled, stations were packed with people milling uncertainly about looking for their trains, and no one seemed to know what was happening. I began to get anxious about whether I would arrive in time for the séance. Eventually I managed to get a train to York, but it was very late, and the suburban train to my destination was even later, travelling at snail's pace and stopping at endless stations. I was panicking by now, and was trying to phone the circle leader on my mobile phone, which true to form, ran out of battery charge before I could explain what was happening and where I was.

By the time I reached the right station I was frantic, and

raced to a pay phone to call Ron, the circle leader. Predictably it didn't work, and I had to rush round and find another. It must have been through unseen assistance that I finally got through to Ron, and he said he would come to pick me up in his taxi. I waited anxiously in the cold, and when he appeared I burst into tears. The dear man was unflappable, and loaded me into the taxi, saying that they were all waiting for me. So I arrived at the séance in a dishevelled and tearful heap, to be received with great kindness and gentle humour. After a quick briefing, we went up to the séance room and settled down. I was quite nervous at first, never having been to this type of physical séance in pitch darkness, but I was sitting next to the solid presence of Ron, who held my hand most of the time when he was not managing other aspects of the procedure, so my fear quickly abated.

The séance began with a prayer, and we sang familiar folk songs as the medium fell into a trance. He was fastened securely into his chair, and there were a few thumps and bumps as the spirit guides took over his body. As we sang, the voice of his principal guide came through, welcoming us, and was followed by a child guide who cracked jokes and spoke to each participant, putting us all at our ease. I was enthralled, completely captivated by the atmosphere and the sense of the interface of two worlds. While my rational mind was still monitoring events and assessing them for authenticity, there was another, heart-entrancing state of being, which completely absorbed my concentration.

More detailed accounts of such séances can be found on reputable websites such as Zerdin Phenomenal, so I will only focus on the events that particularly affected me personally. Another spirit guide then came through and gave us all a welcome, chatting to each person in turn. He said they had been aware that I had had a terrible journey and had been doing all they could to help me get here. I was touched by this kindly recognition of my discomfiting journey, and was curious to know how they could have known about it. There was some more general talk and information about the nature and purpose of the séance, and how it was as important to the spirit people to prove survival after death as it was to us to be convinced of it.

Then there followed a spectacular display of moving 'trumpets' (large solid cones with phosphorescent rims) and a demonstration of matter passing through matter, as the entranced medium's arm, which was fastened to his chair with strong plastic ties, was lifted high into the air while one of the participants was holding his hand. The most astonishing event for me was the manifestation of an ectoplasmic hand – the hand of one of the guides that used energy from the medium's body to form a living human hand. Participants were invited to hold the hand, and each one exclaimed as to its warm, fleshy feel with nails and veins – a 'real human hand' as someone said. I didn't get a turn to experience this during this particular séance, but on subsequent visits I was one of the lucky ones, and can testify to the incredibly moving reality of the experience – holding the hand of someone who had been dead for nigh on one hundred years. It is something that I will never forget, and is a marker in my mind and soul that spurs me on, knowing that one day I will be on that side of life, not dead, but still a living, conscious entity, still able to communicate with others, to love and to serve.

After the excitement of this part of the séance, a lady communicator come through whose main job was to help loved ones who were waiting on the other side to communicate with participants. Of course I was so longing and hoping that Dad would come. There were several communications, all very moving to those who received them, but none for me. I could not help but be disappointed, although I was glad for those who had received a much-needed contact.

The séance drew to a close, and I resigned myself to having to wait and search longer for my Dad, but just as we were leaving the room, one person, who was part of the medium's home circle, asked me to stay behind. Intrigued, I did so, and was asked to sit by the medium and hold his hand. He fell into a trance again and the lady communicator came through and talked to me for a while. She said that she had someone with her who desperately wanted to contact me. My heart leaped! Could it be Dad? I hardly dared to hope. The lady went on to tell me about her visitor, saying his name was John (that was Dad's name, although he was always called Jack) and that he had not been long on the other side. She said he was jumping up and down, showing her that his legs were working. My eyes filled with tears, as poor Dad had lost the use of his legs at the end of his life and was unable to move from his bed, which must have been so dreadful and fearful for such an active, independent person as he had been. She said he was desperate to speak to me, and with that she let him come through and take over the medium. I have never in my life had such an incredibly profound and deeply precious experience as in that moment.

Suddenly the medium's hand became Dad's hand, and I could feel him there holding my hand using the medium and speaking to me using the medium's body. It was his voice, coming through the medium's voice box, and I recognised him instantly. He was so excited that he could hardly talk, but he reminded me of the little wooden ornament that I had given him to have in his room when he was confined to bed – just before he had to go into hospital for the last time – and that this had been a special exchange between us. I asked him how he was and he said he was very well, and I was glad. He said he was with me, all the time. There was only enough time and energy for a few words, but they were some of the most precious words I would ever hear. When the medium came round – quite bemused and not knowing if anything had happened for me – I kissed him and thanked him with enormous gratitude.

I have been to several séances with that same medium and home circle since, and each one has been as magical and as special as the first, giving me increasing confidence that my beloved Dad, and therefore all my loved ones, are alive and well in another dimension. I can never thank that dear man and his devoted circle enough, or the spirit people who work with them, for making this wonderful experience of life and so-called death possible for me.

My fascination with séances and other means of contacting beings in other realms continues, but I have never found it to be in any way an escape from the ongoing work and processes of everyday life. Although it is an awareness of another dimension to life, and quite often a resource of strength, guidance, help and inspiration for the multitude of circumstances and situations that flow from moment to moment as I pursue the earthly pathway, there always remains the necessity to be fully responsible for one's thoughts, decisions and actions in the present. It is all too easy to be deceived, or to deceive oneself, as to the validity of one's perceptions and intuitions. A balance between logic and reasoning on the one hand and intuition and sensations on the other is a delicate one, which is not simple to maintain.

Although the séances brought me great comfort and hope concerning my Dad and my continuing relationship with him, they did not solve the wounding and problems of the past. The work of forgiveness continues as it manifests in everyday life situations, and the solidification of emotional and psychic damage into the social constructs of my life, the habitual thought patterns of my mind, and the physical structure of my body all still have to be addressed. This, to my way of thinking, is a work of life that gathers up the past into the present moment, and out of it creates the future. Since we live in an experience of the passage of time, we have to work within that, however aware we may be of differing time bands, or of the reality of timeless eternity.

*   *   *   *   *

Watson, my dear friend and companion, passed away on Christmas Eve, 1998. When I first met him he had been seriously ill with heart disease, and without an operation had not been given long to live. He had refused the operation, a triple bypass, as he said that he did not particularly want to live longer than necessary. Two years before he met me, had had lost his partner to cancer, and, I think, had never found a deep love in his heart since. When I met him, I felt that he had a great deal of sorrow locked inside, of which perhaps even he himself was not aware. One of the first things he asked me was if I would be with him when he died. Though I could not guarantee that time would bring us together at that point, I said that I would be there if I possibly could. We did not have an easy ride in our relationship, and it was beset by much strife and difficulty, but it was one of the closest and most profound relationships that I have had with a man. So much happened, and we shared so deeply in the short time that we had together, it is almost as if we knew we had to work fast. Soon after we met, Watson decided to have the bypass operation, and this was something like a preparation, as we did not know if he would come through it successfully. He did, and it gave us a few more years to build the deep love and respect that still endures.

Watson did not live a particularly healthy life-style – being a smoker, and succumbing at times to excesses of alcohol. I knew that it was a manifestation of his pain, and that it was shortening his life, but I was not able to help him to overcome these tendencies. Maybe I felt it was not my place to even try, but simply to accompany him through them. It would have been very difficult to dig deep enough to reach the emotional roots of these addictions, and just as difficult to deal with the physical aspects of them. His health therefore deteriorated steadily over the time that I knew him, although we were able to enjoy many pleasures and outings together in spite of that. When he received a diagnosis of cancer, we knew that death was approaching.

There had been several portents, mostly in the form of his vivid dreams, but the one that stands out in my mind was an encounter with a crow on one of our walks. We noticed the bird sitting low in a bush at the side of the lane where we were walking. Not wanting to disturb it, we walked quietly, thinking that it would fly away as we approached, as we would have to pass close by. However, it remained stationary on its perch, the black form perfectly still and the beady eyes glimmering. I wondered if it was ill, but it did not look damaged in any way. It stared at us as we stopped to look at it, and we were a little unnerved, knowing something of the folklore of visits from crows. As we passed it remained – a brooding black image that filled out minds with trepidation. I do believe that bird came as a messenger, but at that time Watson did not want to believe he was dying, although he knew that he was. He found it very difficult to think or talk about death, and had not talked about it with his partner when she had been dying, but with the help of his dreams I managed to get Watson to talk and share with me about death and dying. He said that his main fear was of leaving me, the one love left in his life. It is difficult to reassure someone that love will go on after death and beyond, for whatever we believe about it, unless one has had experiences of the next world in meditation, or near-death or out-of-body experiences, it is still a great unknown. I expect that I shall long for reassurance when my time to die comes around, even though I have talked about, investigated, and diced with death all my life.

I have written of Watson's passing into the next life in an earlier chapter, so will not dwell on that aspect here. After he had gone, I did have one or two sensations of his presence, but not in the same powerful way as I had with Dad. Watson communicated more through thought, as that was very much the medium of our friendship when we were together. I had arranged his funeral to be held at the church that he attended regularly – where he first saw my father's apparition. It was a small, private gathering with just a few of his friends and one or two of mine who had known him. It was a very cold day in January. The church was freezing, and though I had endeavoured to bring a touch of light and beauty to the occasion with several arrangements of flowers, a heavy sadness hung over the service as it proceeded. It came time for me to offer a short obituary for Watson, in which I made a brief reference to his intellectual accomplishments and his love of words, and then recited one of our favourite poems – 'Crossing the Bar' by Alfred Lord Tennyson.

Crossing the Bar

Sunset and evening star,
And one clear call for me,
And may there be no moaning of the bar,
When I put out to sea.

But such a tide as moving seems asleep,
Too full for sound and foam,
When that which drew from out the boundless deep,
Turns again home.

Twilight and evening bell,
And after that the dark:
And may there be no sadness of farewell,
When I embark;

For tho' from out our bourne of Time and Place
The flood may bear me far,
I hope to see my Pilot face to face,
When I have crossed the bar.

How beautiful I find this poem! As I spoke it with deep feeling, lightness filled the church and I felt Watson's presence, as if something had been lifted from him, as if he was free to move on. I buried his ashes in the woodland where I bury all my beloved cats that pass on, and those belonging to my friends, and any strays that need a decent burial. During the time of our friendship Watson had become an animal lover, especially of my cats, and I felt it was fitting that he should share the same beautiful resting place.

I had one or two strong impressions of his presence when I was clearing up his flat. Once when I was looking for his will documents, I felt him guiding me to them. Another time was when I was clearing up a lot of unpleasant mess that had come about on the last day of his life, when I found him in difficulty. I heard him saying almost in horror, 'Jackie you shouldn't be doing this' as I scrubbed away with the bleach and disinfectant. 'It's got to be done, Watson' I replied in my thoughts, 'and anyway I am used to clearing up after cats!' I felt this satisfied and somewhat amused him.

Other meetings have been less tangible, but have still left an impression on me of his presence, and his continuing love and care for me. One time I was going to an open séance at a well-known college of parapsychology in Edinburgh, and being a bit early, looked though various leaflets and pamphlets while I waited. There was one with a large red rose on the front that struck me, inviting a donation in remembrance of loved ones who had passed away. I picked it up, but feeling that I did not have much money to spare at the time, put it back again. I decided to walk around the streets for a bit of exercise before the séance began, and on my way back, I was amazed and taken aback to see a large red rose, exactly like the one on the leaflet, lying on the pavement right in my path. It was in perfect condition and did not have a long stem – as it might have done if it had been in someone's bouquet. As I bent to pick it up, I heard the following words very distinctly in my head, 'That's from all of us', and I recognised Watson's thoughts. He was referring to Dad, Mum and himself, as by this time Mum had also passed away.

I remembered that when he was still alive and we were discussing his funeral, he had said no flowers, but had suggested that perhaps I could leave just a single red rose for him. I had not kept to this arrangement, and had bought as many flowers as I could afford – to leave for the church afterwards, in memory of him. I had made a special basket of white roses, with red ones in the middle in the shape of a heart, with a little note that said 'to my heart husband'.

Coincidence? Well, everyone needs to make up their own mind about such things. I know what *I* think. I did not get any contact via the séance, but the red rose was deeply meaningful and significant to me.

*   *   *   *   *

After my father died, we all wondered how my mother would cope with life without him. They had been together for so long, and had even celebrated their diamond wedding anniversary. She had always appeared to be the dependent one, letting him make the decisions and run the finances, and mostly deferring to his wishes. However, underneath, a current of strength and determination sustained her, and she gave Dad her unstinting support and love throughout his dying process, in the face of very little warmth and affection in return from him. I think he was grateful to her, but could not show it in a way that would have given her the comfort that she craved. She was eighty-six years old when he died – at the age of ninety. Her sight and hearing were failing and her body was infirm, and this was certainly not the best time of life to create a new direction for herself. She soldiered on remarkably, through loneliness and failing health, retaining her mental ability, and her essential loving generous spirit shining through.

It was a sad journey for all of us – my brother, my sister and myself, and many others who loved her – to see her change gradually from being the caring, trusting person who always looked for the best in others, to being preoccupied with herself and negative in her outlook. No one could blame her for this, but it was hard to watch it happening. My personal feeling about it is that she had repressed so much resentment and anger towards Dad because of the way he had treated her, always hoping perhaps for the signs of his love that she longed for, that when he had gone, the lid was lifted from this and she was compelled to face it. She wrestled for long years with her confusion and regret.

It was almost as if she took on his negative attitude to life and people in general. She also struggled with her Christian faith, and found that her belief system did not sustain her in the darkness of her grief and unhappiness. This did not surprise or shock me at all, having been through much the same myself in the darkness of my own despair, but I found it very difficult to channel to her some of the sustaining light and grace that has so generously come to me in my hours of need.

My mother's name was Grace, and she was well-named, I believe, because in spite of everything she had to contend with along her seven-year lonely road to death's doorway, she still remained the Mum that we all loved, still retained a spark to enliven her old, worn out body. My sister looked after her in the family home, my brother and his wife visited her regularly, and I did my best from the other end of the country with phone calls, letters in huge writing so she could read them, gifts, prayers and visits whenever I could.

I always felt so guilty about leaving her and going back to my home in Scotland, but I doubt if I could have helped her any more by being there is person. She came to stay with me a couple of times on her own while she was still able to travel, which was very courageous of her. I was glad of the time with her by myself, as we had not shared this for many years and I had felt constrained in my relationship with her by my sister's presence. Understandably she was protective of Mum, and since she had to cope with the brunt of Mum's practical day-to-day needs, I did not want to upset the *status quo*. It was all so very different from long ago, as now I had to be Mum's carer, her supporter and her guide. I felt her loneliness, sorrow and confusion of feelings towards Dad so intimately, just as I had done as a child, taking it all into myself, but this time I had a buffer, that strong self, forged in the darkness of my anorexia and the many personal and spiritual connections that I had built up. I give heartfelt thanks that I was able to support my dear

Mum in this way, and bear some of her burden to the hour of her departure.

Towards the end of her life she was in and out of hospital quite a lot, needing more care and attention than could be given to her at home. Hospital was not a happy place for her and she hated being there, but on the other hand when she was at home she was constantly fearful and panicky about her failing body, and was always wanting the doctor to come or the ambulance to be called. I can understand only too well what she must have gone through – that immediate terror when one's body lets one down, and the urgent need and desire for help. Unlike Dad, who for his last spell in hospital had had a pleasant private room to himself and good nursing, Mum had to endure the trials of a geriatric ward where many old and ailing women were living out their last days. Amazingly, she seemed to retain a residue of kindness and interest towards these unsolicited companions, for which I greatly admire her.

Often when I went to see her, she said to me privately, 'Pray I will die, dear.' I think she knew she could say that to me, without upsetting me too much. I did pray endlessly for her, in an agony of longing so much to make things better for her, whether that be by life or by death.

The last time I saw her was in hospital. I had tried to make her comfortable, but could not, as she was too heavy for me to lift, and I had to ask a nurse to come to her. The staff sent me away and I felt my heart was being torn out, seeing my poor Mum so unhappy and me having to leave. I think that she had waited for me to come for this visit, to say goodbye to me perhaps – though she may not have consciously known it – for it was not long after this that my sister phoned to say that Mum had died. It was somewhat unexpected for most of those around her, but in my heart I had known that I had seen her for the last time.

She had been very depressed, and in some kind of peculiar attempt to 'treat' this, a psychiatrist had given her an antidepressant. Personally I think that this was the final assault on her body – yet more toxins added to the cocktail of drugs that she was already taking. But maybe she had wanted that medication, as something to clutch on to. I will never forget her in her bed at home, holding out her hand and saying 'Pill, pill', when she wanted her daily dose of whatever the medics had prescribed for her to try to alleviate her distress.

Thankfully those sad memories and many others were lifted from me when she died, for I knew without doubt that Mum's essential kind heart and desire for spirituality would carry her over to a realm where she would at last be happy and find peace. I did not feel her around in the same way as Dad, and I regarded that as a good thing really, knowing that she was safe in the care of her loved ones on the other side.

I did have one or two messages via mediums shortly after she had died, none of which was particularly striking, but were enough for me to feel that she was okay. However, there was one experience that was especially meaningful to me. Quite some time before she became very infirm, I had bought myself a little gold pendant as a kind of promise to myself – a commitment to my own journey and development. Although it was not of any great financial value, I valued it for what it represented to me.

One day, it fell off its chain yet again, after my clumsy attempts at removing it from my neck to go to bed, and the little pendant disappeared. It is amazing to me how something can fall and vanish from sight in an instant, becoming impossible to find. I have had this happen numerous times before, and also being wont to mislay other items, had cultivated the habit of 'asking Grandpa'. This was something I had learned from Mum. I never knew my Grandpa Bickerton, my Mum's father, as he had died before I was born, but she had told me stories about him, about what a kind and loving man he was, although not the best at business and money-making. I had learned that the family home was frequently untidy, being small premises with six children, and when tidiness was an immediate necessity – for example if a visitor was expected – Grandpa would say 'shove it in there', thus clearing the decks, but filling cupboards and other receptacles with unwanted junk. This resulted in things frequently being mislaid, but Grandpa was very adept at finding them. When he passed away, Mum continued to ask him to help her to find things, and kept in touch with him through this means.

I have always hated losing anything, even the smallest triviality, as this makes me feel quite panicky and out of control. Consequently, quite early in my life, Mum suggested to me to 'ask Grandpa'. I tried out her suggestion, and as time went on I built up an increasingly strong connection with him. This then is the background to the saga of the lost pendant.

I had lost it at least a year before Mum died, and had given up hope of ever finding it again. I thought that, although I had searched high and low several times, probably I had vacuumed it up in one of my obligatory cleaning sessions. Not long after Mum died, maybe about three days, I was finishing my dressing routine by putting on some jewellery, and I took out the chain that used to hold the pendant, for which I had by then substituted a tiny dolphin. As I opened a drawer to get my make-up, something fell out and landed in the drawer itself. At the same moment I felt a rush of presences – two of them, unmistakeably Mum and Grandpa – and to my utter amazement, there was my pendant in the drawer! I could not believe my eyes! I was full of joy and gratitude. The words 'we found it for you' came strongly into my mind, with a sort of smile attached, as if they had really enjoyed the finding. I needed no further proof of my dear Mum's continuing existence and recovery on the other side, but even so I have been blessed with a growing sense of her light and beautiful presence. Her visits are not as dramatic as Dad's, but are just as real, just as infinitely precious. I shall come back to Mum later in this narrative.

Dear Grandpa has found so many things for me that I could not count the number and variety of the findings. Each one draws me closer to him and strengthens our connection, and the sense of his presence becomes increasingly tangible. I am very touched by how sensitive and compassionate he is. Even when I have absent-mindedly put something down and then can't see where I have put it – which throws me into a frenzy – or lost something really insignificant, like an earring stud fastener for example, he will still apply his skill and find it, if it is findable. I have had earring studs turn up in the most unexpected and seemingly impossible places. How on earth did it get there? I ask myself with a grin in Grandpa's direction. He will often find things at my request for other people, too, if he can, particularly if he has some sort of connection with the person.

An amusing incident of this kind occurred when I was on holiday with my sister at Findhorn Holiday Park. We had rented a caravan for a week, and were just settling into the somewhat cramped quarters. She had brought with her a vial of Nux Vomica, a homeopathic remedy, which she relied upon for help with constipation and irregular bowels. This little tube was quite an important item of her equipment, and she was distressed when she could not find it amongst her toiletries. She felt sure that she had packed it. We searched through her case and the shelves where she had put her clothes, handbag, bathroom bag and so on, but the Nux Vomica was nowhere to be seen. I told her not to worry, and that we would go and get some more early the next day. She seemed to remain a bit perturbed, so I asked Grandpa if he could help her to find it, if indeed she had packed it. I went back to my little caravan room and continued sorting out my own things, and it was not long before I heard a cry from my sister. 'What's the matter?' I asked, hastening through to her room. She pointed to the Nux Vomica, which was sitting right in the middle of her bed. 'It wasn't there a moment ago,' she said in amazement. I had to laugh as I thanked Grandpa for yet another of his little miracles. How he had done that one I cannot begin to guess, but he was certainly getting really proficient at moving things around.

* * * * *

A recent opportunity to be part of a transition into the next life was offered to me when my brother's wife, Nancy, began her approach to the doorway of death. I had not been especially close to Nancy in latter years, as living so far apart meant that it was difficult to keep in touch, and she and my brother were well occupied with their own family and friends. Nevertheless I had retained a regard for Nancy, and a fondness based on memories of my childhood when she was kind to me, and she and Chris used to take me out on trips with their boys, my nephews. Of late she did have something of a habit of 'putting her foot in it', but for me that was a tolerable, if occasionally irritating, inconvenience, which could easily be side-stepped. The last couple of years of her life were dominated by a series of visits to doctors and hospitals, and like Mum, by a cocktail of drugs which seemed to do little to remedy her ailments. I felt in my heart that she was approaching the end of her life, although no one discussed it, so I kept her in my thoughts and prayers as best I could. I felt concerned for my brother, too, as like Mum and Dad, he and Nancy had been together for many years, and they were now well past their golden wedding anniversary.

As time went on, I heard via my sister that Nancy had been taken into hospital yet again and was not expected to live much longer. It was just a matter of time before her body would give up life and relinquish her spirit. I was amazed and concerned that still no one had spoken of this to Nancy, to help her to prepare for her transition, and to make good her relationships with her loved ones. Surely she would want to know that she was dying, I thought.

There seems to be an embarrassment and subterfuge surrounding death in our culture, as if somehow it should not happen. This is nothing short of insanity, since death is the one certainty in life which we all share. I decided to set up a little place for her in my house – like Mum used to do with her favourite stones, choosing a particular stone for each person she prayed for. I used a Tibetan medallion and stuck Nancy's name on it. One evening while I was praying for her, I had a vision –

something which I had not had for a long time. It was clear and strong, just like the ones I used to have, and of a quality completely different from imagination or visualisation. It could perhaps be likened to taking part in a real film inside my head. I saw some spirit doctors come down to Nancy in her bed. Then they said that they would like to do an operation. The go-ahead seemed to be given, and they very carefully removed her old, diseased heart, cutting a cord at each of its four sections. Then I was asked to take this old heart and lift it up into the spirit world. This I did, and as it disappeared, a new, brightly shining heart was given to me. I was told to lower it very carefully into Nancy's body where the old heart had been, and then the spirit doctors sewed it in place, reconnecting the cords with the tiniest threads of light. I was puzzled and asked a question. They said that they had given her a new heart for her journey ahead and that it would help her when she entered the spirit world. Then the vision faded. I did not know what to make of this, and later wondered if I had just imagined it all or made it up. I thought it best to keep it to myself and not tell anyone about it.

A few days later, I woke in the middle of the night with a vivid dream about Nancy. I had very painful indigestion. I sat up and wrote down immediately all that I could remember of the dream. Not all the details were clear in my mind, but the most striking element of it was that Nancy and I were together, going into a café. She looked beautifully tall, slim and young – just how she used to be, although she looked waxy pale in colour – and was wearing a lovely close-fitting silky golden dress over another more ordinary sort of garment. I noticed the very slim curve of her stomach, and this was somehow emotionally significant, for Nancy, once so slim and graceful of figure, had become bloated around her middle, and her feet and ankles were swollen and distorted. This must have been so poignantly painful for her, on top of all her other suffering. In the dream she confided to me that she had felt much better in the last few months, but was concerned that she had not thanked Chris enough for looking after her and wanted to take him on holiday.

317

Having recorded my dream as best I could, I turned my attention to the pain of my indigestion. It was much worse than usual, and I stayed sitting up, wondering what was causing it. As my mind wandered back over the dream, I wondered if I had been wakened to pray for Nancy, and as soon as this thought came to me, I felt sure that she was with me in my bedroom. I concentrated on her and asked if I could help. She seemed to convey that she was anxious about dying, so I said to her in my thoughts, 'It's going to be okay, someone will come for you, and then you just hold out your hands to them and go with them into the Light. Then you go and say goodbye to Chris, and your helper will look after you.' After a while, a sense of peace descended into the room. The pain left me, and I fell asleep sitting up. When I woke and reread the dream and remembered the experience, once again I was tempted to discount it, but I left it there in my heart, just in case.

A few days later, I was practising Reiki healing with a friend, who happened to be quite psychically sensitive, and who was also training in mediumship. About noon, as we were finishing the session, she said suddenly 'There's someone here!' As she drew my attention, I, too, felt a strong sense of presence, and there was a gentle 'wind' that signalled a visitor from the other side. Seconds later, I knew it was Mum, and my friend said, 'It's Grace.' Mum was full of love – just like I used to know her, only happier and lighter – and she stayed with us a while, giving me her message of 'Love you, darling' and communicating how she loved coming to Reiki healing. Then she let us know that Nancy was in the Light and was with her. A few minutes later the phone rang, and my sister gave me the news that Nancy had just passed away into the next world. It was clear to me that Mum had come for her, and I could not have been more overcome with awe and reverence for the process in which I had been privileged to partake.

* * * * *

I have always felt it to be a great privilege to be involved with death. I have been fortunate, I think, that all the deaths that I have witnessed, or in which I have participated, have been ones of compassion – as with animals given euthanasia to relieve them of suffering, or of a natural dying process, and of the ritual of funerals. I have not had to take on the weight of witnessing murder, holocausts, wars, disasters and other such traumatic ending of life. I am not sure how I would cope with that, but I pray that if it does happen, I will find the strength somehow to call down Light into the situation and for all those involved. When my own death comes, I want more than anything to be well prepared and ready to leave, and pray that those shining ones who have been with me all my life will carry me through to a new life on the other side. The preparation is always now, in every moment, for in a sense all life is a preparation for death. This should not be seen as a gloomy or foreboding injunction, but rather more as an ever present opportunity to create oneself anew.

Death's Mercy

Come death, gentle friend,
Bid the suffering creature that the end
Of agony is nigh.
Tormentor's hand and cruel pain
Have no more power to terrify.
Returning by diverse means unto the Earth
Whose substance gave you form and birth,
Let the light depart your eye,
And rest in ageless mystery.

Each beauteous form
Rising from the ocean of Life
Fulfils its span of years.
Descending again, yields itself
To the embrace of the ever loving Spirit,
In whose awareness is treasured
The Divine patterns of creation,
Each one unique unto itself.

So, gruelling pain, you cannot gain
The power to destroy,
For hidden in destroyer's art
And spectre death of this a part,
Is Life's creative joy.

Jacqueline Kemp
For all creatures

Owls

She called,
A pure note sounding
Across the falling eve.
A little silence, waiting, listening,
Watching for wings
Flitting through the trees.

He answered,
A silent shadow gliding
Through the sombre dark
To the branch where she sat,
In stillness, biding.

Their encounter,
These two creatures of the earth,
Astounding in their beauty
And magnificent design,
As time rolled onward,
Was forever a new birth.

Jacqueline Kemp

Chapter Eleven

My own home

A number of differing threads of experience began to take shape as I lived my life in my own home. On the surface, these threads may appear disparate, but on the deeper levels of my personality, each one represents an area of growth and development. Blended together in the overall story which I tell of myself, they form a significant part of my work of transforming anorexia nervosa.

* * * * *

My mother's death ushered in a new era of my life. This did not take form straight away, as there were plenty of the usual formalities and arrangements to deal with that are an essential part of saying goodbye to someone and taking care of their affairs. In addition, the emotional loss of my mother took longer to work its way through my being than with that of Dad. There was much less shock involved when she passed away, as in a sense it was a completion of the long grieving process that she had been through. In fact it was something of a relief for those of us who loved her that she was at last freed from suffering and could enter into peace. Yet we all missed her greatly, in our different ways. When she was alive, she was still my Mum, the person who had brought me into this world and had given me form and substance, but at the moment she died, I felt myself to be on my own with no parent to turn to. This was more a kind of rite of passage I suppose, and it is difficult to explain the deeper effect that losing her had upon me. It wasn't really a sudden loss, for I had not been able to look to her for help for many years, but it was the feeling that I was in her mind and heart that had created a particular sense of security for me. I know now that this has not changed, and that I am in her mind and heart more than ever, now that she does not have a sick body to impair her functioning, but it has taken me a long time to re-establish that awareness of her care for me, and I still have a longing from time to time for her physical presence.

The matter of her will brought a certain amount of discomfort and tension into the immediate family – my brother and his wife, my sister and myself. I will not elaborate on this out of respect for my departed mother and my siblings, but suffice it to say that we managed to come to an agreement whereby my sister remained in the family home, and my brother and I received our share of the value of the total estate. This took a long time, as the mechanisms of solicitors, executors, banks and the like seem to move very slowly. However, it did mean that at last I had a real hope of moving from my council flat in Hapton into a place that I could call my own home. I had lived for such a long time with the despair of not being able to find a way to escape from that soul-destroying environment that I actually found myself afraid of leaving it. I had learned to cope, after a fashion, and the unknown postured itself before me, offering all sorts of fears and anxieties.

Once my share of the inheritance became available, I set about looking for a new place to live. This turned out to be a task of considerable complexity. Firstly, I did not have very much money to spend, and at my age, and with only benefits and pensions as my income, I was not at all confident of being able to get a small mortgage to augment that sum. Secondly, I was very uncertain of being able to cope with owning my own home, so I needed it to be in a location where I could keep in touch with existing friends and helpers. Fortunately I managed to contact a friendly and helpful solicitor, who gave me good advice and listened patiently to my stream of worries.

After I had made a viewing appointment for the first property, and had gone to see it, I felt that I had taken the plunge and maybe the process wasn't going to be so bad after all. But this was only the start, and after eighteen months of many frustrations and disappointments, I still had not found a suitable property that I could afford. I had found several that I had liked well enough, but the way of the property market at that time meant that the highest offer always took precedence, and my offers were never high enough to secure the purchase. I had so many raised hopes and so many despairs during this period of searching! Along the way, the solicitor who had been helping me sold her business to someone else and moved away from the area, and her replacement proved to be of peremptory and demeaning manner. I felt that I could not continue to do business with such a person, but did not know whom else I could trust.

Yet soon I was extremely lucky to meet a family of husband and wife who were both solicitors, and their two children, one of whom I taught piano for a short while. They very kindly took on the legal side of my quest for a new home, and were endlessly helpful and generous to me throughout the whole process. What a relief this was for me! Looking back I can see that it was yet another grace flowing into my life, just when I needed it so badly, and that through these dear people, the universal source connected up with me. Amazingly, though this has happened time and time again throughout my life, I still find it extremely difficult to have confidence that I can reach out and be met in this way. I am a very slow learner in this respect! Those wonderful life-lines have been cast out to me in umpteen ways throughout my life, some small and barely noticeable to the external observer, others more dramatic and visible and many on the continuum in between.

The search for my new home was about far more than just buying a house. Uppermost in my mind was the urgent desire to escape the punishing environment of Hapton, which had been my lot for so long, and to find a place where I could continue my journey in happier circumstances. Underneath ran the issue of territory, which has always been a matter of primary concern for me as a sufferer of anorexia nervosa. A sense of 'my space' is so crucial to my personal survival that when it is invaded, or taken away, my whole personality goes into a hyper-defensive mode. This can take a variety of forms, the most dangerous one being obsessive body control and compulsive dieting. Other common manifestations for me are obsessive anxiety, intrusive and obsessive thought patterns, panic attacks, withdrawal and hostility. I am sure that there are others!

I can trace the origins of this back to when I was growing up and had no physical or personal space to myself, and where my personality and psyche were invaded by many differing demands and forces. I think that it is also a natural condition of having an introverted personality with an extremely sensitive and reactive constitution. However much I recognise the roots of my extremely territorial nature, it is not something that I have been able to change very much over the years. It is more something that I have had to accept and live with. At certain times in my life, for example when I joined the Community of Transformation, I have had to relinquish my physical and personal territory almost completely, in order to be part of a situation that would help me survive the ravages of anorexia nervosa. This did not mean that I ever gave up my wish or my need for my own space, or that I ever capitulated into conceding that it was not the right thing to want or have. I simply had to set it aside in order to stay alive, and I am sure that I am by no means alone in this. It is amazing what we will do to stay alive, when the chips are down.

This, then, was a major driving force beneath the surface as I searched for a new home. With the little that I had to spend on a dwelling place, it was so difficult to find anything that had a note of accord for me, a sense of 'I could live here and make a go of it'. As each effort to secure a purchase fell through, I became more and more despondent, and a feeling of desperation began to take hold of me. I am not sure how I would have got through this taxing episode of my life if it had not been for my kind-hearted and encouraging solicitor friends. Just going to their house and pouring out my woes and anxieties helped me to continue to pursue my intent.

* * * * *

After more than eighteen months of fruitless attempts on the property market, almost by accident I came across a rather unprepossessing semi-detached ex-council house on a mixed council estate, where over some years, a certain proportion of the houses had been bought privately. I really wanted to get away from council estates, having had such a bad experience in the one where I was living. Although not all estates are the same, and not all people who live on them are troublesome and dangerous by any means, I had accumulated a kind of abhorrence of the very idea of living on another council estate.

However I had not had any luck elsewhere, and this little house did not look too bad. It had everything that I wanted – enough space to organise my possessions, a garage (so that I would no longer have the fear of my car being vandalised on the street) and its own garden to the back and front. I made an appointment to view it, and as soon as I walked in, I knew that I could live there. I don't know how I knew this – maybe it was the welcoming and understanding attitude of the sellers, the pictures of fairies and statues of Buddha in strategic places, the open sky and view of the Forth Bridge from the windows, the attractive gardens and the small pool in the back garden. There was just a sense of goodness about the house. All the rooms felt okay and there were no 'spooky spots' which might harbour unwanted energies. These favourable points outweighed other matters about which I felt dubious – the adjoining neighbour's garden looked like a scrap yard full of old bangers, junk and weeds, and there was an unattractive shopping area just a few minutes down the road. I talked to the sellers at length, and to my amazement they told me to make an offer near to what they were asking and they would accept it. I think that they may have wanted to get out quickly, but for me at this juncture it was a godsend for which I was extremely grateful. After I had contacted my solicitors and the offer had been made, I waited anxiously to see if it was accepted, hardly able to believe that it would come to pass. When I received a phone call to say the offer had gone through, I was thrilled to bits. I had bought a house!

After this momentous event, the actual transaction and moving process took some time. The solicitors of the sellers and my own solicitors did not see eye to eye as to how the negotiations should take place, and there seemed to be endless hold-ups over paperwork, deeds, dates, money and so on. I had managed to arrange a small mortgage to cover the extra amount I needed to buy the house, but this, too, involved lengthy paperwork.

I entered a kind of limbo time. I knew that I had a new home, but I could not seem to make it a reality in my emotional experience, fearing that perhaps after all something would go wrong and the whole venture would fall through. As a result, I did very little about dismantling my existing home and packing up, or organising removals. I regretted this later.

At long last the phone rang and my solicitor, who by now had become a good friend, was on the phone, telling me that she had the keys. The moment I had been waiting for had arrived – the house was mine at last. When I picked up the keys, it seemed to me as if they represented a magical pass to a new life – but of course I had reckoned without my own nature, which I had to take with me!

The first trip to my new home was quite a scary experience for me. On the one hand I was relieved and delighted, but on the other I felt alone and frightened in a new environment. However, I made myself go, and was glad to make contact with my neighbour on the other side, who was a kindly old widower, pleased, I think, to have a quiet single lady as his new neighbour, and not a young family with rumbustious children!

As I acquainted myself with the house, I found that the

previous owner had left me a fairy ornament. I picked it up, and felt a rush of gratitude, and confirmation that somehow and by some means I would make a success of owning my own home. This may seem a simple matter to some, or even to most, people, but for me it was deeply symbolic of taking responsibility for my own life, my own body and my anorexic journey. This has never been a once and for all matter for me, for although the intent has been there for a long time now, every juncture requires a new determination, and indeed every day requires a fresh reinforcement of the decision.

I put the removal process into operation, and began the transition from my old council flat into a home all of my own. I had a couple of weeks in which to vacate my flat, so the transition was not all in one go, which I think helped me to make some of the necessary adjustment. I reflected that it must be a bit like dying. The flat that I had occupied for so many years was no longer my home and my identity had to be retrieved from it and transferred to my new abode. When I was visiting my new house and taking belongings to it, I would often stand and gaze out of the window, thinking 'Is this really mine – my own house with these lovely gardens and garage?' I had never before had these luxuries, and even after more than seven years here, I still give thanks every day for them.

While dismantling my old home in Hapton, many memories came back to me of experiences there – people who had come, cats who had lived with me, my thoughts and feelings, and my growing process. I remembered the process of anorexia nervosa, as I had lived with it in that place – the multiple binges, starving, and endless rationalising of my relationship with food. I remembered how I used to struggle not to eat the food I had bought for my father or sister when they visited – the breathless agony on the edge of a binge in the kitchen when they had gone to bed for the night, the giving in, the shame, the disgust, and having to try to put a brave face on it in the morning. I remembered how when Dad had died I gradually got the binges under control, until it was just Ryvita binges, and how even these had gradually petered out, giving way to a strict but more sensible control over my food, although still accompanied by a gradual decline in weight.

That flat and the immediate surroundings had a long emotional history for me, whereas the place I was going to did not. I found this very difficult, and for a long time I craved the familiarity of the very place from which I had so longed to escape. The physical environment of my flat stayed with me like a living presence for more than six months after I had finally left it, and there was a kind of mourning that went on in a subliminal part of my mind. I can become very attached to places, sometimes more than to people. I don't really know why this is, except that perhaps it is because I am a somewhat 'unearthly' creature. Never having found a sense of home in my own body, those places on the earth where I feel any kind of belonging are very precious to me, almost in a formative way. They give me a root to put down into the Earth, the planet upon whose surface I live out my life.

As I emptied the rooms, and packed up or threw out quantities of accumulated possessions, I reflected on how I had come to Edinburgh with just a minivan full of my belongings, and had somehow drawn all this other stuff to me, almost as if I were a magnet. I remembered the fire at the Cathedral College where I was staying with the community, and how it had consumed all but a tiny remnant of my belongings, and how strange it had felt to have virtually nothing to call my own. My possessions are usually very important to me, as if they were like some kind of clothing for my skeletal anorexic being, yet in the moving process, temporarily it was possible to see them from a different perspective – as a transitory and ephemeral construction around the person that I am.

I cleaned the flat thoroughly, as much as a gesture of thanks to it for sheltering me for so many years, as the desire to leave it in a suitable condition for the next occupant. It felt a bit like wiping a slate clean, but I could never leave the experience of living there behind, as it had become a part of my life's journey. As I closed the door for the last time, I gave a blessing to the flat, hoping that the next person would appreciate it as much as I had done, as a little haven in the midst of the challenging surroundings.

I finally handed over my keys to the council and took up formal residence in my new home on July 4th 2004. I spent my first night there, sleeping on the couch in the sitting room while I finished redecorating the room that I had chosen to be my bedroom. It looked out on to the back garden. The sun looked in through the day and the stars at night. July 4th was my dear friend Watson's birthday and also American Independence Day, so it seemed appropriate somehow that this was also my first day of owning my own home.

By the time I moved I had only one of my old cats left, the two remaining others having passed away only weeks before. I felt very sad, thinking how much they would have enjoyed their new home. My Lizzie, now eighteen years old and very deaf, had always been a nervous cat, and she did not take kindly to moving. My friend, who was helping me, drove Lizzie and me to our house in the van that I had hired. I was clutching Lizzie in her basket on my lap, and she yowled vigorously all the way. Poor Lizzie was too old and nervous to go into the garden and preferred to stay in the room I had set up for her upstairs, but she did gain a little confidence as time went by, and was peaceful and contented, lying in the sun on her chair or in my bedroom.

For quite some time I had been feeding and looking after a stray cat who came around the flats at Hapton. My neighbour on the ground floor also gave him food at her window. I did not feel that I could leave him, as he had become quite attached to me, but I was worried that he would not settle in a new environment and would wander and get lost. He knew his territory in Hapton, and having been a stray for a long time, I did not think he would want to be a house cat.

During the time that I was looking after him there, I had

managed to catch him twice – the first time to get him neutered, and the other when he had an injury to his face. I was doubtful as to whether he would let me get him in a basket again. My neighbour agreed to feed him for a while until I got settled, and I left a supply of food for him. We had all called him Scruffy because of his ragged coat, but I renamed him Joseph in the hope that he would become beautiful if I could care for him well. It soon became apparent that the arrangement for feeding was not working, and I decided that I had to get Joseph, whether I was ready to cope with him or not.

I went back to Hapton quite early one day, telling him in my thoughts that I was coming for him, and if he wanted a better life he would have to let me get him into a basket. To my amazement he was waiting for me, so I dashed into the building, borrowed a basket from my neighbour's son, who luckily happened to be in, then picked up Joseph and popped him into it. He made no protest, and as we raced back to Dunfermline, he put a paw through the basket wire to try to touch me. I was very moved by his co-operation and reassurance.

When we got to my house, I opened the basket in the kitchen and sat down, exhausted, while he explored. I could not believe it when he jumped up on my lap, settled down and purred, sticking his long claws affectionately into my knees as he paddled away, showing me that *he* had adopted *me* as his faithful servant. What amazing creatures these mysterious animals are! Joseph became my dear and close companion, Lord of the Manor, blossoming into a huge, beautiful furry bundle of love, and we had six happy years together in our new home, until cancer took him away.

My lovely Lizzie lasted only three months in our house before it was time for her to go, but I think that she hung on to make sure I got settled. She and Joseph got on fine together, neither one bothering the other, and sometimes they would lie together in the sun. I think he missed her as much as I did when the vet came to the house and Lizzie breathed her last in my arms.

* * * * *

The first months in my new home were ones of sky-high anxiety levels, such that at times I could hardly get my breath. The sense of unfamiliar territory, disorganisation – always a major anxiety trigger for me – and unrelenting piles of paperwork, were almost more that I could cope with. At times I felt that I had made the wrong decision, and was not going to be able to cope. I began to dread the arrival of the postman, the piles of brown envelopes coming through the door, getting up in the morning and feeling so alone with no one to turn to, and picking my way through heaps of boxes all insisting that I unpack and organise the contents NOW. I am not very good at handling a 'pending tray' and feel urgently that I must get everything done right away or else something terrible will happen. I find myself in extreme panic when there is just too much to get done and there is still disorganisation, still matters left unsolved, and still things not in their proper places. I have often wondered why I am like this. I think it is a kind of spill-over from my anorexic drive, that wants to control everything that relates to my body down to the last minute details, so that nothing can be left to chance which can potentially cause me to lose my hold on my shape, my identity. Primarily this was, and still is, directed at eating. Yet eating is so central to life and so many aspects relate to it either directly or indirectly that a fierce control over eating spreads out into a fierce control over life – or rather the attempt to control, for life is not ultimately controllable.

However much we as a human race would like to believe it, we are not masters of the universe. While I think that there is much more possibility than most of us generally realise, in terms of directing energies and thoughts to achieve and manifest that which we desire, complete success is never possible. There are so many of us wanting to achieve and manifest our desires, and not all our aims are compatible. Other considerations include the awareness that there are vast arenas of energy fields and influences upon us that we are only just beginning to recognise and investigate. Such matters interest me greatly, but do nothing to allay my daily experience of anxiety. Over the years I have found that for me the only lasting antidote to anxiety is an experiential awareness of being connected – to the earth, to the spirit world, to people, to animals, to the universe and above all, to myself.

I worked very hard for the next several months to make my new home feel like my place, spreading my influence and personality through it until it began to feel like part of me, an extension of my being. This was so tremendously important to me that I could not let this task rest, and it is still something that I check and adjust every day, almost moment by moment. I know instantly if something does not feel right, something in the wrong place perhaps, or an atmosphere that is uncomfortable. I continually pray and fill my home with Light and blessing, hoping that the dear angels will dispel any negative vibrations that are due to my bad temper and anxiety! I am very protective towards my home. While the environment is not as threatening as it was in Hapton, there are still plenty of potential problems in the neighbourhood, so I do my best to protect my home with positive thoughts and prayers. I feel that I have been fortunate so far, in that there have not been any serious incidents, but I do not yet have complete confidence in my spiritual security system, and I am still beset with anxieties concerning the safety of my property.

It was not long before I realised that I had not escaped completely from the trials which I had encountered in Hapton. When I had come to look at the house, I had noticed the untidy garden and somewhat dilapidated appearance of the adjoining house next door and had remarked on it, but the sellers assured me that the occupants were friendly and helpful. I suppose at the time I did feel a bit dubious, but I so desperately needed a place in which to live that I was prepared to accept the property in spite of this rather off-putting element of its surroundings.

In fact, the problems of living next door to a neighbour

whose life-style is the complete antithesis of my own have been complex, and became a major source of distress and anxiety. However, it is neither expedient nor enlightening to elaborate much upon them in this book, as I believe that the most important issues lie much deeper.

I wondered why, why do I have to live in places such as this where I cannot find the peace, beauty and compatible people that I long for? Isn't it enough to have to carry the suffering of anorexia nervosa for all my life as long as I have lived it? Why do I have to bear the additional burdens of low income, reduced living conditions, poor neighbourhood, depressing environment, and so on? It is easy to feel sorry for myself. Certainly, there are millions who are much worse off by far, and I am very much aware of that, but this does not take away the questioning. Maybe that is appropriate, for the questioning drives me onwards to seek deeper and deeper into this condition which has been labelled anorexia nervosa.

I am at the point now where I see the manifestation of my outer life as part of the illness, and the effort to interpret it as an all-encompassing spiritual journey. Consequently, alongside all the resentment and anger that I feel about the stressful and disturbing situation surrounding my home, there is also the recognition that it is a demonstration of a part of myself – an untransformed, undeveloped, chaotic area of my total personality that is demanding my attention. It would constitute a classical analytic labelling to call it my animus. However, I do not find a great deal of meaning in that, and prefer to see it as a type of life energy whose direction and expression were suppressed and discounted from an early age.

I think that when I was a young child I saw my father as the source of power, as my mother, although an intelligent and spiritual woman, had virtually given away her true identity in order to serve his needs. To the perceptions of my young mind, the power personified by my father as masculine gave me no recognition, no space to be myself, did not respond to my essential needs of affection and affirmation, and actively put me down and humiliated me, albeit unwittingly. In the masculine world then, I simply could not exist as a real person, and the only avenue of survival was sickness, which was amply reinforced by my mother. This powerful early conditioning affected every aspect of my life negatively, especially the context I am discussing now – my inability to harness masculine energy in my personality and to direct it towards finding a place in the public (masculine) world.

During the era in which I grew up, society was more overtly male-dominated. Although the suffragette and feminist movements had brought the rights of women to the forefront of social consciousness in Britain, there was still a pervasive attitude that women were not as able as men to carry out work related to the public domain. Particularly in religious organisations, where traditions generally change more slowly, the concept of woman as the helper of man, and man as the head of the household, remained firmly entrenched. Even if not directly articulated, such concepts powerfully affected the way that society and personal relationships operated.

Since that time, (the 1950's and 1960's) there have been momentous changes in gender awareness and scientific knowledge of human physiology and psychology. There have been noticeable changes in the balance of masculine and feminine energies, and in the roles of men and women, which in some respects has led to a greater freedom of self expression for both sexes. Nevertheless, old attitudes die hard. There still remains a strong element of machismo running through all strata of British society. This seems to be increasingly manifested in women as much as it is in men.

My mother and father, being both affected by the prevailing social attitudes and the influence of their religious beliefs, could not help but convey this to me as the format for my identity.

The disturbance in my current home environment, which I perceive as a threat, constantly reminds me of all this. I feel that I want to get away from it as fast as possible, but comparable to the situation of my early years, I cannot. I am trapped with it, or so it appears to me, and consequently the stress and the despair engendered by it all are considerable. I have at last, reluctantly, begun to think, 'What can I make of it, then? What is it teaching me?'

There are many opportunities for learning and self-development in a situation such as this. As I was writing about it, I wondered why I had focused on it so early on in the chapter about my new home. I think that, although there have been many happenings, sad and joyful, pleasant and unpleasant, since I have been here, the stress of constant disturbance in close proximity has been ongoing and carries a high emotional charge for me. The relentless barrage of invasive noise and mess resonates with the destructive invasiveness of my father's negativity – a miasmal atmosphere which I was obliged to breathe throughout my early life and into my late teens. It is one which has been difficult to approach creatively, and one for which, in spite of all my efforts, there has as yet been no resolution. Essentially it is about human relationships, that arena of life which is so crucial to our ability to survive in this world, both psychologically and physically. Central to my experience of anorexia nervosa was an inability to form functional and emotionally nurturing relationships with people on all levels, and it is still something which I find very difficult and challenging. Consequently, dealing with conflict and potentially explosive situations cuts across all levels of my being and deeply into my anorexic stance – from the roots of being unable to incorporate masculine energies into my persona successfully, to an inability to be assertive and deal creatively with anger, and to a spiritual challenge to wrestle with the requirements of what it means to live a daily life of love, kindness and integrity.

The most difficult situations are often the ones from which we learn the most. However the lessons once understood and absorbed are worth their agony weight in gold. I still have to deal with my own prejudice, and my readiness to judge and condemn people. This is one of my distancing tactics, a way in which I can avoid looking honestly at myself. It prevents me from seeing the good in people whom I find challenging. Furthermore it prevents me from learning the lesson that life is offering

Sometimes I think that if I had a man living with me, life would be easier. Perhaps he would stand up for me, and deal with difficult interactions with the world. Perhaps people would treat me with more respect. Why, though, should I have to look to a man to fight my battles for me? I need to earn my own respect and dignity, but it is far from easy. Anorexia nervosa singles one out somehow, and an anorexic woman alone needs a lot of courage to survive not just her illness, but the world at large, too.

In contrast to this very perplexing, and still unsolved, situation, my relationship to my garden and its inhabitants has been a constant source of healing and of joy. Before I came to live here I had never had my own garden. We had a large garden at my childhood home, and Dad kept it well, but it was *his* garden, and none of the rest of us was allowed to do anything except help him from time to time with what *he* was doing. Until I was able to buy my own house, I had always lived in flats or in some kind of communal premises, so having my own little patch of earth was like a dream come true. In fact, the back garden was part of what attracted to me the house and gave me the impetus to purchase it. Both the front and back gardens had been nicely landscaped by the previous owners, and there was a large tree at the bottom of the back garden with a small pool close by it. This seemed nothing short of fairyland to my soul, which had been starved for so long in the wilds of Hapton. The first morning I woke up in my own home and looked out of the window into my own garden, I was overwhelmed with delight. I say 'my' garden, but I really see my involvement as stewardship – of a tiny portion of this planet's surface where I make my home.

It is something of a conundrum that while I find incarnation so heavy and excruciating, my love of the earth and her creatures is intense and penetrating. The love that the earth has for me, giving me the substance of my body and the generosity of provision, penetrates me with a kind of joy that is also a very great pain. The natural world as I find it in my garden – the plants that I tend, the grass that I mow, the soil that I fertilise, the birds that I feed, the visiting hedgehogs, hawks and crows that I love, and many more wonders – is always a source of stability for me, soothing my panic and comforting my anguish, uplifting me with laughter and enticing me out of myself with fascination.

For me, and probably for most people who suffer from anorexia nervosa, there is a profound disturbance of relationship with one's own earthly frame, and while this cannot always be healed completely in one lifetime, there is solace to be found in relationship to the many and varied forms of the creatures that one comes across, both animal and vegetable. Creatures of the earth do not assess and judge my physical appearance, whether I am fat or thin, how much I weigh, whether I am labelled beautiful or ugly. For them, I am just me, and it is how I relate to them that gives me the measure of my worth. To treat all living things with kindness, respect and compassion is a deeply penetrating and challenging intent, and in the estimation of the earth's creatures, the degree to which I live up to it is my worth. Working in my garden is one of the few places where I can lose track of time. I want to go on and on working in it, even when I know that I must stop because my body is complaining, or because I have remembered something else that I have to do.

Over the years, I have shared so much of my garden with my dear friend and companion, Perry, that it has really become *our* garden. I cannot go out in the garden without being aware of Perry, and all that we have shared together there. I have never been good at sharing – on a really equal basis, that is – and would be unlikely ever to be able to share a living space with anyone successfully, but gardening together has gradually become one of the truest experiences of real sharing that I have ever had. While in other respects our relationship has been at times fraught with impasse and tension, the garden works its healing magic every time we are together there.

The garden also attracted another friend – a feline one – who arrived one freezing cold winter and started to hunt the birds and steal scraps of food I left out for the crows. In order to deter him from his predatory activity, I left food out for him, some of Joseph's leftovers, and a bit more. It was not long before the little cat, who is now my lovely Coco, made it very clear that he wanted to come in and stay. I was worried that Joseph would not approve, and that they would fight, but although they were never close friends, a mutual tolerance was established, maybe because they both realised that they had come in their hour of need and found comfort.

Another stray cat, much more ragged and wild, later took up residence in my greenhouse, where I had made a cosy box for any visitors. He stayed as my guest for several years, coming and going as he pleased, and accepting without much hesitation the generous bowls of food that I left for him. It humbled me to see the way this old fellow jumped out of his bed and hastened over to his dish, usually gobbling up all the food with relish. I worried about him a lot, and asked neighbours to feed him when I was away. Sometimes he would disappear for weeks, and then reappear as if nothing had happened, to take up his routine again. It was a sad day when he fell ill, and I found that he had feline AIDS, and had to be put to sleep. I had called him Jackson – which used to be one of my own nicknames – and he will always have a place in my heart as my garden cat.

I think I can say that I love the garden as much as I love any person. It is a different kind of love, but just as strong and enduring. It is the love that is healing, for in my anorexic state, self-hatred presides over my experience of myself, but when I love truly from my heart – not out of need but more out of recognition – then that love permeates my being and soothes the fire of self-hate that rages so strongly through me. In the garden, I feel closer to the divine, and the divine draws closer to me.

Another aspect of having my own home which had a stabilising effect was having to look after it. Although I had had to look after my council flat in respect of keeping it clean, furnished and decorated, most of the major necessities of upkeep were carried out by the council. This was a blessing in many ways, as it saved me the worry of dealing with repairs, contractors and the like when I could barely have coped with it. I was also fairly lucky in that the flat had been renovated and was in a 'good' stair – in other words, one where the occupants generally looked after the property and did not go around vandalising everything in sight. This meant that the Council had more of a vested interest in maintaining it, and repairs and maintenance jobs did get done, even though there was usually a bit of delay. With my own house, however, I had to organise and pay for everything that needed doing, and this caused me considerable anxiety and indecision as to who to ask to do what.

As time went on, I began to feel very grateful to the people, usually men, who came to my house to do jobs. On the whole, I was fortunate to find reliable and reasonable trades persons, with whom quite often I was able to have a good conversation. Not only did the work get done, but also the visiting joiner/plumber/serviceman eased the sense of loneliness that I experienced so sharply after I moved. I was a bit surprised that I could relate on an acceptable level to these people, and still am. Relating to people is not my strong point and never comes easily, and I can agonise for hours or even days, as to what I should say or what I should not have said, and so on. Healing can come on so many levels. I doubt if any of these folk would have considered themselves to be a healer. Yet their very willingness to come to help me and to give generously of their skills in order to do a good job, and to interact with me in a friendly way, have offered me a significant level of healing. It has, to some degree, built up the shattered remnants of my self-confidence. Occasionally, there have been incidents where a con-trick has been visited upon me, or some kind of extortionate charge been made, but surviving these thankfully infrequent unpleasant events and discovering that I managed to negotiate my way through them somehow, have also given me a positive message.

* * * * *

Since my mother died, my sister Sylvia and I have become closer, and I believe that having my own home has facilitated this. Sylvia did come to visit me in Hapton a couple of times, but it was such a difficult place to entertain anybody and I don't think that she felt comfortable there. Yet the first time she visited my new home, she liked it immediately, and said she felt at home. In the early days of my efforts to establish myself in the new location, that was a good sign. Throughout the time when I was growing up at home, my sister was almost like a second mother to me, and I am sure that Mum was glad of her help in looking after the hyper-sensitive and sickly child that I turned out to be.

When I became anorexic, it must have been very difficult for Sylvia to see the little girl that she had loved and cared for turning into a depressed, obsessive skeleton. It was a dreadful time for all of us. My illness caused a separation between Sylvia and myself, and there was degree of tension and misunderstanding at times, but now I feel that a certain amount of distance has been necessary for us to become closer in our later lives. Although Sylvia has always been very kind to me, I felt that she could be a little possessive at times. I worried about this. I had many fears of being controlled, submerged and obliterated by my family, all of which found expression for so many years in my terror of food and putting on weight.

After I had been living in Scotland for several years, Sylvia and I began to develop a better understanding of each other, and to draw closer again. This was not without a fair bit of hard work on my part – in terms of self-honesty, facing my fears, establishing my own personality, and a good deal of prayer and spiritual work, too. I am sure that she also worked hard in her own way to re-establish the sisterly bond between us. It is not something we talk about. That kind of conversation has not been a habit in our family and is probably uncomfortable for her. I think that it is more to do with a tacit mutual acknowledgement, and the growth of an inner recognition of the true nature of each one of us. This is a very precious thing, one which continues to develop and to bring healing to me, and I hope to her also. We have shared many visits at my home, and each one has been blessed with those special touches from the angels. This lets me know in my innermost being that, while she and I may be very different in our outlook and our way of going about our lives, there is a current of real love between us, that is rooted not only in the realm of human interaction but also in the world of spirit. Latterly we have been away on holidays together to Findhorn, a place for which we share a common love, and both visits have had their magic touches, and those angel wings have brushed by so many times.

My brother Chris' wife, Nancy, died quite recently, and although this is a very sad and difficult time for him, it has provided opportunities for me to draw closer to him again. Since he left home, when I was about three years old, I have never been as close to him as when he was the big brother who comforted me and took me out. His own life, involving his work, marriage, and family of children and grandchildren, took him far away from my experience of life. Although I did not realise it for many years, this was a great loss to me, and had a profound effect on my relationships with men.

I feel that if I had not gone through so much with anorexia – the intensity of suffering, and the unending quest for self-knowledge and development – I would never have been able to be a support to Chris in his bereavement, and would never have had the amazing opportunity to assist Nancy with her dying process. I would never have *chosen* to have anorexia nervosa in order to be of service in this way, but one has to bow to the greater wisdom of life that brings about such things, almost unbeknown to our everyday self which struggles with life's daily challenges.

During October 2010, both my brother and sister visited me together. This was a completely new experience for all of us. They did not stay for many days, as we had wondered how we would all cope with our routines in my little house with only one bathroom, but it was just long enough for us to feel that we would like to do it again. All of us have various health problems and need to take time and space to attend to our ageing bodies.

It was a lovely visit, and in spite of uncooperative Scottish weather, we had a really good time, and were able to do very enjoyable things together. We even went out for a meal – something I have not done for many years. Chris loves going out for meals, and as it was his first visit, I did not want to disappoint him. Luckily there is an excellent vegetarian buffet restaurant in Edinburgh, which I thought that I might be able to cope with, and it turned out to be a good experience for us all. We had the added bonus of some delightful live classical guitar music – yet another of those little angelic touches, in my understanding! As I ate my food, I reflected on the amazing anorexic journey that I have travelled which had made this experience possible for me. In times past I had guiltily sneaked into this same restaurant and bought several items, which I gulped down surreptitiously, hidden away in a corner. Now I was enjoying the company of my brother and sister, feeling gratitude for the food I was eating, and was free from any kind of agonising longings for the shelves of delicious-looking cakes and desserts. I can but bow down in gratitude and amazement for the processes of love, life and grace which had brought this change about.

*   *   *   *   *

Since I have been in my own home, I have had very little in the way of 'adventures' in relationships to men – those encounters that would habitually stir up a lot of feeling in me. I have to admit that I am thankful for this! Such expeditions are never comfortable, and at worst provoke a great deal of anguish, and are extremely disturbing to my stability.

While I have grown closer in my heart to those men in my life who are my friends, particularly my long term companion, Perry, I have found that I have very little wish to engage in anything which would entrap my emotions into thinking that I was in love. Learning to love is an entirely different matter for me. The sense of recognition and appreciation of the person, without feeling that I need him or want to possess him, is a welcome departure from the tortuous tangles that used to destroy all my efforts to draw closer to the male form of humankind.

However, there have been a few temporary 'flashes in the pan', which, although very brief, have caused me a great deal of discomfiture and heart searching. I think that these are worth mentioning, because they reveal both the distance I have come, and how far there is still to go.

Throughout my life, I have been interested in spiritual healing. I have sought out healers from various different disciplines, mostly for my own condition but latterly to pursue a desire to be a healer myself in a more directional way. Today there is more respect for, and research into, disciplines which may be classed as 'energy medicine', such as Reiki, crystal healing, and dowsing, to name but a few. There is also a growing recognition that these modern methods of healing, which reflect a more general awareness of quantum theory, are joining hands with methods rooted in ancient wisdom and spiritual traditions, for example, Wicca, Christian prayer and laying on of hands, Buddhism and Ayurvedic medicine. This interface has always fascinated me, and the desire to learn more motivated me to sign up for an introductory course in Barbara Brennan healing. Barbara Brennan was one of the pioneers of modern energy medicine, being a very gifted healer herself and also a highly trained scientist. Her book 'Hands of Light' had influenced me greatly when I read it several years ago, and at that time I was very keen to study her course in healing, which was a four-year course, held in the USA. Unfortunately I did not have the money to pay for it or to support myself while studying it, so I gave up the idea. When recently I noticed an introductory course in Barbara's methods that was to be held in Scotland, I decided to give it a try.

The healing centre was lovely, in a beautiful part of Scotland. I booked bed and breakfast there for the duration of the course, which gave me extra contact with the course leader and the surroundings. I felt welcome there, almost at home, although I was quite unwell for much of the time. My body is difficult to manage whenever I stay away from home. I really need to eat the same things at the same time in order to stay relatively stable, but this is rarely possible when I am away. Breakfasts are often at a later time than that which I am used to, and this means that I invariably become constipated, leading to an array of uncomfortable symptoms such as headaches, bloating, indigestion, panic and self-hatred, which can become incapacitating if allowed to go on. An enema kit has become an essential piece of equipment, but in accommodation that does not have *en suite* facilities, the process of using it can prove embarrassing and complicated! A dive to the bathroom is the order of the day, and not easy to explain to puzzled course participants. I did not book an evening meal, as I was not sure how I would cope with food that my body would find unfamiliar. Instead I had small picnics of fruit and oatcakes by the river.

Overall, I found that I was enjoying the course, and I managed to participate in everything in a fairly positive way. I am still not good in groups, but I was surprised that I got on well with all the other people there, and was happy enough to work with anyone. So far, so good, I thought! I had decided that if I liked the course and felt good about it, I would sign up for the year-long certificated course, and make this my particular brand of healing.

However, I was so unwell on the last day that I began to doubt whether I would have the stamina for all the travelling involved and the longer duration of the practical classes, so I arranged a consultation with the instructor, Hans, to discuss this. We agreed that it would be better for me to come periodically, perhaps once a month, for healing for myself from him. I think that somewhere deep down I felt disappointed in myself, for here I was ending up as a patient again, needing to spend lots of money on treatment, when I had hoped to develop a skill which would be both a form of service and a means of earning a living. Maybe I did not acknowledge this sufficiently to myself to protect myself from what followed, and to steer myself in the right direction. Instead, I had just lapsed back into what seemed familiar.

During the course I had felt very drawn to Hans. His warm, affectionate and fun-loving nature captivated me, and the feel of his body was somehow comforting. Physical contact was necessarily part of the course, and there were lots of hugs going round amongst all the participants. It was with a certain amount of sadness that I left when the course had finished, and I realised that I was looking forward with anticipation to my appointment for healing. When this came around, I had decided to stay overnight, so that I would not have to make the long journey there and back in the same day. I was hoping that this would give me a little extra time with Hans and his partner, whom I also liked very much.

I arrived for the healing with a sense of expectation and trepidation, and upon entering the room with Hans I realised that everything felt quite different from when I had been there before. Of course I should have expected this, as the energies of a group will be much different from those of a one-to-one situation, but I had not taken this into account, and I felt disconcerted.

The healing itself was also disconcerting, and I found it

much more physically invasive than the gentle techniques that we had practised during the course. Soon I felt rather unsafe, and withdrew into a passive, unresponsive, unassertive mode which is a typical dysfunctional defence system for me. At one point, I think I did manage to tell Hans that he was hurting me, which I suppose constituted at least some effort on my part to define myself.

After it was finished, I felt vulnerable, and strangely tired, and Hans comforted me in his usual warm and affectionate manner. Perhaps this was the trigger point that started me off thinking that I was in love with him. I did not notice it immediately, but in the evening, when we were all sitting together in the dining area, I felt I wanted to be close to him. I did not say of course, but maybe I should have done so.

The next day, I made another appointment before I left, and I felt I could hardly bear to wait out the time until I could come back – an all-too-familiar danger signal! It was not until I got home that I realised something quite devastating had happened to me.

I could not stop thinking about Hans, imagining conversations with him, longing for cuddles, and fantasising about situations in which I would be involved with him. Fortunately I was able to observe this going on within myself, and recognise the pattern, but this did not mean that I was able to stop doing it immediately. I wrestled with it, long and hard, before I finally managed to divest myself of the projection that I had placed upon him. To make this whole situation more complicated, there had been an odd consequence of the healing (I can only presume it was that) whereby I had had a terrible pain round about my middle. It was not located in my body, but a little distance away from it, perhaps at the level of my solar plexus. The only other time I have experienced this as strongly was when my father died.

My stomach became very bloated, feeling like a football, and I was deeply depressed, angry and suicidal. Many times I thought of writing to Hans, but I was aware of my habit of writing long emotional letters, and how they were rarely received with any confirmation or response – hardly surprising I suppose. I am glad to say that I managed to prevent myself, albeit with some difficulty, from indulging in this unsatisfactory effort to solicit a response from the object of my affections.

Eventually, I did write a very brief, factual type of letter to tell him what I was going through. Predictably, there was no response. I tried an email, and another email – no response. I could have phoned. Why didn't I? It was probably because I expected the same kind of discounting of my feelings – but in direct interaction – and also because the more desperate and tormented I feel, the harder it is for me to reach out and make contact.

At the same time I was going through an exercise in past-life memory with my spiritual director Ruth White, and at length it came to my mind that somehow I had remembered a rape and pregnancy situation and projected it on to Hans. As soon as I realised this, my stomach went down and the emotional trauma surrounding him left me. Was this an aspect of the healing he had done for me? I could not tell, and as I then felt unable to return to continue the healing sessions and discuss this with him, I never found out. I think the main reason for not going back was that I did not receive any response at all to the communication of my pain. Maybe he did not receive my messages, or maybe he was just too busy to respond, but even a few words would have made a difference. It was an all-too-familiar situation to me. A lack of response to my tentative offering made me feel that there was no point in pursuing the treatment.

Later on, I decided to go back and spend a night there for bed and breakfast, prior to meeting my sister at the airport for a holiday together. When I met Hans again, it was as if nothing had ever happened, but I did feel a certain inner constraint, and avoided talking about my experience. He was his usual warm and affectionate self, and I think that maybe I felt a degree of regret that I had not pursued the healing sessions. However, when I went back a second time for bed and breakfast, I felt that, although he was friendly and courteous, I had ceased to exist for him. The rapport had gone and our exchanges felt forced. Underneath, those feelings which I had experienced remained unresolved for me, although divorced now from him. When it was time for me to leave, he was not there. I felt sad, and that things were unfinished. Maybe I was still hoping for something.

Before I booked a place on his course, I had sought a 'sign' about it – to be shown whether or not it was to be the pathway ahead for me – and I thought that I had received confirmation. Yet signs can be only what we read into them, and of course, one can always be wrong.

The other sortie into imagined romance was with yet another therapist, this time a cranio-sacral practitioner. I had been receiving cranio-sacral therapy as part of specialist dental treatment – to attempt to adjust the angle of my jaw and improve my bite – and I was really sad when the woman who had been my practitioner for some time closed her clinic in order to take up another form of employment. She was really the only person I had learned to trust to handle my body in the way that cranio-sacral therapy requires. I had begun to look forward to her gentle but firm and penetrating touch, and her kind and understanding manner. It was quite a major loss for me when she left, a kind of mourning in my body for the loved and trusted touch. She had recommended me to someone else, and for a while I went to him for treatment.

He also was a very kind and gentle person, and I really liked him, but unfortunately I grew to like him too much. He was one of those rare men with whom I felt physically comfortable straight away – usually I am indifferent, or even actively hostile. This would have been fine except that the nature of cranio-sacral therapy makes it easy to interpret it as intimacy, even when one knows it is not. In addition, his method of working seemed to provoke in me much more of an emotional response than I had encountered before, and all these factors put together conspired to trigger my 'in love' feelings. Fortunately, I became aware of this almost immediately.

'Oh no, not again!' I thought wearily, 'surely I must have learned by now that it gets me nowhere!' Half curiously, I watched myself going through the usual thought patterns, and I went along with this for a while, hoping that maybe this time I could work through it with the practitioner. However, I began to feel that I hadn't really got the energy for it, for with the combination of various events – an extremely harsh Scottish winter which made getting to appointments impossible for a time, a bout of debilitating illness on my part, a move of clinic location on his part – there was a lack of the continuity which would have been necessary for me to process the feelings in relationship with him. Also, whether it was real or imagined I cannot tell, I detected a reserve from him that withheld from me the kind of response that I was looking for.

I put out a tentative feeler, a Christmas card with a poem about the natural world that I had written specially for him. He did not even acknowledge it, so unless he did not receive it, I felt that it was a signal that for whatever reasons, he could not or did not want to respond to me at that level. Thankfully, I found that this was all I needed in order withdraw the 'love' and process the feelings on my own. I am getting quicker off the mark in dealing with this emotional state, but the underlying trauma that perpetuates it is obviously still not completely identified and resolved.

* * * * *

In spite of the many blessings and positive features of having my own home, I have not been happy here. I really wonder if I would be happy anywhere that I called home, for since the stress, conflict and unhappiness of my early life was the womb of my anorexic illness, and I tend to create, or somehow uncannily discover, similar circumstances wherever I try to settle and make my home. Always the desperate feelings of being oppressed, invaded, threatened and trapped eventually emerge in whatever are my home circumstances. Even though I have come a long way in recognising the origin of the distress that inevitably arises, I have not so far been able to overcome it and find peace of mind in my home. This causes me a considerable amount of despair, for it seems that wherever I go, no matter what I do, those feelings will always be with me.

Methods and therapies that promise release from the grip of such feelings have not worked their magic for me. There is not much point in protesting to those who promulgate them that their particular brand is not universally effective, as there would be all those accusations such as 'you haven't tried hard enough', 'you give up too easily', 'you have not done it properly' and the like, which only leave one feeling more despairing, guilty and useless. I think that some wounds lie too deep, beyond the reach of 'methods', and are only accessible to a wisdom and healing that comes from somewhere beyond the human realm. Such healing can be mediated by a human being – even by oneself – and I have read much about this kind of miracle, yet have been unable to apply it to, or experience it, myself in this circumstance.

Perhaps I have to be content with the slow pace of the painful miracle of my ongoing transformation. While I am preparing food in my kitchen, I can be aware that what used to be 'dangerous' food is in the fridge and a bar of organic chocolate is at hand as a treat for a guest. I no longer have the least desire to stuff any of it guiltily into my mouth, and I realise that a miracle has happened, and is still happening.

A miracle is said to be an event due to a supernatural agency. I tend to think of it as the working of natural laws of which we are not normally aware. We all have the ability to attract, mobilise and metabolise energies beyond our own, either from entities that dwell on other planes of existence other than our own, or from universal energy of differing frequencies which we can draw into our own being or our environment. Thus, we are all capable of working 'miracles'.

Since I moved to my house and became a home owner, my self image has undergone a disconcerting change. When I came I was in my middle fifties, and I estimated that my appearance must be reasonable for a woman of my age. Though not in the best of health, I had a little energy for activities that I enjoy, such as gardening and walking, and following one or two social pursuits. Now I have become a Senior Citizen, and often feel like one! My health has become very difficult to manage and I am often extremely weary. I feel unhappy about my appearance and generally I perceive myself as an ageing woman. This is something that is very hard for me to get used to and to accept.

The further I come from looking like a young girl, the less hope I have of ever receiving what I need to make me come alive. There is nothing intrinsically wrong in being and looking old, but sometimes one feels it is almost a crime. It can make one feel invisible and an object of ridicule or pity, especially by the young. I have fought all the way, but one cannot hold back the passage of time, and though there are ways of staying young – cosmetic, psychological and metaphysical – I do not feel that I can find access to them. Some of them, such as facelifts and cosmetic surgery, are very expensive. Even if I could afford them, I am not sure that I would want to put myself through such drastic procedures. There are plenty of less invasive, more health-promoting ways of preserving one's appearance, but as I have come to learn, to live a healthy lifestyle and have access to health-promoting treatments and products, a considerable amount of money is necessary. I am not sure if one can be poor and healthy these days, in the current atmosphere and demands of our Western society.

I had hoped that my move from the council flat to my own home would bring about an improvement in my health, since I expected that the environment would at least be a little more congenial and that I would be less stressed. However, it has not turned out that way, and reflection upon the whys and wherefores causes me much bewilderment.

Not long after I had settled in, I developed a mysterious

illness that seemed to be related to my teeth. In spite of many visits to doctors, consultants, dental specialists and various complementary therapists, there has never been any definite diagnosis. I have undergone several types of treatment for this illness, but none have proved to be effective in curing it. The symptoms are many and varied, and the details of my attempts to recover from it are a story in itself, some aspects of which seem particularly relevant to my anorexic journey.

I have never had good teeth, and dentistry of one kind or another has been a constant feature of my life. In an earlier chapter, I mentioned the orthodontist who was very kind to me and with whom I formed a special attachment. Orthodontic treatment at that time was not particularly advanced, and although my teeth were somewhat straighter after the treatment, I have learned recently that the actual procedure did more harm than good. Later, I had further orthodontic treatment, from a different dentist, and this, too, had detrimental effects, from which I now suffer. Added to this, I am hypersensitive to many dental materials – which have been causing a slow poisoning of my body systems, recently leading to some extreme reactions and persistent illness, and problems with my jaw.

I have wondered why there are so many traumas associated with my mouth. It is one of the key places in the body where we express who we are, and communicate with others. Both of these aspects of being human were severely damaged in me at an early age, so emotional problems were added to inherited structural problems of my jaws, wreaking havoc in that highly significant area. I have always felt ashamed of my mouth and my teeth, and this has certainly not improved as I have grown older. I always longed for a lovely wide smile and even white teeth – like I saw on models and in toothpaste advertisements.

Whatever goes into my mouth and what comes out of it is a matter of great anxiety for me. A mouth is place of interface, where one energy emerges and integrates with a greater one, or where energy from the greater field is taken in to an individual entity. This interface is one with which I have always had

354

trouble. I do not trust what goes out or what comes in, and feel I need to keep a strict control over the flow, monitoring every movement. Thus I feel that my interaction with the environment in which I find myself is always under threat, and I am hyper-vigilant about it all the time.

During the later stages of the 'tooth illness', I had to have some front teeth extracted, owing to fact that very old crowns had been concealing diseased roots. This was a major decision for me, with which I wrestled for a long time. I hoped that my health would improve. Unfortunately it did not, and in fact seemed to be worse, in spite of using various detoxification treatments. Added to this disappointing outcome was the new challenge of wearing a denture. It was hell. The pain and the discomfort were equalled by the awful feeling of ugliness, and the sense of 'no return' which rang a death knell to my deep longing to feel young and attractive, something which I have never yet felt.

Wearing a denture also seemed to stir up some of my old anorexic tendencies. Having front teeth missing made me feel vulnerable, as if that which guarded the entry of my mouth had been broken open. At the same time, the hard plastic of the denture felt like an invasive object that had been forced into my mouth. It gave me a very great sympathy with horses, most of whom are compelled to wear a bit and bridle whenever humans ride or drive them. The presence of the denture in my mouth while trying to eat radically affected my sensations connected with food. This, coupled with the pain, illness and complicated psychological associations, served to make food feel like a punishment, and even the small amount that I used to enjoy became distasteful. I was so preoccupied with the drama connected with my mouth that incredibly, I did not notice that I was losing weight. It is incredible to me because throughout the years that I have suffered from anorexia nervosa, I have been intensely aware of the tiniest changes in my weight and shape. This time, I had lost a considerable number of pounds before I noticed that my watch strap was loose. At first I thought that this was because it was getting old and that I needed to buy another one. Taking a closer look at my wrists, I imagined that they looked thinner than usual, and decided to weigh myself. I was shocked by the low reading on the scales, and felt a curious mixture of alarm, relief and joy. That old anorexic urge is never very far away from me. I am glad to say that this time, I was careful to take steps to ensure that I did not lose any more weight. However, regaining the amount that I lost has not been possible for me.

The last seven years have presented me with many difficult questions. What is the message of the illness? What is its purpose? Where is it taking me? These questions are not easy to answer, but deep inside myself I feel that I am approaching a major threshold and the illness is a guide.

* * * * *

My own home has been a place of mixed blessing. On one hand it has stimulated a certain kind of growth and development, along with a deepening awareness of just how deeply anorexia nervosa is woven throughout the fabric of my life, on all levels. On the other, it has been a period of difficult adjustment to advancing years, and a struggle with failing health, loneliness and anxiety. It has provided me with a base from which I have been able to examine and develop my relationship with my departed parents, and also from which I have been able to relate more deeply to my brother and sister. It has provided a personal space for dealing with hidden conflicts and difficult relationships, the solace and comfort of a lovely garden, and the companionship of animals. It is the place where this book has been written. I am deeply grateful for my home, whatever it has brought to me in the form of joy or sorrow. I am grateful for its warmth and shelter, its elements of beauty, and above all, I am grateful because it is *my* home.

Crones

Oh wise and beautiful crones,
Life's labours writ upon your bones,
Sorrows etched on furrowed brow,
The once smooth cheek now wrinkled jowl.
Smile and laughter add their creases
And heavy lid eyes behind the glasses
Watch the young ones stepping in to life
Some clouded early by its strife,
Some fresh in innocent belief.

Less polarised now, woman and man
In advancing years that cross life's span.
The sexual diamond closes in.
The two draw near to one again,
But woman must look forever young,
The chant of youth cult anguish wrung
From droopy breasts and saddle bags,
Expanding tum and bottom sags.
Endless treatments, surgeon's knife
Can't bring the young girl back to life,
But only hide the grief.

Dynamic crones, no moans and groans,
The life force surges through the one who owns
Her right to be a vibrant soul,
Pursuing that which makes her whole.
Computers, mobiles, surf the net,
No time to be an old girl yet!
Flirt with the boys, life's just begun,
The menopause can be good fun!
Courses, study, PhD,
Yoga, jogging, learn to ski,
Who wants to grow old gracefully!

Jacqueline Kemp

Chapter Twelve

Discussion

As I draw towards the close of this narrative on my life with anorexia nervosa, I want to enlarge upon and discuss some of the topics that I mentioned earlier. After so many years of searching for the causes and a cure for this illness, I am not sure that I am any nearer to pinpointing a definitive answer. There is only a matrix of probabilities and possibilities. I do not see my family situation or the pressures of society as the cause, although both were certainly contributory factors. Neither is the cause to be found in my personality or my physical body, although these must have held predisposing factors. I believe that former lifetimes must have shaped my destiny in this incarnation, but again this would be unlikely to be the single deciding factor. Would a soul deciding to incarnate say to itself, 'I'm going to develop anorexia nervosa'? Somehow I don't think it can be quite that simple. I have wondered if I became confused somewhere along the line between physical size and aura size, trying, as it often feels, to cram a large spiritual being into a small physical container. Anorexia nervosa is an *illness,* and not 'just a dieting fad' or other derogatory description, of that I am sure. It is an illness of wide-ranging generative elements and of far-reaching effects. It is an illness of the personality, and of the soul. It is representative of a sickness in our society, the human race and our planet itself. As an entity in itself, it has a message for us all.

Anorexia nervosa has pervaded most of my experience of being alive. I cannot now imagine what it would be like to live without it. Although the intensity of its symptoms has tempered and my understanding of its meaning has expanded, over the years I have lived with it – almost fifty to date – the essential driving force of it is still the same. How would it be, I wonder, not to feel so huge and ugly, so bloated and tight in my body, so weighed down by horrifying flesh? My body has felt like a straightjacket all my life. How would it feel to be set free from this? The prospect is rather frightening.

Anorexia nervosa has challenged me to search without ceasing for the essence of what I believe about life and being alive. I have searched earnestly and with intense dedication to find myself – the nature of who I am in body, soul and spirit. I could never identify precisely what guiding force has helped me draw myself from a place of extreme derangement and physical collapse to a place of being able to maintain a relatively creative lifestyle with a growing awareness of the meaning of life's processes. The degree of recovery that I have so far achieved has been brought about, as far as I can tell, by becoming increasingly attuned and respectful of the Self that inhabits my body, and holding on for dear life to my commitment to allow this Self to fulfil its purpose on earth at this time. Also, because I have life, I feel that I have a duty to live it as best I can, for the sake of, and the service of, my fellow creatures. While I am here I want to give what I can, even if it is only a little, to contribute to the overall evolution of planetary life. Those ideals work out on my home territory and in my daily life, mostly in unobtrusive ways. To me they are bread of life, where spirituality is tested and where personal growth is taught and nurtured. So often I wonder 'What's the point of all this?' Yet I have to be content not to know the answer, and to carry on.

My beliefs, concepts and attitudes are constantly being challenged, and are changing in response to new understanding, and although this is not at all comfortable, I believe that it is a good thing. Truth is not a fixed entity but is an abstract concept, which manifests itself in constantly changing attire. As I lived with anorexia nervosa, dark flood waters engulfed me again and again, and much of what I imagined to be solid tenets of reality came crashing down. The person whom I thought myself to be, going about my ordinary life day by day, crumbled to a heap of ashes, leaving a naked trembling self, cringing before the forces that tore through me and battered the bulwarks of my perception of my identity. The confines of normality were burst asunder, and underneath my usually retiring and quiet presentation of myself, a violent process of unfettering was taking place, erupting from time to time in a tempestuous storm. I scraped the edges of existence, balancing on a knife edge between life and death, afraid to live and afraid to die. In a paradoxical way, the truth of my self is both changing and unchanging. The unchanging eternal spirit constantly manifests in new forms, and every moment is a new beginning.

I believe that the anguish I suffer is an authentic participation in the total human experience, just as much as are pleasure and joy. Whatever I suffer in a transformative way – as distinct from accepting the position of victim – is a contribution to the transformation of the enormous burden of suffering which humanity has built up for itself through processes of cause and effect throughout its existence. I do not think that suffering should be an aim in itself, but if it comes about, it can be put to work for creative purposes. This of course is no easy matter, and may well require a supreme effort of the soul on the part of the sufferer.

The work of facing up to one's shadow self – the largely unconscious, untransformed parts of the personality – and thus avoiding projecting it on to whatever person or situation presents as a suitable 'hook', is in my view a work of great significance and great courage. It is not a soft option, or a case of being selfish or self-preoccupied, as has at times been offered to me as a description of my process. Every action and behaviour begins with thought, so to scrutinise one's thoughts and take responsibility for them is the beginning of self-control, which stems from real self-knowledge, and is distinct from repression or restriction. To realise how much of ourselves we project on to other people, groups of people, animals, situations, our gods, and even upon the Earth itself would be the beginning of a realisation and reclamation of the true potential of humanity. In these times this is not just a convenient pastime for the rich or a necessity for the mentally ill, it is an urgent, crying need for all of us to undertake, to save our race and our earthly home before it is too late. To the eminent psychiatrist who accused me of 'making a career out of my illness', I now reply, 'What other choice did I have, and what better choice could I have made?' Anorexia nervosa has become for me a great teacher and a profound intercession, a living sacrifice in which each painful breath of life is a prayer for all people and creatures who suffer.

The fact that food and eating have been such a torment in my life does not now seem strange to me. When our whole world is so totally unbalanced in the sharing of resources, and especially in relation to the distribution of food, it seems inevitable that many of us in so-called 'developed' nations will encounter suffering in one way or another in our relationship to food. I do not mean to say that one should seek food-related suffering in an attempt to help the situation, for this is not a way forward. A right relationship to food in terms of its spiritual and biological qualities, and a reverence and gratitude for its provision is, in my understanding, the way forward to compassionate sharing across the globe, and healthy nourishment of one's own body. Those of us who have the privilege to live in countries that have plenty of food are not necessarily well nourished in respect of the whole spectrum of the needs of a human being. Our poverty of soul and social consciousness may be abject; our relatedness to the earth upon which we depend for our sustenance may be well-nigh obliterated. Our sense of community is so decimated that a breeding ground can be generated for acts of appalling cruelty and arrogance, where people strike out blindly and violently in a frantic effort to break through the hard shells of isolation and deeply concealed fear. A tearing hunger gnaws at the heart of humanity, and only those who dare to face up to its shattering pangs can in any way transcend the crippling effect of the socialisation in a 'civilised' society, and begin to become fulfilled – filled with the totality of their true selves.

In my starvation and binges, I felt – mostly in a barely-conscious way – that I was identifying with such extremities, in some way entering into the suffering of the starving and the overfed, people and creatures alike. After years of trying to conform myself to 'normality', I found that I really did not want to be 'normal' – whatever that was supposed to be. I was never very certain where I began and ended, and the idea of us being individual blobs of humanity, jostling each other on the surface of the earth, did not satisfy my questions about my experience of the intense participation in all kinds of distress which anorexia nervosa brought to me. My desperate need to authenticate my experience led me on a long search, a pathway still continuing, and though it has led me into deep dark waters, I think that now I am grateful to this great dragon of anorexia nervosa, for saving me from shallow self-gratification and superficial dabbling in the processes of life. Had it not been for anorexia, I might well have chosen an 'easy' way, as at heart I am comfort-loving and not someone who likes to blaze a trail.

I think that all sickness comes to us with a message of some sort. It may not be a simple matter to follow this message to its root and to discern its wider implications, but to regard it as just something to be cured is to miss its hidden gift. Every conviction I have ever had about the reality and meaning of anorexia nervosa as it has manifested in me is gradually being validated, and as this happens I become more and more true to myself, and more present to others. To take a small example, I was deeply convinced that certain foods were dangerous to me, although many people including professionals and spiritual authorities tried to persuade me otherwise. In the earlier years of my anorexic journey there was much less awareness of the detrimental effects of refined foods, additives, colouring, preservatives, pesticides and so on, and also of the mechanism of food intolerance and allergic reactions. The whole world could have told me I was wrong, but in my heart I knew that while my body craved certain foods, with such an intensity that filled my mind and drove from it every other thought, when I ate these foods, I sensed that they were poisoning me. In more recent years, nutritional research has gone a long way to proving the interrelationship of food with body and mind, and the devastating effect of toxins in dietary-related diseases and psychological conditions has received increasing attention. As with a warrior fighting for her life, such confirmations of my intuitive knowledge of my body were like a battle won, and were a soothing balm to my integrity. I have learned never to disregard any sensation, symptom, perception or intuition, but to treat it as something to be decoded and explored, no matter how bizarre and unacceptable it might seem. Not all these messages need to be acted upon – some may be discarded, or filed away in my mind for later reference – but having been deaf to myself for a long time, I know that to ignore my own signals leads me into peril.

A gradual, increasing respect for my journey, and a growing sympathy for the poor old body that has faithfully carried me through life, helped me to develop an interest in health and nutrition. Even while still hating the dungeon of my flesh, I began to make conscious efforts to recognise and respect my body as the house of my spirit, and to provide it with wholesome food. I realise now that I can never be 'normal' in the way I relate to food. I will never be able to eat whatever I feel that I want, just when I want it, in any kind of situation or emotional state. My body requires a highly specialised fuel, and I see that I have to understand more and more how to deliver that to it, and how to purify my consumption of food and my attitude to it. I need to be relaxed and quiet, so that I can attend to the process of eating and monitor the validity of my start/stop signals. I also need to be in a peaceful environment, without noise and disturbing vibrations. It is not always possible for all these conditions to be met. However, I do sometimes eat under conditions that are not ideal, and although these days I can generally manage to cope, very often my body will complain afterwards – letting me know that I have overstepped its limits.

I now see the eating of healthy food to be a great privilege, one which should not be taken for granted. The act of eating is a sacred participation in the energies of the earth and spirit that give life to the food, and I offer gratitude to the people and creatures that formed it for me. So many millions of people and creatures are starving in this world, or do not have access to healthy food and fresh water. I make the eating of my food a prayer for them, and an intention to be of service in whatever way I can. This is the only way I can make sense out of eating.

The issue of food in our culture today has come a long way from the true purpose of providing the body with what it needs to sustain itself in a healthy condition. On many levels it has become an emotional battleground, a consumer racket, an elaborate art form, a political stronghold of power, and there is a whole galaxy of artificial consumables masquerading as food. We are lured to eat too much by delectable images of food and pernicious advertising extolling the 'fringe benefits' of various types of produce – a suggested sexy encounter linked to a brand of canned drink, for example. In the next moment, we are told we are too fat, and are invited to compare ourselves with the seductive images of gorgeous models, deemed to have the perfect figure, or even those bordering on the anorexic outline. Television programmes show us how to make beautiful gourmet meals and elaborate dishes, and then 'how to eat sensibly and lose weight'. Government authorities presume to tell us what we should weigh, define for us our 'recommended daily allowances' of nutrients, and tell us how much fruit and vegetables we should eat, while the penetrating chime of bells announces the arrival of the ubiquitous ice-cream vans that sell coils of sweet white stuff and all sorts of other items which could barely squeeze into a rational definition of food. Vast arrays of packets of ready-prepared food in supermarkets are labelled with all sorts of information, often in print so small that you can hardly read it with your glasses on. Such information may well be meaningless to those who have not had the good fortune to study science and nutrition, and may not necessarily be a useful guide to the purchaser as to whether the food is suitable for them. No wonder so many people suffer from so many food-related illnesses and psychological conditions.

Many of us do not have any sense of connection to where our food comes from or the way it is produced, which in my view is a kind of deprivation. There is something so nourishing about seeing food growing on organic farms, where there is respect for the environment in which it grows and for the creatures which share that space, and then eating a meal prepared from the produce. When I was growing up, food seemed to be much simpler, at least on the everyday level, in our home. Whatever contribution my dear mother made to my anorexic manifestation, she did make a concerted effort to cook and provide healthy meals. She did not buy a great deal of packaged food (there was a lot less available at that time) and most of our meals were home made. When I used to go shopping with her for food, there were many small shops where she knew the shopkeeper and assistants, and one felt that there was a closer relationship to the actual food in its original state. A certain supermarket, which is now a huge chain, was then just a small shop amidst the others, with sawdust on the floor and assistants in white coats with muslin hair covers who weighed out butter and cheese and the like, and patted the butter into shape with wooden utensils. A milkman came round with a cart delivering milk, and we took the empty glass bottles back to the dairy. One cannot prevent the forward arrow of time, or undo the changes which come as a result, but I sometimes wonder how much of 'progress' is really that at all, and how in its worship and service we have lost something fundamental to the balance and wholesomeness of human life. Maybe in due course we will perceive and embrace the need to apply the intelligence and creativity which drives breathtaking advances in technology and harness these powers for the nurture and the preservation of the earth and all its inhabitants. I do hope that this realisation will come soon, rather than after it is too late.

Behind the scenes of food and all its ramifications there is a maelstrom of power struggles and political intrigue. Food is that essence of survival upon which the whole created order depends, and has thus been a focus for the survival of the fittest since the dawn of life on earth. The fear of not having enough food or of becoming food for another organism is partly what drives the evolutionary force and the formation of species. From the earliest days, humans have competed for food supplies and have fought to control the territory that is the source of that supply. Today the power struggle goes on, generally in more sophisticated forms in the Western World, but spilling over as eruptions of war and violence in other parts of the world. The subject of control of what we eat is a massive iceberg of which we see only a small part. Other writers have made far more extensive exposés of it than I ever could. I will mention here just a couple of examples for illustration; the debate over genetically modified crops and the issue of diet as an alternative to medical drugs.

The GM crop industry is potentially massively profitable, and in spite of evidence coming in that growing GM crops leads to an increase in the use of toxic pesticides and offers no gain in yield, tolerance or nutritional benefit, large GM seed and agrochemical companies put undercover pressure on governments which have been refusing to use GM seeds. Despite the fact that GM crops have still not been tested for safety in the human or animal gut on a multigenerational basis, or for safety in respect of the biosphere, in some countries GM produce has been allowed on the market without any safety studies and without labelling. In the Third World, GM companies can establish rights to the seeds they develop, and once having set GM crops as the norm, can force the farmers to depend upon them for every crop they grow, including the pesticides and herbicides that are required to ensure that the seed flourishes. The political ramifications of this are enormous and complex.

While most of mainstream medicine asserts the importance of a healthy lifestyle, very few doctors have in-depth knowledge of nutrition and nutritional supplements. The focus is for the most part on 'curing' illnesses with the use of drugs, and pharmaceutical control of information and practice is stronger than ever, with many mainstream journals partnered with drug companies, and ever-increasing limitations imposed upon the manufacture and sale of nutritional supplements. Amazingly, leading medical schools still do not have Professors of Nutrition, and do not provide significant training in this discipline. This is in spite of the increasing number of important studies in the relationship between academic performance in children and what they are eating, the relationship between criminal behaviour and diet, and the effect of dietary intervention in mental illness – to name but a few areas where there are advances in nutritional knowledge. When such encouraging research and results could lead to enormous savings of money and effort for the government and the whole population, and could potentially relieve or alleviate the suffering of so many people, one wonders why there is so little validity accorded to this arena of development, and why there are so many efforts being made to discredit and suppress appropriate research of high quality. In my view there can be only one answer – power and money, and thus, access to ensure the comfortable survival of those in control.

In the face of so many negative trends and horrifying spectacles, so beloved by the media, and which can make us feel utterly helpless and hopeless, it is vitally important to search for and to focus upon all those wonderful uprisings of the human spirit that bring forth heartening and uplifting efforts to restore the earth to balance and productivity. Compassionate aid is given to geographical areas of suffering and distress, and many organisations care for wildlife and work to save endangered species. There is a growing trend to treat domestic animals with respect and humane care, and to address issues of abuse of all kinds. Efforts are being made to educate people in ways of relating to each other with tolerance and understanding and to build bridges between people of differing cultures and religions. The needs of children are becoming better understood, and their education is now beginning to cover a wider scope, with interpersonal skills, study of food production and preservation of the ecosystem being included in the curriculum. There are a great many shafts of light emerging in our troubled world.

I am particularly encouraged by the work of the international permaculture movement. In this planet-orientated organisation, a wonderful variety of ways are emerging to produce food sustainably, to conserve resources and develop alternative sources of power, to transform desecrated land into beautiful, productive places, and to create a worldwide network of people who care deeply about their planet and about their relationships with each other. I am also so grateful for the work of the multitude of charitable organisations – local, national and international – that seek to bring compassionate aid to people and animals, and to empower communities to overcome the misfortunes and challenges that befall them. All over the world people are becoming more and more aware of our interdependency upon each other and upon the environment in which we live, and are responding with those magnificent inspirations of creativity and nobleness of heart of which the human entity is capable. I love to read or watch reports and documentaries about this movement. It makes my heart lift and gives me hope.

There is one further strand of human experience that I feel I should mention, particularly because of its superficial resemblance to anorexia nervosa. This is the phenomenon of 'living on light' – when a human being chooses to abstain from all food, and often drink as well, for an extended period of time. This can stretch into years, and yet the person remains healthy and at a stable weight. I had come across this once or twice when reading about devotees of religion both in the West and the East, but had thought that it was in the realm of those

371

rare spiritual masters (including women) who achieve a kind of awareness not commonly experienced by the general population. However, recently I came across a book by a scientist who undertook this discipline for himself as a matter of research and curiosity, and who was willing to undergo scientific and medical testing to validate the authenticity of his endeavours. While pursuing this path, he became aware of a considerable number of other people who felt called to the same way of living. It seems that such an apparently miraculous existence is not just the province of the advanced mystic, but is accessible to certain people who are living everyday lives.

Although not a new phenomenon, this appears to be a new possibility of existence in the human frame that is gradually gaining more general accessibility. Although it may resemble anorexia nervosa, it is not a variety of the illness, because if practised correctly, it does not result in deterioration and poor health or disturbance of mind. It does not stem from a negative relationship with the body and to food, as does anorexia nervosa, but very often from spiritual leanings or a desire for health and freedom from food. However there are inherent dangers in this way of way of living, and while some people who have undertaken the discipline have thrived on it, others have not been able to continue it, or have become ill as a result.

When I first read about this, I was curious, and felt intensely attracted to the book. The whole idea of it both drew me and repelled me. Having finished reading the book, I feel that this route of human development is not right for me personally, and that my work is to establish a harmonious and reverent relationship to my body and its food. However I am certainly left with many questions. Is this a new evolutionary pathway for humanity? What would humans who did not eat or drink look like, a long way down the line? Our bodies have evolved for dealing with food, and if they did not have to do so, what sort of body would evolve in its place? Would animals continue to eat each other, or would they, too, evolve to live on light? So the questions go on and on, and are definitely matters for further deliberation. I wanted to bring this matter to the attention of readers, as I feel that while it is such a fascinating arena of investigation, it should be regarded with great caution by anyone with anorexic tendencies.

Today, anorexia nervosa is recognised as a mental illness, and receives much more attention that it did when I first made acquaintance with the condition. There are a variety of help networks and treatments available, and websites where sufferers can contact and encourage each other. However, from what I have seen and heard, the effectiveness of such help is questionable. At the very worst, certain websites actively encourage sufferers of anorexia nervosa in their starvation endeavours, and users can compare emaciated images and dieting successes to spur each other on. Perhaps some anorexics find a kind of comfort and solidarity in this, and if so I do not blame them, for there is still so much misunderstanding of the condition. However, I fail to see how such exchanges can bring any true healing to the suffering soul within a tormented body.

While there are places where a person suffering from anorexia nervosa can find real support, effective treatment and understanding, some treatments proffered seem to me to be little short of a kind of torture, and I am left wondering if those subjected to them find any lasting relief from their devastating illness. I suppose it depends on how severely the sufferer is affected by anorexia nervosa. As with other illnesses, it can affect a person briefly, as a passing shadow which can be dealt with in a reasonable space of time, whereas others can be blighted for life by this terrible disease, or even die from it. I am sure that had I been incarcerated in one of those institutions that force-feeds the patient, or deprives them of even basic conveniences in order to brainwash them into eating, or keeps them prisoner and requires them to put on a certain amount of weight by eating calorie-laden food, I should not have survived. I am sure that I would have killed myself. However, I appreciate that such drastic treatments may well have saved the lives of some people suffering from anorexia nervosa.

The decision to force-feed an anorexic patient against her wishes, in order to preserve life, can be a very difficult one to make. A recent case of a young woman, a medical student gravely ill with anorexia nervosa, came before the High Court after an urgent application from her local authority that her position should be protected. Her parents believed that their daughter had suffered enough and should be allowed to die a dignified death. She had been in palliative care for some time. The judge outlined the difficulty in balancing the decision between life on the one hand, and personal independence on the other. He acknowledged the impossible position of her parents, and the fact that the treatment involved carried significant risks, with only modest prospects of success. He accepted that even if short term progress could be made, there was a high chance that long term difficulties would remain, and that a resumption of treatment would deprive the patient of an imminent and relatively peaceful death. Emphasising the grave significance of the almost equally competing factors, the judge ruled that it was lawful and in her best interests to be fed, forcibly if necessary.

While the body is in a condition of starvation, it seems that a person may not able to respond to psychotherapeutic treatment, and in these cases, such urgent and compulsory measures may need to be undertaken to attempt to prevent the patient from dying. Refeeding may 'buy time', by prolonging the life of the sufferer so that psychotherapeutic treatment can be given at a later date. Where a person voluntarily consents to refeeding and cooperates with the process, it is usually done by gradually expanding the range of foods that can be tolerated, under the supervision of a specialist dietician, until a regular balanced diet can be accepted. The use of specialised dietary supplements does not seem to be common unless the sufferer has sought advice from a clinical nutritionist. Personally, I have found a great deal of help in the recovery of my health, through careful use of food supplements coupled with endeavouring to establish a balanced diet, in consultation with a qualified clinical nutritionist. In my opinion, a body which has suffered from starvation and food-related abuse needs a very high quality nutritional input with targeted nutritional treatment for any deficiencies.

I am so thankful for the journey that I have been privileged to take, which, while being indescribably painful, has brought me untold benefits of many kinds, and healing of which I could never have dreamed – right from the early days, when I was either a walking skeleton or cramming my mouth full of 'forbidden' food.

What, then, is the message that anorexia nervosa brings to us? For each person who encounters it, as a sufferer, carer or observer, it will have a unique significance. However, as a message to our culture, I believe that it shows a protest against a materialistic view of existence that treats the human body as a commodity – to be used either by its owner or by others – and a society that values its members in terms of what they look like and what they can produce. The being within craves loving recognition, respect, acceptance and a valued place as part of a community, simply because it is alive. As a message to our species, it juxtaposes those who choose to starve with those who are forced to starve, and asks us to address urgently the underlying dynamics of both. If we cannot see beyond the walls of our skin to our interconnectedness with each other and with all life, we become trapped inside ourselves, fearful for our individual survival, and out of control of our destiny. The arrogant vision of humanity as the dominant lord of the earth and its resources, free to exploit and abuse in whatever way suits its fancy, is fast coming to an uncomfortable exposure. Anorexia is one of the many messages asking us what human life on this planet is really about, and what we want it to be about.

In conclusion, I am asking myself the question 'Where now?' I can never stand still with anorexia nervosa; there are only two choices, onward into deeper and broader learning and healing, or back down the slippery slope of disintegration. I often grumble and complain about this. Why can't I have a comfortable life? Why is this driving force behind me all the time? Maybe that dragon and I are not yet truly united, and until we are, we will wrestle.

I end this account with the sincere hope that the reader has found something, however small, to strengthen, encourage and bring light upon their journey. I offer you the blessing of the Universal Source in whatever way brings you inspiration and joy.

*   *   *   *   *

The Magic Dragon

'How thin can you be?' said the dragon to me,
Puffing a cloud of smoke,
'Come with me
And I'll take you to see
Some beautiful super-thin folk.'

Swirling, seductive, sinuous clouds,
I could not resist that mist,
It drew me in
To the world of thin
And the dragon's feet I kissed.

'Behold my servant' said the beast to the world,
'She shall now obey my will.
For the least infringement she will suffer
With a feast of food to glut and stuff her,
Rend her soul in hell.'

To me the dragon smiled and said
'Well done my faithful one!
I will reward you,
All shall applaud you,
You and I shall wed.'

Thus the marriage was consummated
With glorious blinding desire,
Intoxicating,
Self love-making,
But the dragon at heart was a liar.

Torturous slavery, year followed year
Until I lost hope of release.
I could only long
To undo the wrong
In a grave marked 'Rest In Peace'.

My life sentence I endured
As if in a golden cage,
And as time passed
I grew aghast
As the years ate up my age.

My devotion though caused circumstance
Impossible and strange,
Dragon brought me many gifts,
And as I healed his wounded rifts
He began to change.

Accustomed now to company,
We walked side by side.
Amazingly
He taught and saved me,
At times my help and guide.

So we journey onward,
Inseparable become,
Who is who no longer clear,
To understand replaces fear,
Our destiny as one.

Jacqueline Kemp

Flames

O flame of desire,
Roused once again,
Yet only to burn with searing pain
And return flickering to thy depths?
O fiery flame,
To me my shame,
Cannot thy passion be abated?

O flame of love,
Thy steady blaze
Must surely melt the structures of my being.
I cannot bear thee,
Wilt thou spare me,
Let me lie in peace?

O flame of deepest agony
With tongues of grief and tears,
Leave thee but one corner untouched
Wherein I can store my fears,
One place where I can hide alone
And cease to feel the woe
That, touching thee
Burns into me,
A suffering to bestow.

O fiercest flame of jealousy,
Thine angry fire,
Consuming with pride and hatred
Will not be satiated.
Ignited by need
And fanned by greed,
Thine only fuel is pain.

O thou glorious Heavenly Flame
Which dances up towards eternity,
Draw my flames into thyself
And make their furnace thine.
O Living Flame, the fire divine,
Who didst set thy taper to my heart
My passions to refine,
Thy white hot fire is love's employ,
It comes forth not to destroy
But only to unite in joy.

Jacqueline Kemp

A Gaelic Blessing

Deep peace of the running wave to you,
Deep peace of the flowing air to you,
Deep peace of the quiet earth to you
Deep peace of the shining stars to you,
Deep peace of the infinite peace to you.

Adapted from ancient Gaelic runes

Suggested further reading

The list below contains a small selection of the many books that have provided me with information, inspiration, and support.

Anorexia Nervosa and Eating Disorders
Hilde Bruch, *The Golden Cage,* Open Books 1978
Peter Dally and Joan Gomez, *Obesity and Anorexia Nervosa: A Question of Shape,* Faber 1980
Sheila MacLeod, *The Art of Starvation,* Virago 1981
Dr. Jane Morris ed. *ABC of Eating Disorders,* Blackwell Publishing Ltd. 2008
Susie Orbach, *Hunger Strike,* Faber 1987
Angelyn Spignesi, *Starving Women: A Psychology of Anorexia Nervosa,* Spring Publications 1988
Marion Woodman, *The Owl Was a Baker's Daughter: Obesity, Anorexia Nervosa and The Repressed Feminine,* Inner City Books 1982

Food and Nutrition/ Medical
Patrick Holford, *The Optimum Nutrition Bible,* Piatkus 1997
Patrick Holford and Hyla Cass, *Natural Highs,* Piatkus 2001
Patrick Holford and Jerome Burne, *Food is Better Medicine than Drugs,* Piatkus 2006
Richard Mackarness, *Not all in the Mind,* Pan London, 1976
Lynne McTaggart, *What Doctor's Don't Tell You,* Thorsons 1996
Charmaine Shepherd, *Is it all in Your Mind? 10 steps to resolving the underlying causes of anxiety and depression,* ISBN 978-1-4478-9415-5
Martin J Walker, *Dirty Medicine; Science, Big Business and the Assault on Natural Healthcare,* Slingshot Publications 1993

Psychology and Spiritual Psychology

Dr. Marion Ashton, *A Mind at Ease,* The Overcomer Literature Trust 1969

Conrad Baars, *Born Only Once,* Franciscan Herald Press 1975

Conrad Baars and Anna Terruwe, *Healing the Unaffirmed,* Alba House 1976

Jean Baker Miller, *Toward a New Psychology of Women,* Beacon Press 1977

William Bloom, *Feeling Safe,* Piatkus 2002

William Bloom, *Modern Spirituality,* Piatkus 2011

William Bloom, *Psychic Protection,* Piatkus 2010

William Bloom, *The Endorphin Effect,* Piatkus 2005

Doc Childre and Howard Martin, *The Heart Math Solution: Proven Techniques for Developing Emotional Intelligence,* Piatkus 1999

Ram Dass and Paul Gorman, *How Can I Help?,* Rider 1989

Adele Faber and Elaine Mazlish, *How to Talk so Kids will Listen and Listen so Kids will Talk,* Picadilly Press 2001

James A Hall MD, *Jungian Dream Interpretation,* Inner City Books 1983

Bill Harris, *Thresholds of the Mind,* Centerpointe Press 2007

Bill Harris, *Managing Evolutionary Growth,* Centerpointe Press 2007

Carl Jung, *Memories, Dreams and Reflections,* Flamingo 1985

Carl Jung, *The Archetypes and the Collective Unconscious,* Routledge 1991

Alice Miller, *The Drama of Being a Child,* Virago 1987

Alice Miller, *For Your Own Good,* Virago 1987

Winifred Rushforth, *Something is Happening; Spiritual Awareness and Depth Psychology in the New Age,* Turnstone Press 1981

Frank Lake, *Clinical Theology* ,Darton, Longman and Todd, July 1986

Frank Lake, *Tight Corners in Pastoral Counselling,* Darton, Longman and Todd, 1981

Kay Pollack, *No Chance Encounter,* Findhorn Press 1988

Dale Spender, *Man Made Language*, Routledge and Kegan Paul 1985

Paul Tournier, *The Strong and the Weak*, SCM Press 1978

Barbara Walker, *The Women's Encyclopaedia of Myths and Secrets*, Harper and Row 1983

Barbara Walker, *The Crone*, Harper and Row 1988

Marion Woodman, *Addiction to Perfection; The Still Unravished Bride*, Inner City Books 1982

Science

James Gleik, *Chaos*, Abacus 1993

Steven Hawking, *A Brief History of Time*, Bantam 1995

Bruce Lipton, *The Biology of Belief*, Cygnus Books 2005

Lynn McTaggart, *The Field*, Element 2003

Rupert Sheldrake, *The Science Delusion; Freeing the Spirit of Enquiry*, Coronet 2012

Gary Zukav, *The Dancing Wu Li Masters; An Overview of the New Physics*, Harper 2001

Beyond the Grave

Stewart Alexander, *An Extraordinary Journey; The Memoirs of a Physical Medium*, Saturday Night Press Publications 2010

Helen Greaves, *Testimony of Light*, C W Daniel and Co. Ltd. 2002

Helen Greaves, *The Wheel of Eternity*, Neville Spearman Ltd. 1995

Elizabeth Kubler-Ross, *On Death and Dying*, Routledge 1973

Raymond Moody with Paul Perry, *Reunions*, Little, Brown and Co. 1994

Sogyal Rinpoche, *The Tibetan Book of Living and Dying*, Rider 2002

Jane Sherwood, *The Country Beyond; The Doctrine of Rebirth*, C W Daniel and Co. Ltd. 2002

Brian Weiss, *Many Lives, Many Masters*, Piatkus 1994

Roger Woolger, *Other Lives, Other Selves*, Doubleday 1999

Health and Spiritual Healing

Barbara Ann Brennan, *Hands of Light; A Guide to Healing Through the Human Energy Field*, Bantam 1990

Barbara Ann Brennan, *Light Emerging, The Journey of Personal Healing*, Bantam1993

Deepak Chopra, *Ageless Body, Timeless Mind*, Rider 1993

Marie de Hennzel, *The Warmth of Your Heart Prevents Your Body from Aging*, Rider 2011

Olga Kharitidi, *Mater of Lucid Dreams*, Hampton Rhodes Publishing Company, 2001

Olga Kharitidi, *Entering the Circle*, Thorsons 1997

Thich Nhat Hanh, *The Miracle of Mindfulness*, Rider 1991

Ruth White with Mary Swainson, *The Healing Spectrum*, Neville Spearman Ltd. 1986

Ruth White, *Walking with Guides and Angels*, Piatkus 1996

Animals and Spirituality

Elizabeth Fulton and Kathleen Prasaad, *Animal Reiki*, Piatkus 2010

Monty Roberts, *The Man Who Listens to Horses*, Arrow Books 1977

Jenny Smedley, *Pets are Forever*, Hay House 2011

Gordon Smith, *The Amazing Power of Animals*, Hay House 2008

Irene Sowter, *Tails to Tell*, Tudor Press 1992

Ancient Wisdom

Alice Bailey, *The Externalisation of the Hierarchy*, Lucis 1981

Alice Bailey, *A Treatise on White Magic*, Lucis 1997

Lawrence Gardener, *Genesis of the Grail Kings*, Bantam 2000

Lawrence Gardener, *Bloodline of the Holy Grail*, Element 2002

Lawrence Gardener, *Lost Secrets of the Sacred Ark*, Element 2004

Zechariah Sitchin, *The Twelfth Planet*, Avon 1978 and the following *Earth Chronicles*

Ecology
Maddy Harland and William Keepin, *Song of the Earth,*
Permanent Publications 2012
Richard Heinberg, *The End of Growth; Adapting to Our New Economic Reality,* Clearview Books, 2011

General Interest
Thomas Ashley-Farrand, *True Stories of Spiritual Power,*
Saraswati Publications 2001
Alick Bartholomew, ed. *Crop Circles; Harbingers of World Change,* Gateway Books 1992
Brian Bates, *The Way of Wyrd,* Century Publishing 1984
Eileen Caddy, *Flight into Freedom and Beyond,* Findhorn Press 2002
Renata Caddy, *Encounters with Babaji; Master of the Himalayas,* Findhorn Press 2002
Lenedra Carroll, *The Architecture of all Abundance,* Piatkus 2005
Carlos Casteneda, *The Teachings of Don Juan; A Yaqui Way of Knowledge,* Penguin 2004
Masuru Emoto, *The Secret Life of Water,* Beyond Words Publishing, 2006
Masuru Emoto, *The True Power of Water; Healing and Discovering Ourselves, Beyond* Words Publishing, 2005
Louise Marie Frenette, *Omraam Mikhaël Aïvanhov,* Suryama 1999
Gitta Mallasz, *Talking with Angels,* Watkins 1979
Kyricacos Markides, *The Magus of Strovolos,* Penguin Arkana 1990
Francis Ripley, *Visions Unseen; Aspects of the Natural Realm,* Findhorn Press 2007
Cyril Scott, *The Boy Who Saw True,* Rider 2005
Michael Werner and Thomas Stöckli, *Life From Light, Clairview Books 2007*

Other titles from Augur Press

The Voice Within by Catherine Turvey

ISBN 978-0-9558936-3-6   £5.99

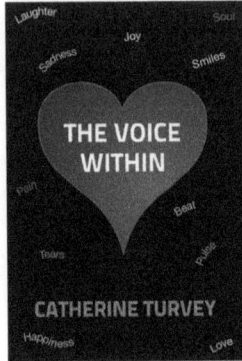

"Creative writing is a wonderful way to express and deal with all sorts of emotions and feelings related to the real world we live in, and everyday life. I was inspired to put all my work together in a book, when family and friends requested copies of my work to keep or to show others. I felt that if my few words could help people in any way by bringing comfort, hope, or encouragement, then why not bring it together for all those who would be interested?"

These poems are the work of a gifted child.

Order from your local bookshop, amazon.co.uk or the Augur Press website at www.augurpress.com

Now Is Where We Are: *Poems from the Priory Hospital* by Hilary Lissenden

ISBN 978-0-9558936-7-4   £6.99

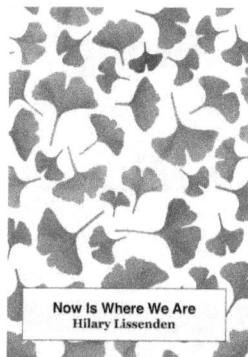

"That there is a link between psychiatric illness and creativity seems widely accepted, although not completely understood. The 'black dog' of clinical depression has kept me intermittent company since my early teens, and I have often written prolifically while recovering from periods of depressive illness."

Once read, these poems will always be your companions. By turns they move and delight with their beauty, wit and depth of fellow-feeling. These are the real thing.

Dr Iain McGilchrist
Consultant Psychiatrist, The Priory Hospital
Former Fellow in English Literature, Oxford University

Order from your local bookshop, amazon.co.uk or the Augur Press website at www.augurpress.com

Beyond the Veil

ISBN 0-9549551-4-5   £8.99

Fay

ISBN 0-9549551-3-7   £8.99

Emily

ISBN 978-0-9549551-8-2 £8.99

a trilogy by Mirabelle Maslin

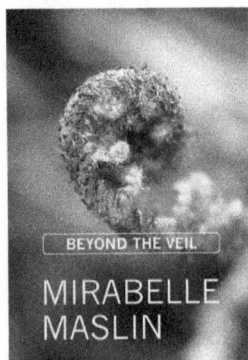

Spiral patterns, a strange tape of music from Russia, a 'blank' book and an oddly shaped walking stick ...

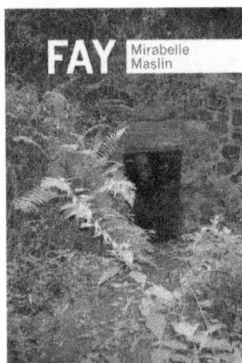

Fay suffers from a mysterious illness. In her vulnerable state, she is affected by something more than intuition ...

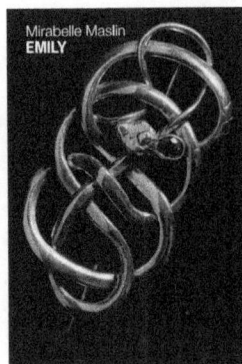

Emily meets Barnaby. Sensing that they have been drawn together for a common purpose, they discover that each carries a crucial part of an unfinished puzzle from years past ...

Order from your local bookshop, amazon.co.uk or the Augur Press website at www.augurpress.com

Field Fare
by Mirabelle Maslin

ISBN 978-0-9558936-8-1   £6.99

Deep in the Cheshire countryside, Philip Thornton
has created 'Field Fare' - a hotel with a special
reputation for its game dishes. The building
contains a secret, known only to Philip.

Feeling lonely while her husband, Grant, is away,
Teresa dines at 'Field Fare', and Philip entices
her to sample a unique cordial. When Teresa
confides about her experience to Carrie, her young
hairdresser, she learns that Carrie has had a similar
encounter.

Could there be more? Concerned, Teresa
approaches her friend, Monica. Aided by Grant,
they devise a plan....

For all other titles from Augur Press
please visit

www.augurpress.com

www.ingramcontent.com/pod-product-compliance
Lightning Source LLC
Chambersburg PA
CBHW031422270326
41930CB00007B/536